PRAISE FOR *CHIEF CULTURE OFFICER*

"McCracken argues persuasively that the missing ingredient is sensitivity to culture, and that this is not such a mystery, but one that companies could do with. [*Chief Culture Officer*] is impressive. . . . The first half of the book is a tour of modern pop culture, intelligently observed."

—*Irish Times*

"A business book for *Entertainment Weekly* subscribers."

—*San Antonio Express-News*

"If big businesses are going to prosper in a time when the Internet allows people to discover how brands fail, they need to learn the ideas, motivations and emotions that influence people's lives. . . . McCracken's message is insightful and stylishly argued."

—*Delta Sky Magazine* (4 star review)

"One of those rare books that made me snap to attention . . . a fresh take on the impact of culture on the corporation. . . . McCracken is an astute observer of human behavior and an entertaining storyteller, and his book offers ample examples of people who take on the role of CCO and what can be learned from their experiences. . . . Grant McCracken gives readers a perfect blend of popular and more obscure cultural trends, great storytelling, and practical application, and in the process makes a strong case that he is this generation's Chief Culture Officer."

—Jack Covert, 1-800-CEO-READ

"The title of this book is a lie. It's not merely for companies that decide they need a Chief Culture Officer, or even just for those who aspire to that job. It's for you. Right now. If your job involves marketing, inventing, selling or simply investing in companies that make stuff, this book is a must read."

—Seth Godin, author of *Tribes* and *Purple Cow*

"In *Chief Culture Officer*, Grant McCracken highlights the increasing importance of cultural understanding for brands that wish to remain relevant—and profitable—in the protean flux of the modern marketplace, as he carves out a new role for the 21st century corporation. The best marketers can hope for is to create something that resonates so strongly it becomes part of our cultural fabric. This book is an indispensable tool for achieving that goal."

—FARIS YAKOB, Executive Vice President and Chief Technology Strategist, McCann Erickson New York

"Building on decades of eye-opening research into the culture of consumption, Grant McCracken demonstrates why many companies get blindsided by cultural factors that were hidden in plain view, and offers a compelling argument for why they need to bring cultural expertise into their executive suite. Here's hoping more corporate executives hear his call."

—HENRY JENKINS, author, *Convergence Culture: Where Old and New Media Collide*

"Many people first glimpsed the strange dignity of marketing in the writing of David Ogilvy or Peter Drucker or Ted Levitt. This book has the power to engage a new generation, by showing that the engine of the world's wealth is culture as much as it is economics. For those who are open to its thrall, *Chief Culture Officer* will change the trajectory of their lives."

—JOHN DEIGHTON, Brierley Professor of Business Administration, Harvard Business School

"Grant McCracken has cracked the holy grail of what's next to blend talent management, corporate strategy, and trendspotting, and his storytelling style captivates and educates. I am blown away."

—MARIAN SALZMAN, partner and chief marketing officer, Porter Novelli

"Grant McCracken, once again, sees clearly the patterns in which innovation, enterprise, and smart people can influence change, create value, and respond to popular culture, where real people experience choice. The book is terrific and spot on."

—Richard Grefé, CEO, AIGA | the professional association for design

"This is a marvel of a business book: highly entertaining, original, and provocative. Entrepreneurs who want to understand their customers, target market, and the cultural dynamics that shape the business world—which is to say all entrepreneurs—need to read it."

—Ben Casnocha, author of *My Start-Up Life: What a (Very) Young CEO Learned on His Journey Through Silicon Valley*

"Marketing gets failing grades when it comes to understanding and using culture. In *Chief Culture Officer*—a delectable cultural soup that is sure to stir your taste buds—Grant McCracken makes a compelling case that culture will be marketing's next silver bullet. I whole-heartedly endorse his call for bringing culture-thinking into the company."

—Philip Kotler, author of *Chaotics: The Business of Managing and Marketing in the Age of Turbulence*

HOW TO CREATE A LIVING, BREATHING CORPORATION

CHIEF CULTURE OFFICER

GRANT McCRACKEN

BASIC BOOKS
A Member of the Perseus Books Group
New York

Hardcover first published in 2009 by Basic Books,
A Member of the Perseus Books Group
Paperback first published in 2011 by Basic Books

Designed by Jeff Williams

The Library of Congress has catalogued the hardcover as follows:
McCracken, Grant David, 1951–
Chief culture officer : how to create a living, breathing corporation / Grant McCracken.
p. cm.
Includes bibliographical references and index.
ISBN 978-0-465-01832-1
1. Management—Social aspects. 2. Popular culture—Economic aspects. 3. New products—Social aspects. 4. Organizational change. I. Title.

HD30.19.M33 2009
658—dc22

2009038736

Paperback ISBN: 978-0-465-02204-5
E-book ISBN: 978-0-465-02010-2

For Pamela

CONTENTS

CONTENTS

INTRODUCTION

LEVI STRAUSS, THE JEANS AND APPAREL MAKER, MISSES hip-hop. The penalty: $1 billion.[1]

Quaker pays too much for Snapple. The penalty: $1.4 billion.[2]

Facebook claims 7 billion photos as its own. Embarrassment and recantation follow.[3]

These corporations, like most, were bad at reading culture, bad at staying in touch with culture, bad at working with culture. And it cost them dearly.

By "culture," I don't mean corporate culture. And I don't mean "high culture," the world of refined taste. By culture, I mean the world outside the corporation, the body of ideas, emotions, and activities that make up the life of the consumer.

It's not that the corporation hasn't *tried* to take account of culture. It's resorted to the advertising agency, designer, consultant, cool-hunter, and guru.[4] Worst case, someone says, "Let's see what the intern thinks." (Now a million-dollar decision rests on a twenty-year-old.) But culture is too important to be left to an outsider (or a twenty-year-old). When there's $1.4 billion at stake, it needs a Chief Culture Officer.

The corporation has learned many things in the past one hundred years. It has mastered most of the mysteries of organizational behavior, operations management, human resources, communication, marketing, and finance. Until it masters culture, it makes the world needlessly mysterious. It multiplies risk.

Culture matters for reasons good and bad. First, it is the place to discover advantage, opportunity, and innovation. The Four Seasons, Patagonia, Starbucks, Nike, Red Bull, Target, Method Soap—each is a culture play. Each found value in culture. Each *extracted* value from culture.

Second, culture is the breeding ground of cataclysmic change, a North Sea out of which commotion constantly storms. Without a working knowledge of culture, the corporation lives in a perpetual state of surprise, waiting for the next big storm to hit. Without a CCO, the corporation has no way to perform this crucial piece of threat assessment.

It's a great puzzle that the corporation should still be trying to solve this problem. We have had 230 years since Adam Smith to find a way to work with culture. Certainly, gifted entrepreneurs and managers rose to address the problem. What was missing was a clear idea, a working knowledge, of culture.

In management literature, there was always a newcomer to elbow culture out of the way. "Objectives!" said Drucker. "Quality!" said Deming. "Reengineering!" said Hammer and Champy. "Excellence!" said Peters. "Strategy!" said Porter. There's always a new guru, bearing a shiny new toy for the C-suite.[5] Poor culture, always the bridesmaid, never the bride.

That's what I want to do with this book: invent an office and an officer—the Chief Culture Officer, the person who knows culture, both its fads and fashions, and its deep, enduring structures. I hope this book will be read by two groups: people inside the corporation who want to make the corporation more intelligent, strategic, and responsive, and people outside the corporation who want to turn their knowledge of culture into a profession and a career.

To the CEO, I say, appoint a Chief Culture Officer. To those poised to become a CCO, I say, "You can do it. I can help."

CHAPTER 1

GETTING PAST GURU

Being Steve Jobs

"HE'S A GENIUS."[1]

"Jobs is indispensible."[2]

"Steve Jobs is the key to Apple success . . . [W]ithout him [Apple's] future is very much in doubt."[3]

People talk about Steve Jobs as if he were one of a kind. Clearly, he is a remarkable man. When we look at what he's done for Apple, cell phones, digital content, the art of design . . . well, he has earned our admiration.

But when it comes to helping Apple navigate culture, Steve Jobs may be less indispensible than we think. With a more systematic approach to culture, many could do what Jobs has done. Let's not be blinded by the "cult of personality." It's good for Jobs. It's good for Apple. It's not so good for the rest of us. We have made ourselves guru-dependent.

Jobs owes some of his celebrity to how bad the corporation is at culture. As long as the competition is someone like Sony's Sir Howard Stringer—the CEO who couldn't bring himself to apologize for "Rootgate" and struggles to grasp new media and youth culture—well, Jobs is bound to look like a genius.[4] As long as culture is ignored by business schools, C-suites, big brands, and consulting houses, Jobs looks great. In the land of the blind, the one-eyed man is king (even in sneakers, jeans, and black turtlenecks).

Many companies depend on a guru: Apple on Jobs, Virgin on Richard Branson, CBS on Les Moonves, Omnimedia on Martha Stewart, Bad Boy Entertainment on Sean Combs. The Securities and Exchange Commission worries about this sort of thing. It says that these companies must warn the investor. Here's what Omnimedia is *obliged* to say about Stewart in its annual report.

> Ms. Stewart's efforts, personality and leadership have been and continue to be critical to our success . . . [T]he repeated diminution, or loss of her services, due to disability, death or some other cause . . . could have a material adverse effect on our business.[5]

But precisely. Martha Stewart is the taste maker at Omnimedia. Her loss would be cataclysmic. But, TV appearances aside, is she essential? Stewart is a virtuoso, to be sure. But her gift is not mysterious, imponderable, or irreproducible. Stewart is not essential.

That's the operating idea of this book: We can reverse-engineer the Stewart sensibility. We can reverse-engineer Jobs's feeling for culture. We don't need gurus. We can be our own barometers. The celebrity CEO would like to play the French monarch and insist, "Without me, you're nothing." The truth is otherwise.

I will know this book has made a difference when the annual report reads,

> [T]he repeated diminution, or loss of the CEO's services, due to disability, death, or some other cause . . . could have a material adverse effect on our business. We have appointed a CCO to diminish the risk.

We will scrutinize the likes of Jobs and Branson and see if we can reverse-engineer their abilities. How do these people do it? What's the secret of their ability to read culture? And could we do it ourselves?

Steve Jobs's parents sacrificed heroically to send him to Reed College, a small liberal arts school in Portland, Oregon. But he wasn't happy. He couldn't see the point of his studies, and after six months he dropped out.

Jobs didn't leave Portland and he didn't leave Reed. He stayed on campus as an unregistered student, walking, thinking, noticing. One of the things he noticed was that campus posters were particularly beautiful. A little investigation told him that Reed had a good calligraphy department, and Jobs decided to take a class, his only class. He promptly fell in love with the art form. "It was beautiful, historical, artistically subtle in a way that science can't capture, and I found it fascinating."

And not just fascinating. When Jobs designed the first Macintosh computer, ten years later, his Reed training came back to him. And the rest, as they say, is history. Without his calligraphy course, Jobs says, "the Mac would have never had multiple typefaces or proportionally spaced fonts." And he says, "It's likely that no personal computer would have them. If I had never dropped out, I would have never dropped in on this calligraphy class, and personal computers might not have the wonderful typography that they do."[6]

Thanks to Jobs and that course, Apple was unique in the tech space. It cared about beauty. And this gave it a strong connection to the creative community, which in turn supplied the corporation with a passionate, supportive base. Apple enthusiasts were so dedicated to the brand they helped fund each new Apple experiment, embracing, without much complaint, even the odd Apple failure. Competitors like HP and IBM lived in a ruthlessly commoditizing marketplace filled with consumers who were "brand disloyal" and aggressively "price sensitive." Apple lived in a magic bubble with brand evangelists and huge profit margins. Jobs had found a way to connect to the creative community. He had found a way to read culture and speak to it.

Jobs wasn't a CCO but certainly he acted like one. The lesson: Connect to our culture and we will follow you anywhere. And Apple is now so spectacularly in touch with parts of our culture, it seems almost in control of it.

But the problem is not always a guru who exerts undue influence and claims undue attention. Sometimes the corporation has a CCO on board, a stowaway who deserves more influence than she has.

MARY MINNICK

For much of the twentieth century, Coke was the defining brand of American commerce and culture, fashioning the image of America at home, distributing the image of America abroad. Coke even helped create our idea of Christmas. (We think of Santa Claus dressed in red and white because these are the colors of the Coca-Cola Company.)[7] Coke was everywhere. Coke was it.

That was then. Now Coke struggles to stay in touch with American culture. The value of the brand fell some 20 percent between 1999 and 2006.[8] Consumer taste and American culture started running away from Coke, not toward it. Niche players like Gatorade and Red Bull were creating new drinks. Coke wasn't it. Consumers were rethinking what a "drink" was.

Mary Minnick might have been CCO to the rescue. She joined Coke straight out of business school in 1983. But despite the fact that she was a Coke "lifer," she was alive to the new directions drinks were taking. She was particularly interested in the noncarbonated drink. (She created Fruitopia.) At Coke, this made her the apostate. A manager told her, "You've pushed too hard, you've alienated everyone in North America, your passion for non-carbs [non-carbonated drinks] has gotten in the way of what's right for Coke, and nobody wants to work with you anymore."[9]

Still, Sergio Zyman and Neville Isdell, the most senior managers at Coke, believed Minnick was the person who could push Coke from "soda-centric" to the "cutting edge of consumer trends."

God knows, she tried. She vented impatiently, complaining that Coke's intelligence was "superficial." She launched a coffee drink called Blak and a green tea drink called Enviga. She brought in Wieden + Kennedy to create a new ad campaign called the "Coke Side of Life."[10] By her departure, Minnick had created an "enduring pipeline of innovation."[11] Despite these encomiums, she left, forced out.

When it came time to appoint the new CEO, Coke passed Minnick by. Instead, it chose Muhtar Kent, who has a bachelor of science degree in economics from Hull University in England

and a master of science degree in administrative sciences from London City University. Kent managed the Coca-Cola system in Central Asia and Eastern Europe. This is another way of saying, and I say this with all due respect, that Kent knows relatively little about contemporary American culture. He is by all accounts a smart and charming guy. But American culture? Perhaps not so much.

Let's be clear. Without a connection to culture, Coke is merely carbonated water and syrup. Without culture, it's just a fizzy drink. So culture counts. Let's be clearer still. The fundamental terms of the Coke proposition are changing. The carbonated soft drink is now contested by new ideas of what a drink should be (Snapple, Gatorade, Poland Springs, Vitaminwater, Red Bull). In the traditional case, culture matters. In the present case, it matters more.

At a crucial juncture, Coke had the good sense to make Minnick the head of marketing. But when it came time to making her CEO, it blinked. It ignored the one person in the corporation who seemed to grasp the new world of the noncarbonated drink. Indeed, Coke appears to have searched its empire until it found someone who didn't. Now, to be fair, a corporation doesn't need to appoint a master of culture as CEO. (Though it is hard to imagine knowledge that matters more to a company like Coke.) But when a company has a local genius, it should count its blessings and do the right thing. If it has a Mary Minnick, it should make her CEO. And if can't do that, it should appoint a CCO.

GEOFFREY FROST

In the 1990s, Motorola was a force to be reckoned with. The StarTAC clamshell was the "it phone" of the moment. (*PC*

World called it "the first mobile phone to establish that design matters as much as functionality.")[12] But by 1999 the company was struggling. Before long, it was in free fall, losing $6.5 billion in 2001–2002. Motorola appeared trapped between a Nokia that was big enough to outmuscle it and new Korean players like Samsung and LG that threatened always to be more innovative.

Geoffrey Frost joined Motorola in 1999. He found Motorola products "stodgy." Having worked at Nike, having built campaigns around Michael Jordan and Tiger Woods, he knew something about being attached to the moment. By the late 1990s, Motorola seemed entirely detached from the moment.

It wasn't that Motorola was incapable of innovation. Periodically, things would come spinning out of the lab with "it" status written all over them. And Motorola the company would find a way to strip them of the qualities that made them thrilling. Every corporation practices "death by committee"—when the time servers, the bean counters, and the naysayers set upon a new idea with their steely knives and murder it in its crib. By the late 1990s, Motorola was very good at death by committee.[13]

It wasn't long after Frost got to Motorola that he was wandering the Chicago lab and discovered a technology, a handset concept, and it was beautiful. A colleague recalls, "From the beginning, once you picked up the Razr and used it, you never wanted another phone."[14] The question was how to protect the nascent Razr from death by committee. Frost was cunning. He kept the Razr below the radar. He concealed it from the corporation. He didn't put it in the business plan. He reached out to the "best, brightest, craziest and most passionate people" he could find at Motorola. And when someone asked how much money this new phone was going to make, Frost said, in effect, "Oh, it's not going to make money. It's a brand builder."[15]

The Razr proved to be the little phone that could. It launched in 2004 to modest expectations. Motorola projected sales of 2 million units. By the end of 2005, the Razr had sold 20 million. By the end of 2006, it had sold 50 million. Geoffrey Frost had saved Motorola.

Like Minnick, Frost gave the corporation a chance to escape its own gravitational field. Once more Motorola was making a phone the consumer "had to have." Frost knew we don't win contemporary markets by adding a feature or shaving the price point. The trick is to make innovations that make people blink with surprise and perhaps shiver with desire. Frost understood that phones are something more than a means of communication, a function, a utility. In our gadget-crazy culture, they are charismatic or they are destined for the "commodity basement," where competitors slug it out for profits measured in pennies over cost. No one wants to live in the commodity basement, not when the alternative is so glorious. (When it first appeared, the iPhone was making $250 in profit per phone.)[16]

Tragically, unexpectedly, Geoffrey Frost died in 2005. And for a while Motorola continued to flourish. Ed Zander, then CEO, remembered Frost fondly, saying he'd helped make the brand "cool again," "renew[ing] and reinvent[ing] Motorola." But with Frost gone, it was as if the navigational equipment had been ripped out of the corporation. It was going somewhere, but no one quite knew where. The "death by committee" contingent got their mojo back, and by 2007, Motorola was once again losing money. By 2008, things were so grim Motorola wondered whether it should *sell* its cell phone unit. By 2008, Ed Zander was gone as CEO.[17]

With Frost's passing, Motorola seemed to return to the form of the late 1990s. It forgot that phones must be wonderful. It forgave death by committee. It let the bean counters have their way. It forgot what Frost knew so well, that "it" status is a miracle of calibration that comes from a fleeting seal between the culture and a corporation. Because our culture is turbulent, the seal cannot last. Innovation is the name of the game. Poor Motorola. It clung to the Razr until it was just another phone on the shelf. Ignominy of ignominies, eventually we could get a Razr by signing a two-year AT&T contract. The Razr was being given away.[18]

CCO AS A PROFESSION

Corporations live or die by their connection to culture. And sometimes they have the good fortune to have a Steve Jobs, a Mary Minnick, or a Geoffrey Frost. In a more perfect world, they would have a CCO to supply cultural intelligence as a matter of course. This is better than forcing the corporation to rely on the whim and the ego of a virtuoso.

Most people now acting in the capacity of a CCO have come to this position not through professional study but by biographical accident. David Ogilvy, the founder of Ogilvy & Mather, had been a chef, a sales rep, a farmer, and a spy. Splendid. Any of these is an excellent window from which to learn about culture. Together they are the stuff of deep cultural knowledge, an anthropological foundation of special value. Neil French, now creative director at the ad agency WPP, was a bouncer, waiter, rent collector, singer, and manager of the band Judas Priest.[19]

Sometimes people know the culture that matters because they have lived it for several years. Phil Knight, the founder of

Nike, had been a runner. He knew runners. He was connected to the community. No research was called for. The market was mostly guys like him. Icebreaker, the New Zealand firm devoted to adventure clothing, was founded by Jeremy Moon, himself an adventurer. Anne Rice, the author of spectacularly successful vampire novels, grew up in New Orleans (where, she says, "the dead walk alongside the living").[20] Lance Jensen of the ad agency Modernista says his brilliant advertising successes of the 1990s came from the fact that he was the audience he was talking to. In all of these cases, someone can act as a CCO not because he has studied contemporary culture but because he comes from that culture. He knows it in his bones.

The problem with this approach is the "best by" date stamped on knowledge. Our community carries on without us. In the early days, we can update our knowledge without much effort, but eventually our knowledge wears out. We have lost our "seal" with culture.

The other problem is that we must finally transcend the community from which we come. Eventually Phil Knight had to talk to nonathletes. Eventually Lance Jensen had to do ads for people who were not like him. Eventually every CCO has to know about the whole of culture, and not just the part of it he or she knows from personal experience.

This is, finally, an issue of professionalism, of systemizing our knowledge, of getting organized, of going beyond our own preferences and comfort zone. Unofficial CCOs may rely on particular knowledge, on "hunches." They may feel things in "the gut," as if culture were a probiotic enterprise, after all. But the professional CCO has a breadth and a depth of knowledge. The CCO has to know the whole of its waterfront, not just his or her favorite patch or point of origin.

A student I taught at Harvard now manages an investment fund. We had lunch one day and he took me through a "day in the life." I was amazed to see how disciplined his approach was. Greg, let's call him, never made an investment without scrutinizing and then recording his assumptions. At routine intervals, he checked his assumptions. And when he was wrong, when his investments failed, he did an autopsy. Where did he go wrong? What assumption was mistaken and needed replacing?

Most of us don't admit error. We proceed from hunch to hunch. When we're right, we like to think our genius is confirmed. When we're wrong, well, the less said the better.

This is not the stuff of professionalism. We wouldn't tolerate doctors who relied on divination. Judges may not justify decisions on the grounds that it "feels right." Engineers may not reassure us that bridges are trustworthy because "I know it in my gut."

The C-suite has higher standards. We are entitled to know that the CCO is working to the same standards that our CIO brings to the corporation's information technology. Standards, knowledge, continual learning, the ability to process massive bodies of data and possibility, the ability to spot the crucial development in a perfect storm of possibilities—this, and not intuition, is the work of the CCO.

CHAPTER 2

STEALTH CCOs

THE CHIEF CULTURE OFFICER DOESN'T YET EXIST. BUT THERE are people who act like CCOs and we can learn from them.

DAN WIEDEN FOR NIKE

By the mid-1980s, the running boom was giving way to a fitness craze, and Phil Knight, founder of Nike, wanted his company to take part. Knight didn't much believe in advertising, but competition with Reebok was fierce, and he had begun to work with a small shop in Portland, Oregon, called Wieden + Kennedy. Dan Wieden, Portland native and second-generation ad man, proved an essential asset.

It was Wieden who coined the slogan "Just do it" in 1988.[1] Most slogans are about the brand ("Coke is it."). They may make a promise ("You can do it. We can help."), or they evoke a mood ("Bilbao, now more than ever."). Rarely do they tell the consumer what to do. But "Just do it" was imperative, impatient, presumptuous, and, well, a little rude. This was not the sort of thing consumers had heard before.[2]

Acting as unofficial CCO, Dan Wieden had looked into the life of the consumer. He saw someone struggling to get off the couch into fitness, someone suffering aches and pains, someone tempted by excuses. In "Just do it" Wieden found the three words that allowed Nike to intervene. Acting as unofficial CCO, Wieden had found a way to help Nike ride the fitness wave.

Wieden is the author of a 2001 Nike ad called "Tag."[3] This TV spot features a young man on his way to work in a big city. It could be Chicago, New York, or San Francisco. (It is in fact Toronto.) All of a sudden, he feels a hand on his shoulder. He's been tagged. He's it. Pedestrians scatter. Plazas empty. The chase is on. He almost tags one woman as she enters a bus. He almost tags another but she dives into her car. He almost tags a policeman as he pulls away in his cruiser. Our hero is a wildebeest, charging wildly, hoping for contact. Finally he comes upon a hapless guy in the subway, the only man in the city who doesn't know the game is on. Tag. Now he's it.

Frame for frame, "Tag" is probably the most exciting ad ever made. It had the drama of the chase scene in *The French Connection*. It won the admiration of the industry and a Cannes Lion Grand Prix.[4]

But it's an odd ad. It takes twenty seconds before we understand what's happening. For a while it's just people running around on a plaza, forcing us to puzzle things out on our own. Advertising is famous for its simplicity, repetition, and sometimes sheer stupidity ("But wait! There's more! Act now! . . ."). In the world of advertising, twenty seconds is a client-provoking eternity. Wieden dared tinker with the rules.

For all that, "Tag" is a straightforward piece of advertising. It is playful. It makes Nike the friend of spontaneity and urban athleticism. It brings the viewer off the couch to the edge of his seat, the very point of the Nike proposition. Every commuter would love to see the tedium of travel exploded this way.

Certainly, every athlete (and Nike is filled with athletes) would love to see the city as a competitive space.

And there were deeper resonances. Since the 1960s and the era of the be-in, the city was being proposed as a platform for spontaneous expressive events. Street theater was now agitating public life and the pages of *Time* and *Life*. In the TV show *Mork & Mindy*, Robin Williams brought the idea of improv to American living rooms. Americans were giving up the Northern European idea that public behavior ought to be guarded and expressionless. They were beginning to tinker with the notion that the world could hand you a proposition and you would "go with it."[5] (I remember being thrown a "ball" by a passing mime in Hyde Park in the late 1970s. I threw "it" back.) Some of the raves that became so popular in the 1990s had precisely this quality: perfect strangers assembling "just in time" in abandoned warehouses. Somehow culture by accident was more interesting than culture that was planned.[6]

"Tag" also resonated with ideas of order that were less theatrical and more scientific. The physicists sent to the desert during World War II to create the atomic bomb stayed on in Santa Fe, New Mexico. They were interested in how complex order could issue from simple rules. The game of tag is based on a very simple rule, and, sure enough, it makes the disorder of city life give way to pattern. Somehow culture that was "emergent" was more interesting than culture that was organized.[7]

"Tag" evoked a third trend we might call the "generous stranger." For many of us, first notice came in the form of a bumper sticker that read "Practice random kindness and senseless acts of beauty," a phrase so influential, it now has its own Wikipedia entry. Several thousand years of cultural practice and religious teaching had encouraged us to think of generosity as a personal gesture that passed between known parties. The "generous stranger" trend suggested it was better when things passed between perfect strangers. Hollywood picked up the theme belatedly and not very successfully in a couple of films: *Pay It Forward* (Mimi Leder, 2000) and *Serendipity* (Peter Chelson, 2001).

With the help of digital technologies, "generous stranger" projects were (and are) suddenly everywhere. Bookcrossings has people conceal books somewhere in public for other strangers to find.[8] In Geocaching, people search for caches using GPS coordinates posted online, and when they find the cache, they take one thing and leave another. In Phototagging, disposable cameras are left in a public place and the finder is asked to take one photo and pass the camera along. In Where's George? people register dollar bills, put them back in circulation, and ask finders to record the bill when it passes through their hands.[9] It wasn't always clear why this was interesting. Somehow it just was.

Howard Rheingold took things a step forward with *Smart Mobs*, encouraging people to meet together in public, to freeze for a moment in Grand Central Station, shop in slow motion at Wal-Mart, or act out letters in department store windows.[10] Rheingold's book appeared in 2002, which puts the book and the ad in production at roughly the same time. Both could hear our culture stirring.

Max Weber, the German sociologist, believed that as the Western world grew more rational, routinized, and commercial, a disenchantment beset us. The personal, the traditional, the sentimental, the human scale, all of these were diminished. "Tag" and its companion trends seemed to offer a restoration.

Apparently, even strangers can make the city more playful and less predictable. With "Tag," Wieden helped Nike re-enchant the world.[11]

And that's all very well. But of course Nike is not a philanthropic organization. It sells footwear. And here "Tag" performed brilliantly. It helped Nike fight off competitors who believed that the game was merely about "sports performance." "Tag" gave Nike what Theodore Levitt, god of the Harvard Business School, called "meaningful distinction." As Levitt said in *The Marketing Imagination*, "All else is derivative of that and only that."[12]

And some people think it's just an advertising campaign.

LANCE JENSEN FOR VOLKSWAGEN

In the 2001 ad "Pink Moon," Lance Jensen showed four people in their twenties driving with the top down in a VW Cabrio through the silky darkness of a summer evening, music supplied by Nick Drake. They arrive at their destination, a house party on the beach. It's a great party, radiating exuberance, ringing with laughter. But the friends don't get out. They exchange a look—and drive on.[13]

In a spot called "Synchronicity," a man and a woman drive through city streets. At the fifty-five-second mark, the man says, "That was interesting." And that's the whole ad. Two people in a car and the phrase "that was interesting." "Really," we hear a little voice within us say, "Interesting or really quite weird?" On the second viewing, we notice that the things outside the car are moving in unison. Windshield wipers, basketballs, and traffic signals all seem to have rhythm. Another viewing and our suspicion is confirmed. Things *are* moving in unison. *What?*[14]

Gerd Klauss, president of Volkswagen North America, wasn't crazy about "Synchronicity." He called it "obscure." The agency said, "Precisely. It's *meant* to be obscure." It was designed to demand reviewing.[15] And what we saw in subsequent viewing was another case of emergent order, a world magically marching in unison, exhibiting fleeting, spontaneous patterns. Jensen and VW had joined Wieden and Nike in a re-enchantment of the world.

Jensen and Wieden were seeing something happen in contemporary culture. They knew consumers were getting more sophisticated when it came to watching TV. Acting as unofficial CCOs, they could hear something rustling in our world. Academics and intellectuals were inclined to take another view. It was fashionable to suppose that consumers were dupes, stupefied by the wasteland of popular culture, mesmerized by media and marketing, and incapable of thought, imagination, and, most of all, choice.[16]

Convention said popular culture was diminished culture. Commerce created conformity in consumers and uniformity in societies, and it distracted us from the higher callings of art, literature, and religion. It was giddy when it ought to be serious. It was frivolous when it ought to be solemn. It was manipulative when it ought to be plain dealing. The intellectuals agreed: Culture touched by commerce was "dumbed down," "hollowed out," "flattened," "impoverished," "bankrupted."[17]

American scholar Lewis Mumford offered this vision of the world created by commerce:

> A multitude of uniform, unidentifiable houses, lined up inflexibly, at uniform distances, on uniform roads, in a treeless communal waste, inhabited by people of the

> same class, the same income, the same age group, witnessing the same television programs, eating the same tasteless pre-fabricated foods, from the same freezers, conforming in every outward and inward respect to a custom mold.[18]

Mumford's vision was played out by novelists Richard Yates and John D. MacDonald, by folksinger Pete Seeger, by economist John Kenneth Galbraith, by John F. Kennedy appointee Newton Minow.[19] This became the intellectual's favorite thing to say about popular culture: that culture touched by commerce must be diminished by it.[20]

Henry Jenkins, professor at MIT, was perhaps the first to spot the new development. He found active, participatory viewers, not passive couch potatoes. These viewers were mastering the nuances and the grammars of TV. And when Jenkins sat down and talked to media consumers (a strategy the old school carefully avoided), he discovered a mixture of motives. These consumers kept an ironic distance even as they cultivated a passionate interest. They were both mocking and fond. But most of all they were participating. Consumers were rewriting scripts and second-guessing directorial decisions even as they were feeling the protagonist's pain. There was no "dupe" here.[21]

Steven Johnson helped explore Jenkins's discovery several years later in his book *Everything Bad Is Good for You: How Today's Popular Culture Is Actually Making Us Smarter*.[22] Johnson discovered new complexity in TV shows and popular fiction. He examined ordinary prime-time TV dramas and discovered a tangle of plotlines. These shows were—gasp—actually difficult to follow.[23] The trend has grown apace. J. J. Abrams is one of the most active TV producers, having had a hand in *Felicity*, *Alias*, *Lost*, and *Fringe*. The *New York Times* says his storytelling style "demands total commitment from audience members, requiring that they keep up not only with complicated single-episode plotlines . . . but also with fiendishly intricate narratives . . . that can take an entire season—or seasons, plural—to play out."[24]

Some new shows had nuance. They invited alternative explanations and left things unsaid. They did not insult the viewer's intelligence, but threatened actually to augment it. Somehow this wasteland culture was now producing TV entertainments that had some of, if not all, the hallmarks of culture of the kind intellectuals approved of. How very, very vexing for the intellectuals. And then a flood of scholarship, as historians, economists, and every kind of scholar began to examine the facts of the matter.[25] And now it was clear. The "diminished culture" argument made a lovely story. But that's all it was, a story. It was indeed very like a myth, a narrative our culture had decided to tell itself about itself. Under closer, dispassionate study, the problem was clear. This argument so oversimplified and in places falsified the facts of the matter that if these "critical" scholars were to make the argument about another culture and not their own, they would be laughed out of the academic world.

Culture was not caught in downward cycle. There was evidence that a virtuous upward ascent had been set in motion. Smarter viewers encouraged smarter culture. Smarter culture encouraged smarter viewers. For Generations X and Y, this development had become a badge of pride. Being good at popular culture became a generational marker. For boomers, popular culture might have been a guilty pleasure. For younger generations, it was a rich, more complicated joy.

This was the opportunity Lance Jensen took up. He was writing for the new, smarter audience. "Pink Moon" and "Synchronicity" were not difficult for the usual reason—because the agency wanted to produce something "edgy" to win industry awards and admiration. They were difficult because difficult was now the smart, strategic thing to do.[26] Jensen was doing for Volkswagen what Wieden was doing for Nike: reaching into culture to find a way to speak to culture. Thus did two "mad men" act as CCOs.[27]

ALEX BOGUSKY FOR MICROSOFT

When Google said its unofficial motto was "Don't be evil," everyone knew what *that* meant: "Don't be like Microsoft." By the first decade of the twenty-first century, Microsoft had dug itself a very deep hole. It was infamous for using its massive size to swamp smaller companies. It treated business-to-business partners badly and consumers with disdain. The software was bloated with features and inclined to crash. Microsoft didn't seem to care. Microsoft's attitude toward Google was characteristically aggressive. Of Google CEO Eric Schmidt, Microsoft CEO Steve Ballmer is reported to have said: "I am going to fucking bury that guy . . . I'm going to fucking kill Google."[28]

Microsoft had helped create many things: Silicon Valley, the computer industry, the personal computer, the disintermediation of American business, and the digitization of American culture. Not bad for a decade's work. But it acted with such bully-boy arrogance, no one wished it well. Microsoft helped start the party. Now everyone wished it would leave.

The company seemed especially tone-deaf when it came to culture. The spellchecker on Microsoft Word would correct you if you misspelled Phil Mickelson, Donny Osmond, Alan

Greenspan, or Steven Spielberg. But it didn't seem to notice if you misspelled Jim Jarmusch, Christopher Hitchens, Ron Popeil, or Dale Earnhardt Jr.[29] Poor Microsoft, bullying when it paid attention, clueless when it did not.

Microsoft had to do *something*, and what it did was hire Crispin, Porter and Bogusky, one of the hot shops in the advertising world. Creative head Alex Bogusky is regarded as a miracle worker, a meaning-maker of extraordinary gifts. As *Fast Company* says, "Bogusky can give it—and take it away," citing his work for the Cooper Mini and Burger King and against smoking and against the Hummer.[30]

Still, the world had its doubts. Microsoft's reputation was a meteor so deeply buried it wasn't clear that even CP+B could extract it. The agency had put itself on the line in the process. Success would confirm its genius. Failure could well bring ruin.[31]

The first CP+B spot featured Jerry Seinfeld replaying himself from his show *Seinfeld*. "Jerry" was a guy too smart for his own good. Episode after episode, he and George tried to beat the system, only to watch their efforts gently spin out of control in a slow motion Rube Goldberg disaster. Everyone was horrified, except, of course, Jerry and George.

Bogusky gave Jerry a new sidekick, Bill Gates, and dropped the two of them in a splendidly odd little world called Shoe Circus. A family gathers outside the store window in learned reverence for the shoes within, and churros (aka the "Spanish donut") are given a starring role. Seinfeld suggests that Gates try wearing his clothes in the shower. Gates turns out to be a Shoe Circus Clown Club card member. Jerry offers the prediction that computers will someday be "moist" and "chewy."

Astounding! Shoe Circus actually managed to make Microsoft seem more human and more companionable. Bogusky hadn't reinvented Microsoft by any means, but he had successfully lodged a "minority opinion." It was just a start, but before CP+B a start had seemed unthinkable.

The second stage of Bogusky's work was "I am a PC," a series of ads that feature ordinary people, apparently shot without the benefit of makeup, good lighting, or art direction. It's just one cheerful soul after another saying "I'm a PC," including a four-and-a-half-year-old girl called Kylie who edits a picture of her fish, Dorothy, on camera.[32] These ads looked homemade, handheld, low-res, and they helped Microsoft tunnel out of its hated citadel.

Here's how: Our culture has been predicated on a simple distinction between the mainstream and the avant-garde. The mainstream is supposed to be conformist, unimaginative, narrow, and controlling. The avant-garde is supposed to be rebellious, risk-taking, creative, and reckless. It's a pretty crude distinction, but in our culture it has proved a highly influential way of thinking.[33] (It's on this assumption that cool-hunters and trend spotters have made their way in the world.)

Along comes Apple. Steve Jobs and company say, "Perfect! We'll play the avant-garde. PC can be mainstream." And so was born the "Mac vs. PC" campaign, started in 2006 and crafted by the agency TBWA Media Arts Lab. "Mac vs. PC" showed Apple to be hip, gentle, and patient (as played by Justin Long) and Microsoft to be small-minded, smug, and annoying (as played by John Hodgman). It was a huge success. Microsoft was now trapped in a game of "I'm rubber, you're glue."

What to do? Like Wieden and Jensen, Bogusky was alert to the changes taking place in his culture. He noticed in the 1990s that this two-party system exploded. In addition to the mainstream and avant-garde, a new "third space" was opening up. Driven by the great fragmentation of taste and preference in the last quarter of the twentieth century, this consisted of a very large group of people who didn't define themselves as hip or mainstream. They just were.[34]

Bogusky and Microsoft said, "Perfect! We'll play third space. Apple can be avant-garde." Thus did Microsoft tunnel out from under Apple's hipster image and into the new world of the unaligned.[35]

Let's give Microsoft its due. It may not have understood contemporary culture, but it was smart enough and brave enough to hire someone who did. And Bogusky—well, Bogusky is a genius.

A. G. LAFLEY FOR P&G

When A. G. Lafley became the CEO of Procter & Gamble in 2000, the company was a powerhouse. Founded in 1837, P&G created national advertising, the soap opera, and brand management. It was a house of big brands, including Tide, Folgers, Cascade, Pampers, and Swiffer. Its managers were wooed by corporate America and many went on to greatness: Jeffrey Immelt to GE, W. James McNerney Jr. to 3M, Meg Whitman to eBay, Steven Case to AOL Time Warner, and Steve Ballmer to Microsoft.

But the new CEO was not happy. Lafley believed his company was a little slow, insular, and self-congratulatory. He wanted to reinvent P&G for the twenty-first century. "Speed and agility," he said, "matter more than heft."[36]

And this is why a couple years ago Lafley made a pilgrimage to Venezuela. He climbed a steep set of concrete stairs to a cramped apartment to interview homemaker Maria Yolanda Rios. As the *Wall Street Journal* reported, "For an hour, Mr. Lafley sat in the corner of Mrs. Rios' kitchen, where bright yellow paint peeled off the wall, and listened to the young mother. [Rios produced] 31 bottles of cream, lotion, shampoo and perfume and placed them on the embroidered tablecloth. She has two lotions for her feet, one for her body, one for her hands and another for her face. 'It's her entertainment.' Mr. Lafley said."[37]

It was a telling moment for American capitalism. Lafley was saying, in effect, "These creams and lotions are not what we say they are. They're whatever Mrs. Rios says they are. If she treats them as 'entertainment,' we must treat them as entertainment. Let's stop listening for what we want to hear." The most powerful man in this most powerful company was saying, "It's not about us. It's about her."[38]

Lafley is insisting the corporation take the larger view. In his recent book, *The Game Changer*, Lafley wrote, "P&G needed to look at consumers more broadly. It tended to narrow in on only one aspect of the consumer—for example, their mouth for oral-care products, their hair for shampoo, their loads of dirty clothes and their washing machines for laundry detergents."[39]

Lafley disliked the way this approach "extracted" the consumer out of her life, focusing P&G on what was important to the company, not the consumer. Lafley said, in effect, *See the whole person.* "P&G has since learned to understand and appreciate her and her life—how busy she is; her job responsibilities; the role she plays for her children, husband, and other family members; and her personal and family aspirations and dreams."[40]

This is the role of CCO, to dolly back far enough to see the consumer in her life, in her culture.

Actually, CCOs move in two directions. They go *inward* toward the consumer more than anyone else in the C-suite. They come to know what these lives feel like to live. But CCOs also move *outward* to capture the bigger picture. Dolly up. Dolly back.

Wieden discovered new ideas of fitness; Jensen, new ideas of media; Bogusky, new ideas of hipness. But what Lafley was proposing in his "Venezuelan discovery" was something more fundamental: Go. Ask. Forget what you know, and listen. It's not about us, it's about Mrs. Rios. And once you find her, pull back and capture the whole of her world.

SILVIA LAGNADO FOR DOVE

Sometimes the work of the unofficial CCO is not to discover culture, but to help create it. Thus did Silvia Lagnado and Unilever create the Dove "Campaign for Real Beauty."

Unilever is another juggernaut in the world of marketing. It is a transnational enterprise, operating on all continents, active in India, Africa, Latin America, and Southeast Asia. Long before it become fashionable to talk about a global economy, Unilever—part English, part Dutch—was active just about everywhere.

Dove was a "beauty bar," competing with Ivory, Jergens, and Nivea. It promised to make women more beautiful by moisturizing their skin. No mysteries here, surely. What could be more obvious than beauty?

Still, Unilever decided to take a look. The global brand director for Dove was Silvia Lagnado. Her first discovery was unsurprising. "Young, white, blonde, and slim" were the almost universal characteristics of women portrayed in advertising. Lagnado's next discovery was still more interesting. Only 2 percent of respondents in a worldwide study believed themselves to be beautiful.[41] Perhaps "beauty" was not so obvious after all. Indeed, the closer Dove looked, the more it detected what Harvard Business School professor John Deighton calls a "current of deep discontent."[42]

Unilever was doing its cultural due diligence. What did the consumer mean by "beauty"? Apparently a massive social change was under way. The old definitions (young, white, blonde, and slim) were being challenged. Many marketers would have done the safe thing and stickhandled their way around the problem. ("Let's emphasize health instead of beauty.") Dove took a more direct approach: to "broaden [the very] definition of beauty." Less formally, the Dove team was now saying, "Our notion of beauty is not elitist. It is celebratory, inclusive, and democratic."[43]

It turned out that a broader idea of beauty had many friends. Feminists had long disputed the power of taste elites and fashion magazines. As America became more inclusive in matters of race and ethnicity, the old ideas of beauty were clearly too narrow. Parents were alarmed at the rising incidence of bulimia, anorexia, social anxiety, and teen bullying. They wondered if new ideas of beauty might help here. Virtually everyone thought it was wrong that only 2 percent of women thought they were beautiful when evidently so many women were beautiful. (No one was consulting men on the issue, but clearly this is where they stood.)

Dove worked to mobilize these currents of opinion. The company hired the British photographer John Rankin Waddell to create billboards of ordinary women. Passersby were asked whether models were "outsized" or "outstanding." Dove did a series of ads featuring women in plain white underwear. They were not only larger than the average model but much more cheerful. The Dove team quizzed their own daughters about beauty. This produced an ad in which a young girl with freckles was shown with the caption, "Hates her freckles." Perhaps most notably, Dove offered an ad called "Evolution" showing all the ways a model was retouched to make her glamorous.

Dove had discovered a "blue ocean." This is what business scholars W. Chan Kim and Renee Mauborgne call new markets that are relatively undiscovered and free of competition.[44] What's odd is that *this* blue ocean has been with us at least since the 1980s, undetected by marketers; that is to say, for nearly a quarter century. Twenty-five years and no one noticed. Better late than never, of course, and by 2006, the results of Lagnado's discovery were in. The world lavished sales and awards on Dove. Unilever was galvanized. Dove was named one of the ten brands with the greatest growth in the past three years.[45] The "Campaign for Real Beauty" had worked.

CHRIS ALBRECHT FOR HBO

Home Box Office began as a pay channel in the 1970s. Based in Wilkes-Barre, Pennsylvania, it featured boxing and post-release theatrical films. Things began to change in 1995 with the arrival of Jeff Bewkes and Chris Albrecht, CEO and president of programming, respectively. Within a decade, HBO had transformed television. *Sex and the City*, *The Sopranos*, and *Six Feet Under* changed just about everything, including pop culture. At the 2004 Emmy awards, HBO received 124 nominations and 32 awards.[46]

If anyone can claim to have mastered culture, it was Albrecht and Bewkes. But when Albrecht was asked for the secret of their success, his reply was odd.

"We ask ourselves, 'Is it different? Is it distinctive? Is it *good*?' Ultimately, we ask ourselves, 'Is it *about* something?' By 'about something' I mean not just the subject, or the arena, or the location, but really about something that is deeply relevant to the human experience. *The Sopranos* isn't about a mob boss on Prozac. It's about a man searching for the meaning of his life."[47]

Not to be a spoilsport, but *The Sopranos is* about a mob boss on Prozac. Albrecht's account is too general. "Different," "distinctive," "good," and "relevant"—these are the qualities of *everything* exemplary. The HBO secret remains a secret—even from its creators.

A CCO could have given us a more informed account—and a more useful one. *The Sopranos* exploited an emerging convention in American culture. Crime and criminals had been a constant interest in popular culture. But the new mafia genre made crime spectacular. In the hands of Francis Ford Coppola, Martin Scorsese, and Brian De Palma, it became more complex and grand than in the gangster and noir genres.[48] These directors gave us big emotional gestures, beautiful tailoring, male vanity, and operatic violence, even as they fought against type. Michael Corleone was the reluctant gangster in *The Godfather* (1972), Henry Hill was the outsider's outsider in *Goodfellas* (1990), David Chase's Tony Soprano was riddled with anxiety, obliged to rely on Prozac to fight his war on panic.

When asked how he made HBO a success, Chris Albrecht might have said, "Well, we like to take a movie genre and play around with it, especially when we have a precedent, as we did in the case of *The Sopranos*."[49]

HBO looked for innovation everywhere. *Sex and the City* asked what life would be like if women acted like men, treating sex recreationally, partners casually, and footwear with deep respect.[50] The show used a simple transposition, taking the rules from one domain (men) and transferring them to another (women). Like *The Sopranos, Sex and the City* was an experiment in genre busting. Albrecht's answer might have been, "We like to take the rules from one world and apply them to another. We get something familiar from the old, something fresh from the new, and a frisson when the two come together."

But in fact HBO's creative model was just plain puzzling. In 1995 Jeff Bewkes said that the mission was "to jump fully off this cliff . . . It was a real mess. But we just said, 'Forget about it—let's just do great stuff and we'll solve it later.'"[51]

HBO didn't have a plan. It didn't seem to have a model of what was wrong with existing TV or how it was innovating. This made the innovation reckless and undue. When asked how HBO intended to duplicate its extraordinary accomplishments, Albrecht said,

> We have to be more aggressive and take bigger risks than before. We're actively looking for new cliffs to jump off. We're doing things nobody else will do, because they can't chase us into those spaces. We didn't get here by playing by the rules of the game. We got here by setting the rules of the game.[52]

Albrecht's "rule" was blind abandon, as if he couldn't divine the system of his success. He speaks like a man on the run ("aggressive," "risks," "cliff," "jump," "chase"). The secret of success is not "bigger risks." It is to harvest error, to take new risks more strategically. The motto of tech guru Esther Dyson captures the prevailing managerial wisdom nicely: "Always make new mistakes."[53] Taking risks *because they are risks* is an abdication of managerial responsibility.

Management can't be Darwinian. It's not a random evolutionary walk, searching for good options by exploring all bad ones. The point of management is choice. And the point of a Chief Culture Officer is to factor culture into choice. And in the case of programming television, culture is just about everything.

We have opened up a mystery of our own. If Albrecht and Bewkes had no secret system, how did they manage to choose so well so often? I believe the answer comes from Albrecht's commitment to two things: being true to the idea, and being true to the creator.[54] When David Chase said that *The Sopranos* had to be shot in New Jersey, Albrecht consented. This was his way of being true to the idea *and* the creator. Shooting in New Jersey gave the show access to things that could not be found or fabricated in Hollywood. It was a way to get the details right. Most of all, it was a way to escape that "good enough for TV" mentality. (And it puts Albrecht in the tradition of producers and writers like Norman Lear, Steven Bochco, David Milch, Bruce Paltrow, Mark Tinker, Paul Attanasio, Tom Fontana, and David Simon.)

In 1961, Newton Minow said TV was a wasteland.[55] Forty years later, Albrecht and Bewkes made the wasteland bloom. With *The Wire, Flight of the Conchords*, and *Entourage*, HBO continues to turn out TV that wins audiences and critical praise. But some recent productions have disappointed on one score or both: *John from Cincinnati, Rome, Deadwood, Big Love*.

A CCO with a systematic idea (instead of a deep intuition) could help pick the winners and avoid losers, or at least look before leaping.

MILTON GLASER FOR NEW YORK CITY

In the 1970s, New York City was in trouble. The economy was foundering. Residents and companies were fleeing the city. The tax base was crumbling and budgets were bankrupt. Deinstitutionalization had released mentally ill people into the streets. Drug addiction was high. Murder rates were skyrocketing. During the blackout of 1977, there was heavy looting and civil unrest. New York City looked to some people like a city in "irreversible decline."[56]

The assistant commissioner of commerce for New York state, Bill Doyle, decided to do something. He hired Milton Glaser. The idea, Glaser recalls, was to create a new campaign to encourage tourism and raise residents' spirits. Glaser created "I ♥ New York," one of the most successful and duplicated pieces of design in the twentieth century. In fact, "it has become so much a part of the general language [of design] that it's hard to imagine that it was actually designed by someone and did not always exist."[57]

Why was "I ♥ New York" effective? It wasn't because it was beautiful. A student of the Italian painter Morandi, Glaser has done beautiful work, but "I ♥ New York" was plain. And it wasn't because it was "designerly." Glaser has pushed the boundary of his discipline, but his "I ♥ New York" was unassuming. Some design reroutes our admiration from the design to the designer. But here Glaser takes nothing for himself. "I ♥ New York" is so humble that it looks, as he says, like it wasn't designed by anyone.[58]

"I ♥ New York" had its work cut out for it. For New York truly was a city caught in a downward spiral. New Yorkers were withdrawing from the contract that made the city practicable, from the very idea that made it conceivable. Some were so miserable they were actually moving to Connecticut. What was needed was what the information processing theorists call an "interrupt," the moment when our workaday perception stops and we are forced to reassess the world and the assumptions with which we understand it.

"I ♥ New York" forced an interrupt. On first sight, it was anomalous, a sentence with a hole in the middle. To read this sentence takes a special act of information processing. We say the first word but we're forced to *see* the second word. The sentence starts with language and converts without warning into image and then, whoops, returns to language again. It loops the loop.

What does ♥ stand for? Our first guess is "emotion." We say the heart is the organ of feeling. But we don't *think* feeling. We feel feeling. "I ♥ New York" didn't merely say we *love* New York. No, it said, we ♥ New York. And that's something more. "I ♥ New York" says our feeling for the city is foundational. As another order of experience, we need to retrieve it from another place in memory . . . What we felt for New York was ineffable. Plain old "love" wasn't going to do it.

Built into this was another act of cunning. Glaser could have represented "love" with any number of icons, but he chose a corny icon, the ♥. He used the symbolic language of the sailor's tattoo, the kid's drawing, the Mother's Day card, the valentine, and those people who, charmingly, declare their undying affection in that least stable of media, sand on the shore. This heart evoked the most populist face of New York, the crowd-pleasing, democratic, Times Square, Coney Island, "give me your huddled masses" New York. Clever Glaser. Only something as corny and foundational as this would arm New Yorkers against the horror of 1970s New York. Glaser had found a way to move them to say, "Verily, this city is a shit box, but after all is said and done, I ♥ it."

"I ♥ New York" skips media, from language into form, and the form is an icon, and the icon comes from popular culture and the most democratic face of a very democratic city. It forces us to move from language to the heart and from heart to emotion, from any emotion to a deep emotion, from this deep emotion to a feeling so grounded that it could survive even those moments when the city subjected us to chaos, danger, and a crazy person screaming at us on the Upper West Side. "I ♥ New York" wasn't ordinary or workaday meaning management. It wasn't "brand building." It was design triage. It was rescue. And here we may think of Glaser as Superman, speeding to catch up to a falling city, putting his shoulder to the thing, forcing it to stop, bringing it about.

Eventually, New York City would need many additional things to repair itself. It would take a City Hall with new heart and will. It would take mayors as skilled as Rudy Giuliani and Michael Bloomberg. It would take a return tide of investment, people, and confidence. It would take new prosperity, new policies, and new communication campaigns.[59] But none of this was possible if the city's consensus was damaged. This is where design, designers, and a CCO managed to intervene.

How did Glaser do it? What could we learn from him? He says he can't tell us. He says, "Why and how this ever came about is a mystery to me."[60] Right, sure! A guy as smart as this?

Please. One of the first orders of business: Let us decode and capture the genius of Milton Glaser.

BEYOND STEALTH

Lots of people act as stealth CEOs in the corporation. The work they do shows a deep mastery of our culture. There is a lot to know here. I am concerned that some readers will say, "Yes, actually, way too much. I can't learn all this. This world is unmanageably large."

But how can it not be large? The world of culture is a vast mansion of knowledge containing wings upon wings, rooms within rooms. Unmanageable? No. But it does call for a deep and lifelong dedication to knowledge.

No one thinks that finance should be easy. This is precisely why we appoint a CFO and look to her to keep us in touch with everything the corporation needs to know about its financial affairs. No one thinks information technology is simple, which is why we have a CIO, our expert in the field. So it is with the CCO. Culture is a large, complex, and dynamic body of understanding. And this is why we have a CCO.

The alternatives are unappealing. Rely upon a virtuoso? When the head of the advertising firm BBH, Sir John Hegarty, was asked, "What exactly is good creative judgment?" he replied, "You are talking essentially about taste . . . And you can't teach taste."[61] This is what every virtuoso wants us to believe: that culture is a mystery . . . and that the guru is indispensable.

Forgive me, but this is self-serving nonsense. It's the way the virtuosos perpetuate our dependency upon them. In point of fact, we *can* know what culture is and how culture works. Even in the case of HBO, we can peer into the product offering and begin to see what made HBO so very successful. We cannot afford to buy the lie that it's all about "taste" "intuition," or "genius." This knowledge is knowable.

External consultants are a little more forthcoming. They can give us the why and the how of their analysis. But the larger question remains: Should the corporation trust so important a body of knowledge, intelligence, and strategy to a traveling salesman with an attention deficit disorder? We need someone with an enduring knowledge of our culture and our corporation. We need a Mary Minnick who gets the Coke proposition absolutely even as she understands everything else that is taking place in the world. Surely this is too important to be left to outsiders.

The CCO matters for another reason. Without him or her, the corporation is vulnerable to passing fads and fashions, the "stunt" ideas of business literature. The next big business book says it's all "memes." That we need to "go viral." Neural nets! Widgets! Web 2.0! Brand virus! Too often in matters of culture, the corporation is driven by the idea of the moment, as if intellectual churn will somehow help the corporation plot a better course. But of course the result is navigational zigzag.

We need someone on the inside who can canvass these new ideas, separate the wheat from the chaff, and choose what if anything the corporation shall use. Marketing is not a Pachinko machine. People like Geoffrey Frost find a way to save their corporations with exactly the right insight at precisely the right time. The CCO is a profession like others—lawyer, doctor, strategist—a person who thinks long and hard and systematically, considers options, explores alternatives, and makes careful choices. The corporation mustn't gimmick, stunt, or trick its way to market share. Stunts are for Steve-O, not serious, gifted professionals.

CHAPTER 3

CULTURE FAST AND SLOW

IT WAS THE LATE '80S. I WAS SITTING AT MY DESK, WORKING away, minding my own business. A junior academic living in obscurity. An ink-stained wretch hoping for tenure. Think someone out of Dickens . . . with a Canadian accent, eh. My life was about to change.

The phone rang. It was Amy from Harpo Productions in Chicago. Amy wanted to talk about my work on homeyness. We chatted for a while. And that was that.[1]

A week or so later, Amy called again. Would I like to come on the show and talk about my work? I said, "Sure, I would."

Nothing happens in the academic world without the knowledge and approval of the department secretary. I took my news to Barbara.

"Oprah Winfrey?" she asked with reverence.

I nodded.

"You?" she said dubiously.

Barbara made further inquiries.

"On the *Oprah Winfrey Show*?"

"In *Chicago*?"

"On *television*?"

I nodded. Barbara's eyes narrowed. Something was wrong with the universe.

I arrived at O'Hare airport on the appointed day. I'd been told where to look for the Harpo Productions limo, and sure enough, there it was, purring curbside. I stepped inside expecting to have the car to myself, and I was surprised to find someone in place: a woman dressed all in blue. She was wearing a blue Chanel suit with matching stockings. The suit had piping around the jacket and over the pockets, and her hair was pulled back in the socialite manner, held by a little black bow.

A look of instantaneous dislike passed between us. Conversation inched forward. It turned out that the woman in blue was the other expert to appear on the show. She was a New York designer and the author of a recent book on design in the home. As I recall, she said something like, "My publisher has printed an extra 50,000 copies of my book. What about you?"[2]

I had no book and no publisher. I had a photocopy of my academic essay.

"Oh, you know, we're talking about it," I lied shamelessly.

We made our way to a Chicago suburb and stopped in front of an attractive middle-class home. Taping commenced.

The first shot took place on the outside, to show the "experts" entering the home. We were supposed to climb the stairs, hit the doorway, look to the camera, and say, "Hi, Oprah. We're here at the home of the Sullivans, and we're going inside to take a look around!"

The blue-suited woman dispatched the task effortlessly. She hit her mark, dispatched her line, and the producer said, "Perfect. You're a doll."

My turn came. Repeatedly.

"Grant, let's do it once more. But this time could you give it a little more *oomph*?"

I tried a couple more times, but it was clear I was hopeless.

"Can you be more . . . vivid?" the producer asked me.

"Um," I said finally, "you do realize I'm Canadian."

No one thought this was the least bit funny.

The next shot was to capture our reaction to the Sullivan home. The designer strode down the hallway into the kitchen. She said something like, "Well, it's obvious this is a family with no sense of design. None! Look at these curtains. Wrong shape. Wrong size. Wrong color!"

I cast a glance at poor Mrs. Sullivan, who was cowering against a kitchen wall. She was beginning to have doubts of her own. I couldn't watch. I slunk into the living room.

And there were Dan, the father, and Danielle, the daughter, doing what they called the "Pocahontas dance." A couple of days before, they had been to see the Disney movie. Danielle, blonde, sunny, and about six, had "memorized" her own scrambled version of the theme song, and father and daughter, oblivious to the commotion in the kitchen, were now performing it. Dan picked Danielle up, threading her across his shoulders and sliding her back down to the carpet. Danielle sang throughout these exertions, and as she dropped to the carpet, she finished with a joyful flourish.

The designer had swept out of the kitchen and was now, it seemed to me, laying waste to the living room.

She said something like, "Oh, look at this furniture. I mean, really. Everything is pushed to the wall. No sense of *proportion*. *No* sense of placement."

I took this as my cue. I signaled for the camera, and as it swung toward me, I said, "Well, actually, there's a reason the furniture is pushed to the wall. It's to make room for the Pocahontas dance. Would you like to see the Pocahontas dance, Oprah?"

The producer looked around in panic. She spotted Dan and Danielle and cued the cameraman with a desperate, pointing gesture.

Just in time. Dan and Danielle were already exuberantly singing and lifting. It was perfect. Had they known they were going to be performing for national television, the dance might have been anxious or labored. As it was, they were merely sharing a private joy. It was about the sweetest thing you ever saw.

The producer gave me a look of new regard. I might not be good television but I could see what was. The designer, on the other hand, was staring daggers.

We went to a couple of other homes. The designer was predictable. No one in suburban Chicago seemed capable of grasping the simplest precepts laid down by the New York design community. Her job was apparently to mock and diminish. My response was predictable too. I kept suggesting the Sullivan home was something remarkable, that this family had turned 2,000 square feet of concrete and drywall into something happy, homey, and theirs.

The CCO has a core competence: a deep body of knowledge and a strategic feeling for how to apply this knowledge. The designer and I were talking about two kinds of culture. She was talking about fast. I was talking about slow. Both matter to the CCO, but fast culture gets the lion's share of our attention. It is so much more visible, vivid, obvious, and, yes, fashionable. Slow culture plays the country cousin, less interesting, less fashionable. It is punished with neglect. Think of it this way: Fast culture is like all the boats on the surface of the Pacific. We can spot them, number them, track them. Slow culture is everything beneath the surface: less well charted, much less visible. Slow culture is the lesser known half of the CCO competence. But it is equally important.

Homeyness is slow culture. It consists in a set of rules. It specifies our choice of colors, materials, furniture, decorative objects, arrangement, interior design, and exterior characteristics. It is the way we take an ordinary space and give it extraordinary powers. It shows us how to turn a house into a home. It is an enduring, deep-seated aspect of our culture. To find it we have to root it out. We have to visit the home and ask the consumer to talk about it.[3]

As a part of slow culture, though, homeyness gets scant attention. It is too sentimental to interest the designer. (All those doilies, antimacassars, throw rugs, and fridge magnets.) There is no breaking story here, so it doesn't capture the attention of the journalist. Because homeyness is so stubbornly behind the trend, it doesn't interest the cool-hunter or the trend watcher. Even academics have been slow to take a look, and they are puzzled when they do.[4] As slow culture, homeyness is everywhere in our midst and, apparently, everywhere invisible. It shapes Americans' lives but stays below the radar of American experts.

Pity the CCO who ignores it. It is often homeyness that helps decide whether consumers will embrace a new product, how they will use it, what they will use it for, and whether this proves a "keeper" for any given American household. When we follow A. G. Lafley's injunction and dolly back to see the consumer in her or his full complexity, it is often homeyness that comes swimming into view. "Homeyness" is the secret, the very code, of domestic life in America. Get at *this* and we can grasp family life, what a "mother" and a "wife" is, what a "father" and a "husband" is, how the budget is apportioned, and, perhaps most important, why some brands and innovations resonate for the family and others bounce off. (Homeyness can even explain the Pocahontas dance.)

It is topics like homeyness that separate the CCOs who are moved by genuine curiosity about their culture, from those who are merely in it for the really stylish eyewear. There is nothing in homeyness that will make you look hipper to your friends. There is nothing here you can drop into conversation at a party. There is no knowledge here that really works as social capital. No, the CCO wants to know about homeyness because it is part of American culture and that's his job.

I was in Charlotte, North Carolina, in late 2008, and my taxi driver had a copy of *Common American Phrases in Everyday Contexts: A Detailed Guide to Real-Life Conversation and Small Talk.*[5] I paged through it on the way to the airport and thought, "This is a book I have to have." Here are a couple of outtakes.

> You bet your life.
> That's the last straw.
> You make me laugh (never said by someone
> who is laughing).
> Shake the lead out.
> I need a change of scenery.

We know these phrases. We "get" them immediately. But they depend on cultural knowledge. If we were recently arrived from Gambia, struggling to learn American English and hearing these phrases for the first time, we would find them strange. ("I bet my what?") We could call this the Ziva effect, after the character on the TV show *NCIS*. As a trained Israeli assassin, Ziva is smart, beautiful, and dangerous, but when speaking English, she gets the little phrases wrong. She retrieves them from their familiarity and suddenly they are slow culture made visible.

Now consider these:

See you!
I've changed my mind.
Come back anytime.
Care to dance?

Our first reaction is to say, "These don't demand a special knowledge. If we know the terms, we get the meaning." Really? Look again and imagine yourself a taxi driver from Gambia. Culture operates here. We must supply a deeper, slower knowledge to understand these phrases.

Culture supplies us with knowledge we don't know we know, that operates invisibly to shape our understanding of the world. Slow culture is especially hard to see. The CCO who knows only fast culture is just another kind of cool-hunter. American culture is imperfectly and incompletely mapped but there is great scholarship on which to draw. Rutgers sociologist Eviatar Zerubavel gives us a sense of how we organize our cultural categories. English anthropologist Kate Fox explores the rules of interaction. Cornell University French literature professor Richard Klein gives us a brilliant study of how smoking and tobacco insinuated themselves into our culture. (Although smoking and tobacco are ending as a cultural preoccupation, why and how they were important still matters.) Professors George Lakoff and Mark Johnson examine our metaphors. Historian Richard Huber studies our idea of success.[6] Some scholars have made themselves very useful. But the CCO often will have to do his or her own work. This will take Lafley-like excursion into people's homes, to patiently listen for a long while. The CCO has years of ethnographic work in view.

Clever Oprah. When her production staff teamed the anthropologist with the designer, a perfect contrast was created. In the designer, they discovered an expert on the fast culture that shapes the American home. In the anthropologist, they discovered an expert in the slow culture at work there. Out of the tension came a show.

FAST CULTURE

Alvin Toffler published *Future Shock* in 1970. Change, he said, was changing. He wrote, "We have not merely extended the scope and scale of change, we have radically altered its pace. We have in our time released a totally new social force—a stream of change so accelerated that it influences our sense of time, revolutionizes the tempo of daily life and affects the way we 'feel' the world around us."[7]

The decade that followed the publication of *Future Shock* served as proof of its argument. In 1970, China was a socialist economy with Mao Tse-tung at its head. The Soviet Empire stood impregnable. Iran was a pro-Western monarchy. No woman had served as the elected head of a Western government in the twentieth century. By the end of the '70s, Mao was dead and his regime repudiated. Russia was in crisis. Iran was an anti-Western republic. By 1980, eight women had been elected heads of government. Yes, change seemed to be accelerating.

When it came to technology, Toffler might as well have fired a starter's pistol. Intel released its first microprocessor in 1971.

Cray, the maker of supercomputers, was founded in 1972. Magnavox released its first video game console in 1972. Home computers appeared suddenly from Apple, Atari, and Commodore. Philips produced the VCR. Fiber optics came from Corning Glass. Bell Labs installed the first commercial cellular network. In ten years, computing went from big business to small desktops.

In 1970, the family sitcom (*The Brady Bunch*), the western (*Bonanza*), and the variety show (*Ed Sullivan*) were all fixtures of popular culture. By the end of the decade, they were gone, dislodged by an independent film sensibility shaped by the films *Easy Rider*, *M*A*S*H*, and *The Godfather*. The big three TV networks, once the only game in town, now shared the airwaves with cable, specifically MTV and HBO. Comedians went from punch lines to improv. In ten years, popular culture went from a place of mainstream entertainment to something more various and complex.[8]

As if feverishly trying to prove the truth of Toffler's argument, the world was speeding up. It was decentering. It was multiplying. It was churning. And, yes, it was shocking.

But of course the '70s were just the prelude. In the next thirty years (1980 to the present), the "scope and scale of change" has become unimaginable. In American cities, Main Street was dismantled by the big-box "category killers" like Wal-Mart and Home Depot. Digital technologies rewired banking, retail, and entertainment. Scientific research has increased by 40 percent since 1988, and the conversion from science to technology is happening faster. The World Intellectual Property Organization says that from 1997 to 2002, the number of patent applications went from 680 to 5,359, an increase of almost 700 percent.[9] The Internet, circulating 93,000 terabytes of data at any given moment, opened new worlds of content, knowledge, and opinion.[10]

Computer games like Halo and virtual worlds like Second Life literally created new worlds. Social networks like MySpace and Facebook changed the very nature of the social group.

On the economic side, there was still more turmoil. In the words of financial journalist Harris Collingwood, "Idiosyncratic volatility is the signature of our economic age."[11] President Ronald Reagan's reduction of government spending and control added a new dynamism to local and international economies. There was a huge run-up in the creation of value in the dot-com economy, and NASDAQ broke 5100. The roller-coaster ride continued with a sudden collapse in the spring of 2000. NASDAQ lost 500 points in five days. More recently, the real estate market has seen a great ascent and decline. Venerable financial institutions, the great foundational suppliers of capital and advice, have actually disappeared. Wachovia, Merrill Lynch, and Lehman Brothers, as independent organizations, are no more. At this writing, the auto industry is flirting with bankruptcy. Only massive government intervention has stabilized the economy.

Taste and preference, as the economists like to call them, are in a spin. Fast food slowed down. McDonald's started stocking salads. Processed food fell more and more from fashion. People stopped smoking in droves. (Forty years ago, 40 percent of Americans smoked.) Omega-3, soy, and more fiber are suddenly in everything. It became harder and harder to anticipate what audiences wanted. "Television used to provide big-tent programming designed to appeal to a lot of people, with characters and story arcs that would appeal to everyone," says Alan Wurtzel, president for research and media development at NBC. "Now you find audiences are very, very specific."[12]

How fast are things changing? Friendster was founded in 2002, a media darling by 2003, overtaken by MySpace in 2004, falling fast by 2005, and had completely vanished by 2007, managing to run full circle from obscurity back to obscurity in five years. How fast are things changing? Growing up in Hawaii in the 1970s, young Barack Obama saw plenty of racism. And he was struck by how casual, confident, and deeply embedded it was in the world around him. Racist Hawaiians *just knew* Obama was inferior and untrustworthy. A mere forty years later, this "certain" knowledge is a minority opinion. Forty years later, Obama is the forty-forth president of the United States.[13]

If Toffler's remarks were a little hyperbolic in 1970, now they seemed to understate the case. If the future was shocking in 1970, now it was concussive.

Business is alive to the presence and force of this change. We can detect a whiff of anxiety coming off the titles of recent business books: *Faster*, *Blur*, *Out of Control*, *Blown to Bits*, *Fast Forward*, *Speed of Thought*, *The Age of Unreason*, and *Predictably Irrational*.[14] Business thinkers John Hagel, John Seely Brown, Lang Davison, Nassim Nicholas Taleb, Peter Schwartz, and Clayton Christensen ask us to accept disruption and turmoil as the new order of the day.[15] *BusinessWeek* declared the arrival of an "innovation economy."[16] "Creative destruction" went from being an arcane term from a little-known European economist to the title of a book from the head of an American consulting house.[17]

The American corporation rose to the occasion. It made itself more responsive, more creative.[18] It began to downsize, restructure, flatten, delayer, decentralize, outsource, and go global. It became more fluid, more responsive, and more questing, and prepared to reinvent itself continually.[19] But the paradox was inescapable. As the corporation struggled to respond to change, it increased the speed and depth of change. There was no hope of catching up to change. The best the corporation could hope for was to keep it in view.

Culture is a critical part of this change. It is sometimes the cause, as when hip-hop joins us as a kind of music but eventually becomes a style of clothing, masculinity, filmmaking, celebrity, and politics. Culture is sometimes the effect. The rave culture that transformed dance, drugs, and the social experience in the 1990s was driven in part by new technologies. The counterculture of the 1960s was driven in part by a demographic (baby-boomer) tidal wave.

It would be easier for the CCO if culture were a small and discrete player in the world. But culture is hyperactive. Even when not a cause or event, it concatenates so furiously with other factors that no event is culture free. Good luck teasing this apart. The CCO must be good at understanding complexity, because this is the nature of the beast in question.[20]

Fast culture is invasive. Even the "quiet corners" of our culture have let it in. Until quite recently hardware stores were mostly fashion-free. They were staffed by guys called Dave who knew a lot about glue guns and not a thing about fad and fashion. If we wanted white paint, Dave had two choices (really white and not so white). Now Sherwin-Williams sells over two hundred shades of white, including Dover White, Aesthetic White, and Panda White.[21] (To be honest, Dave's a little hazy on the difference between Dover and Panda.)

Fast culture is obligatory. The cable show *What Not to Wear* feels like a Soviet show trial. Participants are mocked for their old-fashioned choices, obliged to admit the error of their ways, and then publicly repudiate their favorite outfits. Redressed and transformed, they are readmitted to the civilized community. We are unkind to people who don't keep up. "When you walk down the street and catch a glimpse of yourself in a window and say, 'Oh my God, do I really look like that?' Well, you do, and you've got to start paying attention. When people don't change, they become caricatures of themselves."[22]

Fast culture is alarming. As usual, the intellectuals are quick to tell us how dangerous fast culture is. They warn us that change must wear away the foundations of our knowledge of the world. It must overwhelm us with choice. It must confuse and conflict us. But this is what the intellectuals always say, and we must take their advice with a grain of salt.

Fast culture is now the great challenge for the C-suite. Every corporation is like a fishing boat, pitching on high seas, wave after wave crashing through the wheelhouse. Circuit City, recently deceased, failed to take advantage of the "Geek Squad" trend that helped lift competitor Best Buy to greatness. A couple of years before, Best Buy had purchased Musicland, just as kids were using peer-to-peer file-sharing technologies to download their music from the Web.[23] Rupert Murdoch, owner of News Corporation and once a dominant force in the media world, now presides over a cataclysmic loss of share value. Property developers were surprised by the loft condo trend that hit American cities in the 1980s. Some responded; others fell. Some advertising agencies grasped what TiVo meant for their business model; others will never catch up.

Fast culture has many origins and the CCO must monitor them all. New cultural developments can come from the worlds of cuisine, sports, music, fashion, moviemaking, Web sites, and new media. Chefs, point guards, engineers, indie bands, Hollywood producers, bloggers, new presidents—any of these can prove a decisive influence. It's a lot to monitor. To make matters trickier still, we can't merely monitor the most famous of these players. The new technologies make it possible for obscure players to punt their influence in from the margin. And all of a sudden, too. (Take a bow, Jimmy Wales, founder of Wikipedia, Craig Newmark, founder of Craigslist, and Arianna Huffington, founder of the Huffington Post.)

Fast culture is a blessing and a curse. It can open up "blue oceans" of opportunity.[24] It can deliver "game-changing" developments.[25] But it also delivers blind-side hits. The CCO who can manage fast culture can earn her income for the year by lunchtime . . . every day.

DISPERSIVE CULTURE

A couple decades ago, our culture seemed to lose its center of gravity and began to run off in all directions. It became dispersive. There were more ideas, more people creating ideas, more ways of living life, more points of view. The real diversity of contemporary culture was not race or gender. It was this and everything else. The center would not hold.

When we were contemplating options for the subtitle for this book, I devised this list:

> synchronized swimming, Target, Simon Cowell, Facebook, Bryan Singer, Chinese soft drinks, Grammys, *SNL*, YouTube, Gucci, Wikipedia, Jeff Koons, Apple, Kanye West, Hulu, Francis Bacon, South by Southwest, Mizrahi, TypePad, Heath Ledger, Nike, Karim Rashid, Josh Friedman, Agent Dinozzo, Manolo Blahnik, *Veronica Mars*, *Arrested Development*, Lil Wayne, Coen brothers, *Heroes*, Hollywood Hills, Tina Fey, reality TV, *Chuck*, Frank Gehry, Claire Bennett, FriendFeed, mashable, Thievery

> Corporation, Twitter, tagging, Henry Jenkins, Milton Glaser, *Monk*, Last.fm, Second Life, Cherry ChapStick, Hannah Montana, *Dexter*, David Simon, Panic at the Disco, iPhone, Xbox, Shoegazers, Andy Samberg, Joss Whedon, *Ellen*, anime, hip-hop, Ollie, cut-and-paste culture, *Entertainment Weekly*, Matador Records, Tim Gunn, Yahoo, Damien Hirst, Audrey Hepburn, IDEO, Ashton Kutcher, *Twilight*, synchronous, SMS, Bollywood, Mickey Rourke, Christopher Guest, Ownage, MMORPG, Rasta man, red vs. blue.

It's a noisy list that names brands, actors, architects, designers, musicians, academics, writers, producers, computer games, fictional characters, generic categories, and slang terms. But the real noise comes from the sheer cultural diversity encompassed here. It is hard to imagine that a single culture can produce Frank Gehry and Hannah Montana, a *Monk* and a *Dexter*, a Damien Hirst and an Audrey Hepburn, an Ashton Kutcher and a Tim Gunn. They are so different that they appear to come from mutually exclusive worlds. Or here's a simpler example. Chances are, dear reader, you use e-mail and the Internet daily. But one in five Americans has never sent an e-mail.[26] We can't imagine their lives. They can't imagine our lives. Ours is a dispersive culture.

In the late 1980s, I did research on teens.[27] I was preparing an exhibit on popular culture for the Royal Ontario Museum and it seemed like a good place to start. My first efforts were sad. As an ardent TV viewer, I expected, vaguely, to find myself talking to the likes of Alex P. Keaton, the character played by Michael J. Fox on the 1982 NBC series *Family Ties*. I was wrong. By 1990, Alex P. Keaton existed only on TV.[28] The "preppy" teen was disappearing. In his place was a world teeming with diversity. I went to the mall and asked a local teen to help identify the new species of social life.

"So what's he?" I asked.

"Ah, he's a rocker. You know, heavy metal music."

"And him?"

"He's kind of a surfer-skater kind of guy."

"And those girls?"

"Oh, man, those are b-girls."

"What about her . . . and her?"

My informant turned to gaze at me in wonder that anyone could be so thoroughly stupid.

"She's a goth and that's a punk."[29]

By the time I had finished the study, I could manage without a "seeing eye" companion. There were some fifteen types of teen. Nothing in my experience as a teen, nothing in the academic literature, had prepared me for this. The category "teen" is itself a relatively recent invention, and for a long time it was structurally simple, containing few options. In the 1950s, for instance, there were only two categories of teen. As one of our respondents put it, "When I was sixteen, you could be mainstream or James Dean. That was it. You had to choose."[30] Without much fanfare, things got more complicated.

We are not just talking about surface variety. These are differences with depth. As I began to talk to b-girls, goths, punks, and skaters, I found myself listening to different values, outlooks, and points of view.[31]

I continued to look in on teen culture during the 1990s, and something interesting was happening. Kids were now joining not one but several groups. Sometimes they would be a goth and sometimes a Rasta man. Multiple memberships were now possible, and it seemed right to think of kids as ships that could up and change their port of call at will (or whim). In my day, you signed onto a single group and you gave it your undying loyalty. At least for a year or two. I went from being a cliquer to a hippie, a shift that consumed the whole of my adolescence.

As we enter the new century, we can see yet another change. Kids do not have multiple memberships so much as multiple selves. They are many people bundled into one. And now we can't tell very much about them from the way they dress. Now they belong to networks (we'll discuss those soon), and this is the new locus of the self. These kids are distributed across social worlds and cultural worlds. The days of a defining social group are gone. The days of fixed membership are gone. Indeed, the very idea of a generation may well be over. It was once possible to talk about boomers and Gen Xers. These were messy categories but useful generalizations. Millennials, the tag most often given Generation Y, sometimes looks like an empty generalization and is not very useful at all.[32]

Everywhere we look we see this kind of multiplication. Not just among the young, but at the other end of the age spectrum where there appears to be a quiet revolution among the elderly. Many resist the stereotypes. People who were once obliged to give up their selfhood as they crossed the threshold of seventy now insist on taking it with them as they go.[33] There may come a time when "old" people will be as diverse and heterogeneous as those of middle age.[34] One told me, "I want to live for myself and not worry quite so much what the neighbors think." Indeed, it is possible that the last years of life may offer new opportunities for self-exploration. In the words of Florida Scott-Maxwell, "Near the end of my life I am myself as never before."[35]

We are a mere century removed from the Victorians. The world that existed one hundred years ago was vertical, divided into groups, defined by class, controlled by orthodoxy and elites—political, religious, and social. At some point in the intervening period, we managed to throw off virtually all these properties.

This plenitude is driven by a hundred little engines. We have more people engaged in creating culture. There are lots of people starting bands, writing scripts, shooting movies, turning out blogs. Let's say the ratio of culture producer to culture consumer was once 1 in 10,000. It is now more like 1 in 100. Many of the new producers are working "without supervision." They are not answerable to studios or editors or critics. They are not aiming for mainstream participation. They do not need to make compromises. Our culture is dispersing because many more people are making it with more technologies out of new motives and with much less constraint.[36]

The symptoms of a dispersive culture are everywhere around us. The social and lifestyle typologies are breaking down. We have seen a steadily inflation of categories. Nine was plenty. Then twelve were called for. And then people just gave up. No typology could capture all the things we were. Award shows are changing. Where once there were a handful of genres, now there are many. There are now forty-eight subgenres of the electronic genre alone.[37] Jon Pareles, the *New York Times*'s chief music critic, says the Grammys "continue to add [award] categories for more niches and subgenres in a delightfully futile quest that's something like mapping an amoeba."[38]

This shift in culture forces a shift in commerce. Chris Anderson, the editor of *Wired*, tells us that we are now dealing with a long tail as we move from mass markets to many little ones. And Swarthmore College author Barry Schwartz believes that more choice makes us less happy. The great new pipelines of commerce—eBay, Amazon, Craigslist, Netflix, and iTunes—are compelling commercial propositions because we live in a culture so thoroughly dispersed. The dispersive effects of technology are only just beginning, as Internet gurus Clay Shirky, David Weinberger, and Don Tapscott have warned us.[39]

The Public Broadcasting Service is a network of stations spread across the United States. There are five big stations that produce most of the content for the system. (WGBH in Boston is one.) And there are around 350 little stations whose job is to broadcast this content. This is pretty much what our culture looked like until about fifteen years ago. There were a few key players, professions, and places, and the rest of us were little stations that didn't produce much of anything. Our job was to pass things along. And then something happened. In the past couple decades, a great transformation took place. It's as if Paula Kerger, president and CEO of PBS, woke up one day in Washington to discover that all her little satellite stations were now producing too.

It is the CCO's job to find a pattern in this chaos. We can assume that dispersion will continue and that it will get worse. The generative engines in our culture will continue to throw off more differences.

CONVERGENT CULTURE

But for all this new variety, there are still moments when a magical consensus will emerge. We decide that for all of our differences, we share a way of seeing the world and defining ourselves. A characteristic style of clothing, language, music, art, and prose springs up. These convergences don't last long but they are interesting when they do. They are fantastic market opportunities, thermals on which to rise.

It's a glorious moment. Suddenly we hear something new and we know the world has changed.

"It's Too Soon to Know" by The Orioles was like Elvis Presley's "That's All Right (Mama)," Aretha Franklin's "I Never Loved a Man (The Way I Love You)," Nirvana's "Smells Like Teen Spirit"—a shock, a dead-in-your-tracks what *is* that?—a sound that was stylistically confusing and emotionally undeniable.[40]

Out of the noise and commotion something comes. Our culture suddenly snaps into a new configuration. A certain kind of music, prose, spoken language, clothing styles travel as one. A tiny but powerful culture is now upon us. It may last a couple of years. It may endure for a decade. But there it is, a moment of consensus. This happens, usually, with each decade, each generation.[41] These convergences are miraculous. And puzzling. How we get from the "disorderly conduct" that is our customary approach (lots of opinions, lots of difference, lots of discordance) to a sudden agreement is not clear. What makes it more puzzling is that we accomplish this consensus without a referendum, explicit discussion, or debate of any kind. Apparently we are all listening all the time. Along comes the right book or video, and we all quietly think, "That could work." And in the blink of an eye, somehow we agree to new marching orders. The good news is that these convergences are scrutable. We can sense them coming. Especially if we are prepared to keep an ear to the ground and to listen for faint signals.

Take the case of the preppy convergence. It's the most recent convergence for which we have full hindsight.

The convergence began to form visibly and publicly around 1980, but if we were well informed, we could have seen it coming ten years before. Doug Kenney founded *National Lampoon* in 1970 with staff from the *Harvard Lampoon*. And we could have tracked the convergence as it began to scale up. *National Lampoon* published parodies of *Newsweek* and *Life*, the *1964 High School Yearbook Parody* (1974), and a well-received issue titled *Buy This Magazine, or We'll Shoot This Dog*. By the end of the 1970s, *Lampoon* circulation had reached nearly a million copies per month. And by this time even the dimmest trend hunter had it on radar.

Sales were one thing. Another clue was the migration of talent. The world started raiding the *Lampoon* community for talent. Kenney left to write movies. Michael O'Donoghue left in 1975 to become head writer for *Saturday Night Live*. Harold Ramis left for *Second City*. P. J. O'Rourke left to write for *Rolling Stone*. The *National Lampoon* spoke with the voice of the ruthless private-school boy. Apparently this was now in demand.

The preppy convergence went to the movies. Kenney created *Animal House* in 1978 and Harold Ramis created *Meatballs* in 1979. The first featured a prep prototype in Tim Matheson; the second, in Bill Murray. The prep also appeared in *Bachelor Party* (1984), played by Tom Hanks. Most famously, the prep turned up in the 1982 NBC series *Family Ties* in the character of Alex P. Keaton. The prep also appeared in the 1982 late-night comedy show in the person of David Letterman, who gave voice to prep form by standing in a window of Rockefeller Center and announcing with a bullhorn, "I'm not wearing any pants."

(Preps loved to be vulgar and clever at the same time. It's a frat thing.)

Everyday language began to vibrate with new phrases: "go for it," "get a life," "get a grip," "snap out of it." These phrases spoke for the new convergence. People were impatient with the old pieties. They were being asked to snap out of their '60s idealism. People were done with that.

Convergences must shake the webs of the publishing world, or they cannot be convergences. One of the bestsellers of the period was Lisa Birnbach's 1980 *The Official Preppy Handbook*. This was two hundred pages of detailed advice on what to wear, where to go to school, what sports to play, what sports to watch, what slang to speak, how to be rude to a salesperson, and how to mix a Bloody Mary. If the *National Lampoon* had supplied the new character of the decade, here were instructions of a much more detailed kind.

The consensus was visible in public life. Suddenly Harvard Yard, never especially presentable in its architecture, appointments, or personnel, filled with glossy teens in down vests, Norwegian sweaters, and Top-Siders, all newly minted by L.L. Bean. Some of them were the children of old money following ancestral footsteps to the Ivy League. But most were kids from Boston University who believed that the Yard was a better lifestyle accessory.

The convergence began to recruit ferociously. A young woman remembers:

> As a teenager [my mom] was pulling *The Preppy Handbook* out from under my [sleeping] cheek. These were the mid-'80s, and I just lapped up all that puppy/yuppie/ J. Crew catalog/Lands' End stuff. I didn't want to live in

> Wisconsin; rather, I wished my parents played tennis and would send me away to Phillips Exeter. In fact, I waged a two-year send-Ann-to-Exeter campaign ("or, hey, Choate would be OK. C'mon, at least consider the University School of Milwaukee!"). I wished we summered on Martha's Vineyard and wore penny loafers without socks. I wanted to ski in Vermont during Christmas vacation like my copy of *The Preppy Handbook* recommended . . . I wanted to live far away from Wisconsin and my family and come home only at Christmas. As pathetic as it sounds, deep in my soul I wished I owned a navy-blue blazer with my school's crest embroidered on the lapel and wore grosgrain ribbons in my hair. I daydreamed about the day when I would go East to college, and I believed I would.[42]

The preppie convergence sold a lot of cars for Chrysler (Jeeps) and, eventually, a lot of SUVs for everyone. It sold clothing for L.L. Bean, Lands' End, J. Crew, Ralph Lauren, and eventually Tommy Hilfiger and the Gap. It sold a lot of furniture for Restoration Hardware, Ethan Allen, and eventually Sears. It sold a lot of watches for Rolex and a lot of cars for BMW. Eventually, it would serve as the foundation for Martha Stewart and her brand of status. It would shape and still shapes what boomers wear on the weekends. Boomers will take this convergence to their grave. It's their look.[43]

Then the tide turned again. Repudiation came on like gangbusters. I remember seeing graffiti on a Tom Cruise movie poster that read, "Die Yuppie scum." Another was Gordon Gecko in *Wall Street* (1987), a film Roger Ebert hailed as a "radical critique of the capitalist trading mentality."[44] The prep hero was now tarnished. (Life soon imitated art, with the fall of Michael Milken, the junk-bond trader indicted in 1989 for violations of federal securities and racketeering laws.) The third repudiation was the movie *Heathers* (1989), in which teens took a terrible revenge against the preps. The fourth was the publication of *American Psycho* in 1991. This was, among other things, a vilification of the prep. At this point, the CCO is fully apprised. The prep convergence is failing fast. But pity us if this is our first warning. CCOs are not allowed to be caught by surprise.

When I was doing research with teens in 1990, almost to a person, they were saying, "Well, I guess you could say I'm a prep, but I don't really think I am." Or, more forcefully, "The last thing I want to be called is a prep." This was coming from kids who were still wearing button-down shirts and Top-Siders. Teens were moving on, some to the emerging subculture of rap, some to a brief revival of the hippie regime; still others were taking an "alternative" turn. We do not have access to this data, but we can assume that sales figures for Ralph Lauren, Rolex, BMW, and the decade's other "flagship" brands fell sharply. Presumably, furniture and textile stores suddenly found it difficult to move their "duck" and "sailboat" motifs. What convergences give, they take away. The prep look lives on at Ralph Lauren and, debased, at Tommy Hilfiger, but it is no longer at the center of things.

Convergence culture is fleeting. But it supplies order, and for the CCO this order is a gift. It is the chance to speak a single language to a very large group. Every convergence culture is a remarkable opportunity, the bluest of oceans. But only if we get there early.

CHAPTER 4

STATUS AND COOL

THE STATUS CONVERGENCE AND THE COOL CONVERGENCE are central for the CCO. They are now foundational parts of our culture, and the great ying and yang of the Western tradition. Both have passed from absolute currency, but they remain active and formative. It's the CCO's job to figure out how they work, and the framework they provide for our understanding of fast and slow culture. Without this framework, we're chasing trends.

STATUS CULTURE

Why do people never live in the living room?[1] They lavish time and money on this room. They agonize over colors, fabrics, drapes, art, and decoration. Then they seal the room away. They might even put up a velvet rope. Or just forbid everyone to go in. Occasionally Bernie, the family Labrador, wanders in. But Labradors don't always grasp the subtleties of American life. What about the rest of us? Why spend money and space on a room we will use only a couple times a year?

The answer is that the living room represents a status message we want to make but don't want to live. Living rooms are designed to show our best choices, our good taste, our feeling for the finer things. And that's the problem. In a room like this, we're obliged to stay "on our best behavior." How very tedious. We would much prefer to be in the kitchen, where we can "just be ourselves."

If we were a CCO in the sixteenth century, status would be the great preoccupation of our professional lives. And this is because status was the great preoccupation of everyone's life. Status was a capital more precious than capital. We know this because the moment people made extra income they turned it into status goods. But status wasn't just about owning the right things. It was also a code that specified how people should speak, whom they should marry, where they should live.[2] Right through the twentieth century, status was the cardinal compass point, the true north, of what people cared about. For the early modern CCO, virtually everything you needed to know about culture was contained in the idea of status.

After World War II, Americans bought clothing, cars, homes, and club memberships with a view to staking status claims. They engaged in competitive spending, in a struggle to change their social standing. And they engaged in emulative spending, to imitate their "betters" in the status system. (The famous photojournalist Margaret Bourke-White shot a series of photos called "High Society in Philadelphia" for *Life* magazine to keep Americans informed of how the "other half" lived.) CCOs of the 1950s watched Americans use their consumption choices to get into the right school, the right club, the right suburb. The car one drove, the scotch one drank—these were determined by status aspirations.

Vance Packard, an influential journalist after World War II, called these Americans "status seekers."[3] The prototypical CCOs monitored status closely. Pierre Martineau studied status in

Chicago. Herbert Gans studied it on Long Island. John Seeley et al. studied it in Toronto. W. Lloyd Warner studied it in Yankee City.[4] Paul Fussell made a good living making fun of American status pretensions.[5] But people secretly bought his *The Class System* to learn about the status code.

All the while, status was actually dying. What used to be a relatively tidy system for ranking people, classes, and consumer goods is now a mess. Classes are hard to identify, and relative status is murky. Take ten of your neighbors, and imagine ranking them. An Elizabethan could do it in his sleep. We're less sure. There are so many different and conflicting grounds to use. We might be able to manage a crude distinction between upper class and lower class. We can distinguish between people who rank very high and very low. But anywhere people cluster, it's quite hard to say.

The French sociologist Pierre Bourdieu thought he had found a way to sort this out. Status, he said, is finally about taste. What one wants, how one chooses, the sophistication evident in one's material world—*this* determines where we stand. Louis Vuitton handbags aren't just there to show income; they are sold as badges of discernment. In France, this may well be true. But in America, taste is in shambles and unclear. Those Americans. So frank.[6]

Once the magnetic north of social aspiration, status is now merely one of the things we care about. Certainly, when the occasion calls for it, we like to think we can stage a persuasive social performance. If need be, we can unrope the living room and treat some high-standing visitor to refined conversation and decorous behavior. But really that's what the living room is for: to say that we *can* do the status thing, not that we *want* to. The CCO needs to know the vanishing status system because you never know when it is going to rear its beautiful head. Status still moves us when it comes to certain kinds of purchases. It matters particularly when it comes to luxury brands, like Chanel, Mercedes, Dior, Burberry, Cartier, Patek Philippe, and, yes, Louis Vuitton. Sometimes status is the wind beneath the wings of a trend. For example, the single-malt scotch trend of the 1990s was driven in part by status consideration, as boomers began to look for a kind of EZ connoisseurship.[7]

What or who demoted status? Part of the problem was that the social elites Bourke-White photographed ceased to act like elites. They bought into American individualism. They came to see the "high society" thing as a threat to their individuality.[8] Besides, American culture wasn't paying them in deference anymore. After the 1960s, elites were scorned as snobs and thereafter admiration was generally "sneaking." There was a brief restoration in the 1980s, as we have seen, but that too has passed. And now it looks as if some people with wealth don't know how to act like elites. It's hard to imagine the likes of Mark Cuban or Donald Trump acting as our social "betters." (Trump may come from second-generation wealth, but that haircut is a dead giveaway. This is a man with no taste.) And there are others with wealth and prestige—Google founders Larry Page and Sergey Brin, say—but by all accounts they couldn't care less about status. Silicon Valley managed to produce vast wealth without producing any kind of social elite.

Our models of admiration have shifted. We care more about celebrities than about social doyens. If *Life* once gave us pictures of polite society, we now read *Vanity Fair*, which gives us photos of Tina Fey, Miley Cyrus, and Bernie Madoff. Celebrity culture has trumped high culture. If once we cared about the affairs of royal families abroad and the Rockefellers at home, now we prefer to follow Brad Pitt and Angelina Jolie. These two are many things, but are they paragons of taste and breeding? We really have no idea.

For some people, culture still means "high culture." This might be defined as what the English critic F. R. Leavis called "the subtlest and most perishable parts of tradition [and] the finer living of an age."[9] It is the kind of culture we absorb through what Matthew Arnold called the "study of perfection" and the pursuit of our "best self."[10] This is culture with a capital "C," represented by elite institutions like museums, ballet companies, symphonies, and art galleries.[11] In its day, this was a potent idea. It helped organize the Anglo American world. But it could not, did not prevail. Popular culture in all its noisy, facile glory won the day. It did so, finally, by proving that culture can be good, illuminating, and subtle, without actually being difficult. Thus did the elites lose a favorite device for sorting the world.

Upward aspiration has been replaced by our search for authenticity. People may admire Martha Stewart for the status advice she gives, but they *love* Oprah Winfrey, a woman who never gives status advice and who, if pressed, would probably say that status is a false god we should not worship. The democratic, egalitarian, energetically anti-status America is winning after all.[12]

Consultants Michael Silverstein and Neil Fiske, authors of *Trading Up*, say the consumer society has turned its back on status. "New Luxury goods, however, avoid class distinctions and are not promoted as elitist. [Instead], they generally appeal to a set of values that may be shared by people at many income levels and in many walks of life."[13]

Taste now belongs not to elites but to the professionals. When furnishing our home we look to the likes of interior designers Victoria Hagan and Barbara Berry. Were they "well born"? Did they go to Vassar? We don't care. It doesn't matter. Taste now comes from experts, and experts come . . . from television. There is something old world about Tim Gunn, but the reason he designs American lives is *Project Runway*. We used to admire things that were old world. This has been trumped by things that are old school. Taste now comes from a mastery of change, not a mastery of status.

The very verticality of our society has changed. It's not clear who sits on top. Is it celebrities like Kate Winslet? Politicians like Barack Obama? Editors like Graydon Carter? Basketball stars like Kobe Bryant? Computer billionaires like Steve Wozniak? Short-fingered vulgarians like Donald Trump? (Okay, not Donald Trump.)

Almost no one these days tries to pass as a member of a group more exalted than their own. This fiction (or "status counterfeiting") was common in the 1950s, but these days it does not interest us at all. For most people, self-presentation is like yard work: We do enough of it to keep the place looking respectable. The idea of devoting much of our concern, most of our income, and all of our aspiration to great status performances is over, the ideological antique of another age.

And what's become of the living room? For a while it was roped off. And in the past ten years it has suffered a still crueler fate. It has been displaced by the "great room" that began to appear around the turn of the twenty-first century. This consisted a single, large, open room, constructed out of three existing rooms: the living room, the dining room, and the kitchen. The great room sprung from several motives. But it was clearly intended to demolish two status places, the living room and dining room. The kitchen absorbed them both. And once Americans were persuaded they could live without their "status rooms," they spent a small fortune excising them from the family home. From 2005 to 2007, expenditures on interior renovation rose about 40 percent to $13 billion.[14] It was the only way Americans could find to live in the living room.

COOL CULTURE

Cool culture is a much newer cultural force than status. It rose as an attack on status. Cool holds status to be an anxious, craven act of conformity, a needy clinging to convention. Cool scorns status as clueless and dopey. It prefers a more thoughtful self-assembly, intelligent choice in music, clothing, and attitude that shows one's autonomy and distance from the group. If status is about standing, cool is about standing free.

Cool came up late but it came up fast. We can see it arise from its tiny origins in nineteenth-century Paris. I reckon the original community was fewer than 5,000 people.[15] This avant-garde had a distinct cultural mission: to break the rules of art and life.[16] They lived in open violation of the middle-class code, the better to scandalize those who conformed to the code, the better to "épater the bourgeoisie." Manet's *Absinthe Drinker* would challenge the competitive Salon partly because this drinker was a creature unfit for the salon of the middle-class home. Horrifying middle-class expectations, this is what "cool" was for.

The avant-garde might easily have been a small band of rebels who had their moment and then passed into obscurity. But the fates were kind. The Paris artists attracted the attention of American artists who came to Paris in such numbers that in 1926 *Time* magazine took to calling the Latin Quarter the American Quarter.[17] Some of the wealth being created in the new world was returning to Paris as the stipends and trust funds with which wealthy families long ago learned to manage the "artistic" child.[18]

Ernest Hemingway's 1926 novel, *The Sun Also Rises*, sold briskly.[19] And with its publication came the avant-garde "meme." Now you didn't have to spend any time in Paris to master cool. You could find Hemingway's book in any American public library, drugstore, or five-and-dime. And you didn't work very hard to "decode" this new social posture. *The Sun Also Rises* reads like a lifestyle manual, specifying how to dress, to live, to speak. Cool had leapt from art to prose, from France to America, and from artists to anyone with a library pass.[20]

Cool scaled up furiously after World War II.[21] The "carrier" in this epidemic was the "beats," poets, artists, and "apocalyptic hipsters" who lived in obligatory violation of the status code. One founder, Herbert Huncke, ran away from home at age twelve and divided his time between jail, freak shows, and the street.[22] The father of the movement, William Burroughs, abandoned a life of privilege in St. Louis and a Harvard education for a life of heroin abuse and destructive self-discovery. He found his Montmartre on Chicago's North Side.[23] But there was no posing as a romantic artist here. Burroughs worked as a bug exterminator and styled himself a criminal.[24]

In the manner of cool, the beats protested the narrowness and timidity of the bourgeois view of the world. Jack Kerouac sought spontaneity in Benzedrine, jazz, and trances. He created "wild form" prose and scorned Allen Ginsberg for his more classical, rule-bound poetry.[25] It was Kerouac's very portable prose that carried the standard. *On the Road* sold fantastically well, recruiting an enormous audience for cool. As Burroughs was to mutter, "Kerouac opened a million coffee bars and sold a million pairs of Levi's."[26]

Cool is one lucky meme. While other social innovations died around it, it went from strength to strength. It was nurtured by one community until it could be adopted and cultivated by a still larger one. It started in art. It moved to poetry and then to prose, and, eventually, as we shall see, to movies and music. An ideological hustler, cool seemed to have an eye for the main chance and its next best move, even as it protested its artistic distance. It may have started as an obscure style in the Paris café, but it was climbing international best-seller lists in no time.

In the late '50s, the avant-garde commandeered popular novels. The best-seller *Bonjour Tristesse* gave voice to the existential angst of the café dweller.[27] Better still, the popular press was paying attention. In 1957, a columnist at the *San Francisco Chronicle* helped popularize the beats by calling them "beatniks." The big magazines, *Time* and *Life*, were offering coverage.[28] Thus did cool find its way into the middle-class living rooms, using mainstream media as its Trojan horse.

Cool captured the attention of the most popular of media: the Hollywood film. It appeared in *Rebel Without a Cause* (Nicholas Ray, 1955), *Funny Face* (Stanley Donen, 1957), *Bell, Book and Candle* (1958, Richard Quine), and *Lolita* (Stanley Kubrick, 1961). The last of these gives us Charlotte, a middle-class creature passionately interested in the poetry reading, the jazz solo, and the African mask. Apparently, beat values were finding their way off the coffee table and into the design scheme.[29]

Cool even found a way to colonize TV. A series called *The Many Lives of Dobie Gillis* ran from 1959 to 1963 and featured a character called Maynard G. Krebs, who wore black clothes, grew a goatee, played the bongos, and used coffeehouse argot to comic effect. The show appropriated cool, to be sure, but it also helped recruit on its behalf. As one young man remembered it, "Maynard had . . . a profound effect on my personal development." It prepared him to read Ginsberg's *Howl*.[30]

The avant-garde impulse reappeared, reworked, in the counterculture of the 1960s, thanks to the intercession of Allen Ginsberg, Lawrence Ferlinghetti, and Bob Dylan.[31] Compared with the streetwise beat who haunted Times Square, hippies were kinder, gentler, more starry-eyed. (New drugs, new vistas, no doubt.) But finally, hippies cared about the very "madness" Kerouac prized.[32] Like the beats before them, hippies violated the middle-class code to a purpose.

To be a hippie, it wasn't actually necessary to make art or music. Some people transformed their lives, to be sure, but others merely grew their hair long and entertained a new set of values. Hey presto. A diffusion miracle was now accomplished. Cool had gone wide but remained cool. It was that exclusive club that anyone could join. And because music was now the preferred medium, the would-be recruit didn't even actually have to read. Cool: the little meme that could.

Measures are hard to find, but we can extract the following numbers from the "hippies" entry in Wikipedia.[33]

1965 1,000, a rough estimate of the number of prototypical hippies living in the Bay area.

1966 10,000, the number of people who attend the Trips Festival organized by Stewart Brand, Ken Kesey, and Owsley Stanley.

1966 15,000, the new estimate for the hippie population of Haight-Ashbury in San Francisco.

1967 20,000, the number of people who attended the Human Be-in, January 14.

1967 100,000, the number of people who visited San Francisco for the "Summer of Love."

1969 500,000, the number of people who attended Woodstock.

1970s millions, the number of people in the postwar baby boom who were prepared to identify themselves as hippies in style of life or thought.

Cool was winning the day. Once the minority enthusiasm of a tiny group of artists in Paris, it had scaled the heavens. It was now an official, massively distributed, crowd-sourced, counterculture, colonizing popular culture from top to bottom. The exact tipping point is not clear, but the transition year might have been 1967. In 1968, Jimi Hendrix held the top spot on the best-seller list with his album *Are You Experienced*. In 1966, the best seller had been *Whipped Cream and Other Delights* by Herb Albert and the Tijuana Brass.[34] These albums appear to come from different cultures. And in a sense they did. Earnest, transformational, bent on cultural and political revolution, hippies would dedicate no art to whipped cream.

Time magazine was increasingly sympathetic. In the 1950s, it had treated beats with ambivalence, but the tone of its hippie coverage was more respectful. One story offers a dignified subtitle ("the philosophy of a subculture"), and the content is sympathetic, in places almost proselytizing:

> If there were a hippie code, it would include these flexible guidelines: Do your own thing, wherever you have to do it and whenever you want. Drop out. Leave society as you have known it. Leave it utterly. Blow the mind of every straight person you can reach. Turn them on, if not to drugs, then to beauty, love, honesty, fun.[35]

By this time, cool and status cultures had been locked in battle for a hundred years. One outcome now looked inevitable. Cool was going to take the day. Status had lost so many battles, surely it must lose the war. As the torch passed from Montmartre to Montparnasse to Chicago to San Francisco, cool was apparently inexorable.

By the end of the twentieth century, the results were in. The winner was obvious. And the victor was . . . compromise. For all their intense conflict, the avant-garde and the middle class had achieved a glorious rapprochement. They had fought so long and hard, they now were one. The middle-class world was shot through with avant-garde liberties, encompassing a new latitude of personal expression and a new order of creativity. And the avant-garde discovered that certain kinds of social order, self-discipline, and instrumentality were, when all was said and done, obligatory. You couldn't live without them.

Both parties won and lost. The status code would never be the same. Its "anchors" had been permanently loosened. Senior white males were losing their hegemony. Social regulations were in steep decline. Cool had come to accept compromises of its own. Some kinds of self-expression were not to be allowed. Certain intoxicants must remain against the law. Certain social experiments, like communes, could only end badly. Capitalism was no longer the obvious villain of peace. Property might be "theft," as Proudhon said, but it was going to endure.[36] Cool also had to accept that personal liberty was probably not going to eliminate social differences or social sameness. A hipster regime was not going to happen.

If the avant-garde artists of Paris had had their way, we would have seen the demolition of bourgeois society. Indeed, public life would now look something like Burning Man, that extraordinary festival that happens each year in Nevada.[37] As it turns out, we hold this festival only once a year. And we stick it way out there in the desert. Like the living room, we felt, somehow, that it was better kept roped off.

Cool is an outsider's sensibility now completely internalized, built into every individual and our entire culture. This feels like a puzzle and a paradox to the likes of Thomas Frank and Naomi Klein, and this is perhaps the best way to see it.[38] But it is anthropologically more rewarding, I think, to see cool as a measure of our culture's ability to absorb conflicting impulses and embrace contradiction. Once so sure of itself, so monolithic, so clear and well defined, our culture is increasingly a house of many mansions, a bundle of conflicting points of view. To everyone's astonishment, it not only survives this complexity but thrives on it. Frank, Klein, and all their new-order orthodoxy to the contrary, we bumble along quite nicely. It's not very elegant, but it is pretty effective. (Elegance, we leave to the French, who prove in return that you have to choose.)

The larger outcome is clear. Neither cultural constellation will ever seize the day and return itself to its once glorious position. For we are a culture with a third term, a restless creativity. If once we were mainstream and avant-garde, now we are a great wilderness, with thousands of little experiments happening everywhere. Point, counterpoint is dead. The struggle between status and cool is over.[39] We are now a culture overflowing with variety and noise.

CHAPTER 5

PRODUCERS AND CONSUMERS

CULTURE WAS ONCE MADE BY A HANDFUL OF PRODUCERS on high and delivered to millions of consumers below. The producers mostly gave us what they thought we wanted. And the consumers might sometimes have disliked the outcome, but there wasn't much we could do about it. We either watched one of the big networks, or we didn't watch TV. We called it mass media because this programming was made for the largest possible audience. Niches were impossible. Tiny audiences were forbidden. Active audiences were unlikely. Power belonged to producers. Consumers did what they were told. And then things began to change. The new contract between producer and consumer is perhaps the most urgent thing the CCO needs to know about. It is one of the most compelling messages he or she has to deliver to the C-suite.

PRODUCER CULTURE: WE'RE ALL DEKTOR NOW

When *NYPD Blue* launched in 1993, it was praised for the work of actor Dennis Franz, new kinds of dialogue from creators Steven Bochco and David Milch, and an ensemble style that built on *Hill Street Blues*, the TV show that ran from 1981 to 1987. But what made it striking for many people was the visual style, the camera work.

NYPD Blue had a restless camera engaged in what sometimes seemed like amphetamine photography. The camera would begin at the rooftop of an eight-story apartment building and scrape downward to the street, and then sprint horizontally to the station house. Where most shows would "jump" from scene to scene, *NYPD Blue* liked to careen between them in real time. Indoors, the camera would fidget and drift, fixing on one detail, then another. The *NYPD Blue* camera might as well have been a kid with ADD. Even when "moored" on an actor, it rocked in place.

Some people called it the "shaky-cam." Others called the style "floaty" or "hitchy." And many frankly hated it. "It makes me seasick!" "It gives me vertigo!" Stop the presses. Or at least the camera. It looked like the motion of a handheld camera but it wasn't. The restlessness was made possible by a camera technology called a "fluid head," which stabilizes the camera even as the camera operator moves it. Gregory Hoblit, the first director of photography, brought it to the show, and Mark Tinker cultivated it.[1]

It turns out the restless camera was the creation of a man called Leslie Dektor, a South African who has lived in the United States since the 1980s. Dektor learned his craft at the knee of his mother, a documentarian. And he honed this craft as a still photographer working in the fashion business. He invented the restless camera while making ads for Levi's and AT&T. The guys on *NYPD Blue* gave Dektor full credit. When directing the camera, Tinker would say, "Hey, dektor over to Sipowitz."[2] Dektor's innovation is now a fixture of television. It's been used across a range of shows: *Homicide*, *Friday Night*

Lights, *Battlestar Galactica*, *Curb Your Enthusiasm*, *Arrested Development*, *Reno 911!*, *TMZ*, and *The Shield*.

I called Leslie Dektor to ask him about his invention.[3] He was very kind. I got the feeling he was expecting me to fail to grasp most of what he said, and I'm pretty sure I didn't disappoint him. There were a couple of pauses in the course of the conversation where I could see him staring at the receiver.

Dektor told me he wasn't trying to create a "technique." He said he was "trying to find the moment. I wanted to get to the moment almost a beat too late. I wanted to give an importance to the moment." The idea is to "discover" what the camera sees, perhaps even to "occupy" what it finds before it.

The trouble with some photography, Dektor says, is that it's "manicured," by which I think he means "premeditated." Indeed, the film camera has many masters: the producer, the director, the director of photography, the camera operator, the editor. Cameras are thoroughly "bossed around." Dektor gives the camera its liberty, the better to get accident, spontaneity, and the ordinary back into the scene.[4] Dektor told me his camera work is

> not about technique. It's about sight. It's about breathing, I don't ever think about it. If someone like me thinks about it, it becomes technique . . . I never know what I'm going to do in a situation. I never let people know what I am going to do with a piece. I want the moment to be the author of the moment, and the actors to be the author of the moment.[5]

I especially liked Dektor's idea that the camera should come to each scene "a moment too late." Surely this was a camera incapable of bullying or inquisition. A late camera comes to the scene breathless, eager, as if to say, "What'd I miss?" This camera is not the boss of anyone. It's ingenious and alert.

I asked Dektor why the camera rocked in place. "I would let the camera vibrate because I wanted to be prepared to make the next move. It's poised for movement. I wanted the frame to be rubbery to prepare myself for the next move. You never wanted it to go rock solid."

Precedent was not on Dektor's side. When the great German film director Fritz Lang went to Hollywood in the 1930s, his style irritated cast and crew. There was no room for fluidity, improvisation, or adjustment. Lang came to the set with every shot specified down to the tiniest detail. And it had to be shot exactly that way. Cameras did not move . . . at all. American directors might be a little more flexible, but even for them the film set was a relatively static place. In the old Hollywood, the world came to the camera, like Gulliver strapped down by Lilliputians. The camera did not go to the world.

Dektor's camera was perfect for the new Hollywood, a world that prizes the mobile, curious, nimble. Jean de Segonzac, director of photography on *Homicide: Life on the Street*, described his style as if channeling Dektor. "Everything was shot fast. The actors would ask me when they'd be on camera, and I refused to tell them. Everyone was in the moment, everyone had to be on. It gave the scenes tremendous energy."[6] Robert Altman counted on "found" drama, things the script didn't anticipate. Actors now expected to be turned loose to discover their characters and the dramatic moment. Directors as diverse as Judd Apatow, Christopher Guest, and Mike Leigh all harvest the gifts of a free-form approach.[7] Hollywood needed a Dektor camera because it was intent upon capturing more in the moment . . . to put more on the screen . . . to deliver more to the viewer.

There was evidence of a richer signal everywhere. In the old world of TV, dialogue could be wooden, predictable, and the abject servant of clarifying the plot. When shows were particularly implausible and unworkmanlike, one of the characters would offer a gloss. (This is the convention Mike Myers made fun of with the character he created in Basil Exposition, the one who is always explaining things in the Austin Powers series.)[8] People didn't seem to mind because good dialogue was for the theater, and TV cared about other things. Detective shows featured car chases. Variety shows had a weakness for men spinning plates. TV was a visual medium, not an auditory one. It existed for the image, not the word. TV dialogue was thin gruel, but that was probably just as well.

Buffy the Vampire Slayer was launched by Warner Bros. in 1997. It was the creation of Joss Whedon, a third-generation TV writer. Perhaps this is why he introduced a new idea: talkative television, which was interested in wordplay, wit, verbal jousting, assumption jumping.

In a episode called "The Pack," Buffy and Giles contemplated a change in her hapless friend Xander. Does he perhaps suffer from some condition? What's happened him?

GILES: Xander's taken to teasing the less fortunate?

BUFFY: Uh-huh.

GILES: And, there's been a noticeable change in both clothing and demeanor?

BUFFY: Yes.

GILES: And, well, otherwise all his spare time is spent lounging about with imbeciles.

BUFFY: It's bad, isn't it?

GILES: It's devastating. He's turned into a sixteen-year-old boy. Of course you'll have to kill him . . . Testosterone is a great equalizer; it turns all men into morons.[9]

In an episode called "The Zeppo," Buffy wants Xander to stay out of harm's way. She instructs him to remain "fray-adjacent." It is impossible, I submit, to imagine an instruction of this kind from Joe Friday, Jim Rockford, or Thomas Magnum.

This isn't Shakespeare, but we can imagine the reaction from the old world of TV. An old-time producer would surely say, "'Fray-adjacent,' that's just stupid! You're going to confuse people!" The new-order producer does a trade-off analysis: Does this delight the viewers I care about more than it confuses the ones I don't care about? We have seen a lot of talkative TV since Buffy went off the air in 2003, including Amy Sherman-Palladino's *The Gilmore Girls*, Aaron Sorkin's *The West Wing*, and Tina Fey's *30 Rock*.

Buffy the Vampire Slayer was also prepared to acknowledge popular culture. Whedon has Buffy say, "I can't believe you would Scully me," and Xander complain that he has been "Keyser Sözed." These are references to *The X-Files* and *The Usual Suspects*, respectively. Popular culture in most of the twentieth century was thoroughly cowed. It was low culture and it knew it was low culture. Quoting, that was for literature, for real writers working in a great tradition. Popular culture didn't ever quote itself. That was just asking for invidious comparison. But for Whedon, "intertexuality" was okay, as it was for a generation of writers, working in a range of TV shows (*The O.C., NCIS, Psych, The Simpsons, SportsCenter*).[10]

If dialogue was getting richer, so was acting. Disney hired Johnny Depp for *Pirates of the Caribbean* because CEO Michael Eisner regarded him as the "sexiest man in the world."[11] But the actor who showed up to play Captain Jack Sparrow didn't seem sexy at all. Captain Sparrow had matted hair, a mincing gate, bad teeth, a braided goatee, eyeliner, weird headgear, a cartoon run, and an apparent disregard for personal hygiene.

Disney was horrified. When Disney executives saw the dailies, they called director Gore Verbinski and producer Jerry Bruckheimer with questions. Why was Depp walking funny? Why was he lisping? Was he drunk? Was he gay? Some Disney executives felt this performance might be a little too magical for the Magic Kingdom.

There were shouting matches. (Bruckheimer says one meeting was the worst he ever endured as a producer.) There were other things to worry about, a budget approaching $150 million, a title no one could agree upon, and whether the movie should be associated with a theme park ride. But the sticking point, the ticking bomb, was Depp's Captain Jack Sparrow. With this much money at stake, putting the hero in eyeliner and a beaded beard looked like a really bad idea.

Success has a way of clarifying the mind. *Pirates* made $46 million in its opening weekend, a ten-day take of $258 million, and a final profit of $655 million. The *Pirates* trilogy has made Disney $2 billion. Hollywood now agrees that without Captain Sparrow, *Pirates* would have been a dreary exercise in genre filmmaking. More to the commercial point, it might merely have made its money back.[12]

Depp remembers, "There was one executive in particular who really went out of their way to investigate what the fuck

I was up to, and after the release of *Pirates*, I got a letter from that executive saying, 'Look, I apologize. I was wrong. You were right. Thank you for sticking to your guns. I appreciate the fact that you didn't listen to me.'"[13]

Hollywood was now abandoning the "clarity contract." By this convention, popular culture took extraordinary pains to see that the viewer was never puzzled or confused. This was one of the reasons that car chases and spinning plates were so popular. They escaped no one. But now Hollywood appeared to be resisting predictable story lines, thin dialogue, and laborious casting. Even with blockbusters like *Pirates*, even with many millions of dollars on the line, cultural creators had new freedom, new expressive range.[14]

What happened? I think it's clear. Popular culture became culture plain and simple.[15] It will be the work of some scholar's career to determine the cause of this transformation. Certainly, artists always wish to make things more nuanced and interesting. And once nuance became possible, it become a competitive advantage. Mass media gave way to multiple media, as the Big Three networks gave way to a world with many cable outlets. HBO flourished. If the marketplace was once hostile to narrative complexity, now it was increasingly obliged to use it. But surely the single biggest driver of a new kind of culture was the rise of Gen X and Gen Y. These generations spoke popular culture as a native language. And they did not like being pandered to. Now there were viewers out there who were smart enough and nimble enough to handle just about anything you could throw at them. The KISS model—"keep it simple, stupid"—was dying.

Our culture used to come from small elites in a handful of cities. It came to us carefully crafted to remove the possibility of confusion. We were very like those fixed cameras that existed before Dektor. We were prepared for anything as long as it was static, overlit, and formulaic. And the comparison carries into the present day. That alert, mobile, eager camera we get from Dektor, it's a lot like us.

CONSUMER CULTURE: THE APOLLO THEATER EFFECT

Were we ever couch potatoes? Perhaps. But at some point consumers of media took on new acuity. MIT professor Henry Jenkins saw this in the 1990s.[16] As we noted in Chapter 2, his work stunned the academic world, contradicting its most heartfelt beliefs. Jenkins discovered that kids raised on TV (and sometimes by TV) appeared to have observant and creative "faculties" that were subtle, complex, and integrative after all.

These kids second-guessed casting choices. (David Duchovny in *Evolution*?) They were mapping *Star Trek*'s *Enterprise*, using minute acts of observation and charming acts of deduction. ("When Bones leaves the infirmary, he always turns right. This must mean . . .") They were still "watching TV" but increasingly they were querying dialogue, camera angles, editing strategies, and directorial approaches. We may call this an "Apollo Theater" effect, after the Harlem venue famous for the crowd's high standards and the candor with which judgment is rendered. At age fourteen, comedian Dave Chappelle was booed off the stage there. The TV audience is increasingly like an Apollo audience. It had better be good or God help the offender.

The appearance of *All Your Base Are Belong to Us* in 2000 gave the world pause.[17] As an Internet confection, a stream of images under a driving sound track insinuated the words "All your base are belong to us" into every medium imaginable: ads, packages, signs. It was funny and entertaining. But it also sent a message: Amateurs had cracked the code of popular culture. Apparently, *All Your Base* was created by kids working on their parents' computer in the family room. Kids or no, they had succeeded in a Promethean thievery, making off with the secrets of culture. Hollywood and Madison Avenue were on notice. Even "rank amateurs" could produce good work, and before long we were graced with machinima: *Red vs. Blue*, *Odyssey* (the Star Trek movie made by fans), and the strong production values of some of the stuff now on YouTube. The consumers of popular culture were beginning to rival the producers of popular culture.

Acuity and authorship brought a new sense of ownership. Chris Carter, creator of *The X-Files*, was at first charmed to see that the fans were so passionately involved, trading alternate plotlines and endings. But we must wonder what he thought of this declaration: "Some in the *X-Files* fan community were disturbed by what they saw as significant characterization and continuity problems in season eight [of *The X-Files*]. They are now addressing this issue by rewriting the episodes to correct the problems."[18]

Adoration was taking a proprietary tone. Increasingly, fans felt the show belonged not to Carter but to them. If we move forward to the present day, we see the producers of *Heroes* and *Lost* engaging with their fans in an active, sometimes playful way. These shows take for granted that fans watch with a ferocious attention to detail and that they will find new uses for dialogue and characterization.[19]

And then the deluge. A vast number of people are now entering the production game. There are more than 80 million videos on YouTube. There are 1.8 million bands offering music on MySpace. There are some 50 million blogs. Not all of this work is good, to be sure. But anyone who makes himself a producer of culture becomes more exacting as a consumer of culture. Moreover, these are people who have the security of day jobs. They are not answerable to editors or viewers. They are making culture to please themselves.[20] And thus is a virtuous cycle set in motion: The more they make, the smarter they are; the smarter they are, the more demanding they become. This is not an unalloyed gift for Hollywood. Recent statements by Jesse Alexander and Mark Warshaw, the creators of *Heroes*, suggested that some fan interest can smack of tyranny.[21] It turns out that some fans build cultural capital out of their knowledge of the narrative, and they resist and decry any departure from that narrative. These fans are not so much "cocreators" of the narrative as its jailer, constantly vigilant for any change, even a minor one.

It also spelled trouble for marketing. As the Internet became more robust and well distributed, the corporate world decided to put the world of branding online. Coca-Cola or General Motors wanted to be where the consumers were. But what happened there was a revelation. When corporations made traditional ads and sent them down the chute of a TV show, there really was no clear way of telling whether people liked them or even watched. In that famous line, only half of advertising works and the trouble is we can't tell which half. Only sales figures served as a measure, and it was a very distant and loose measure, to be sure. But with the Internet, you could tell. And when the first Web sites went up, the numbers came in.

There was a stunned silence in the marketing world. No one could quite believe it. The prevailing assumption had been well steeped in self-congratulation. Big corporations believed people loved them. After all, they had used our brand for years, right? We're part of their family, no? They're going to have to come to our Web site. Just to say hi? But no one came. No one cared.

The consumer was consulted. One said, "When brands get on the Internet, they don't really seem to get the game. They don't understand that this is about interacting with us. They're like that fat, balding guy at a party who talks too loud, drinks too much, stares at the girls, and generally thinks the world revolves around him."[22]

Corporate America, welcome to the new consumer. Brands were discovering they could no longer treat this consumer in the old way, as a simpleton to be talked down to, to be shouted at, to be lectured, scolded, bamboozled, and browbeaten. In the language of the seminal book *The Cluetrain Manifesto*, the consumer culture now had to be more like a conversation between equals.[23]

If consumers now had some of the producer's skills, it was possible to reach out and make them cocreators of the brand. In 2005, Converse invited consumers to customize All-Stars.[24] (The new motto there: "We don't own the brand. Consumers do.") They encouraged them to make ads about Converse in the world. Doritos did the same, and managed to elicit ads of staggering ordinariness, apparent proof that civilians could make advertising as badly as the experts.[25]

In 2006, Chevrolet asked consumers to make ads for the Tahoe. Some people seized this opportunity to mock SUVs as a cause of global warming, as a danger on the highway, and as a source of social injustice. Before long there were dozens of Tahoe ads on YouTube, most of them anti-Tahoe. *Adweek* scolded Chevy for this marketing debacle. But it was clear that this sort of thing was the inevitable price of consumer participation. More participation meant less control. This is what a conversation looks like. Surely no one supposed that you could invite the consumer to talk and then control what he or she said. Bringing the consumer in was going to be messy. The brand was going to have to be less pristine.[26]

The very term "consumer" now seemed wrong. First of all, it offended anyone with an ear for an ecologically sophisticated understanding of things. But more important, being labeled "consumers" put them at the end of the line. The new consumers didn't want to be a bowling pin acted upon by marketing. They expected to be given a little credit, to be asked to complete the ad in their minds, with their skills. And they would like a little something for themselves. Maybe an image or a line. Something they could feed into their networks. Otherwise, as one of them told me, it was like looking at stuff under "plate glass." You just couldn't get at it.

If "consumer" was the wrong word, I wondered if "multiplier" might be a better one.[27] It would encourage marketers to encourage people to invent, personalize, complete the brand for their own purposes, and in the process make the brand more vivid and interesting. By itself the brand is incomplete, imperfect. It remained for the "multiplier" to begin to make free with its meanings, and to circulate these meanings on Facebook, blogs, and YouTube.[28] "Multiplier" had the advantage of assuming an active participant in the branding process.

Fan cultures are especially productive of new content. Consider the case of Bud Caddell. He works as a strategist for a New York–based digital think tank called Undercurrent. That's his day job. But Caddell so loves the TV show *Mad Men*, he decided to contribute to it. He invented a character called Bud

Melman, a mailroom clerk at Sterling Cooper Advertising in 1962. And then he began to Twitter messages . . . in character . . . from the mailroom . . . from 1962. It's all a little confusing but here it is in short form: a real person, Bud Caddell, has created a fictional person, Bud Melman, who he has inserted in the fictional world built by a TV show, from which he, Bud Caddell, really Twitters.

This is a devotional activity. It measures how much Caddell loves the show. And it multiplies the show, adding a character, a narrative stream, and viewer interest.[29] But it made the AMC network uncomfortable. AMC believed that Caddell was not adding but taking. And it asked Caddell to cease and desist. Caddell's reply captures precisely why fan cultures matter.

> Fan fiction. Brand hijacking. Copyright misuse. Sheer devotion. Call it what you will, but we call it the blurred line between content creators and content consumers, and it's not going away. We're your biggest fans, your die-hard proponents, and when your show gets cancelled we'll be among the first to pass around the petition. Talk to us. Befriend us. Engage us. But please, don't treat us like criminals.[30]

The world of marketing is changing at light speed. And this is another reason to hire a CCO. If the corporation is now going to talk to consumers, instead of shout, or lie, it needs to know how to start and sustain the conversation. This means a nuanced knowledge of the consumer, the many different kinds of consumers out there and the depths and facets of any individual consumer. It needs to proceed with a new order of intelligence. As Steven Johnson says in *Everything Bad Is Good for*

You, "For decades, we've worked under the assumption that mass culture follows a steadily declining path toward lowest-common-denominator standards, presumably because the 'masses' want dumb, simple pleasures and big media companies want to give the masses what they want. But in fact, the exact opposite is happening: the culture is getting more intellectually demanding, not less."[31] To live in this culture, to profit in this new marketplace, a CCO is called for.

This may require a complete replacement of the marketing team. In the meantime, it will require the presence of the CCO, someone who knows the culture well enough to engage with it, to talk about it, to contribute to it.

Something funny happened on the way to the twenty-first century: A virtuous cycle was engaged. Smarter consumers made for smarter producers made for smarter consumers. The consumer culture was rising. The days of a simple-minded marketing, of finding and pushing "hot buttons"—these days were over. If popular culture was now culture plain and simple, things were going to have to change at the corporation, especially the C-suite.

And this is why there has to be a CCO in place. Only a CCO has the weather maps to keep track of all this information. Only a CCO can know all the players and the trends that move them. Only a CCO can manage a market like this. Wishing will not make it go away.

CHAPTER 6

BUILDING A SECRET SNEAKER STORE

A SECRET SNEAKER STORE? MY FRIEND JOHN REASSURED ME there was such a thing. In downtown Boston. We piloted his ancient BMW out of Cambridge well enough, but things got more complicated when we got downtown. Part of the problem is, of course, that Boston streets twist and turn. Plus, John and I have a bad habit of talking while driving. It's controversial and someday I know it'll be against the law. We get caught in a conversation and then discover the car has apparently piloted itself for several miles and we're lost. We consult maps and plot a new course. But another topic comes up, and before you know it, it's "Damn, where are we this time?"

John was pretty sure that the secret sneaker store was somewhere near the Christian Science Plaza. And that's hard to miss. (But of course we did miss it, several times.) Eventually we found ourselves in the shadow of the plaza. We even found a parking spot. The search was on in earnest. (I figured being out of the car increased our chances enormously.) The neighborhood around the plaza is forlorn, but in his distracted way John seemed to be zeroing in on something.

"This must be it," he said.

We were standing in front of a convenience store, one of those places that looks like it's got three weeks to live, tops. In the window was a bottle of BBQ sauce and a couple rolls of Bounty, sun bleached and dust covered. Every city has neighborhoods where retail goes to die, little stores appear designed to chew through someone's life savings and then go out of business. Surely, this was one of these.

"Go in," John insisted.

Okay, fine. I opened the door and, sure enough, it was one of those sad little candy and cigarette operations. There was a guy sitting behind a counter, framed by lotto tickets. He looked at me balefully. Two more guys were sitting on a ratty old sofa. They didn't look up.

"Go up to the Coke machine," John said. (Professors herd well.)

I approached the Coke machine and it disappeared. Just vanished. Inside was perfect, clean, and well lit. Racks and racks of sneakers. Shoes as far as the eye could see. I looked at John in wonder. A secret sneaker sanctum. So close to Boston. So near to God.[1]

The secret sneaker sanctum is the new model of culture. It's how we do things now. Culture streams here in all directions. Behind a Coke machine in Boston.

In the 1950s, my mother used to buy sneakers in a bag. Ten pairs to the bag. They were black canvas high-tops, made in Hong Kong or Singapore, copies of the PF Flyer or the Converse All-Star. They were as close to a mere commodity as a shoe could get.

Things have changed. At this writing, the secret sneaker store is now featuring Nike ACG Blazers. They were designed by the London design firm Cassette Playa and launched during the line's "Future Primitive" runway show. The theme of the show was "urban shamanism." The creative director of Cassette Playa, Carri Munden, said her inspiration was "ancient Amazonian hunting rituals adapted by a gang of skaters in a postapocalyptic city."[2] And, no, you can't get them by the bag.

The world of sneakers was once dominated by corporations. In 2003, Bobbito Garcia was saying that he yearned for the days "when street-basketball tournaments didn't double as youth-marketing opportunities for sneaker companies."[3] But now producers and consumers engage deeply with one another. Garcia has since worked as a consultant to Nike, Adidas, and Converse. And in 2007, Nike actually named a version of the Air Force 1 after him: the "Bobbito 'the Barber' Garcia edition."[4]

The world of shoes is a complicated airspace, with inspiration coming from many sources, including NBA celebrities, folk heroes in the world of street basketball, graffiti artists, rappers, the dance community, and kids everywhere. The big brands are here. So are smaller players like One, the sportswear company. Design comes from tiny garages in obscure neighborhoods. It comes from design studios in London and Amsterdam. It comes from skaters sitting on stoops, scratching things into their shoes. News of the latest developments come from the big magazines and Web sites and from many smaller outlets, blogs, and word-of-mouth. Shoes may be purchased at big athletic outlets and of course the secret sneaker store in Boston. Sneakers were even featured in an episode of the HBO series *Entourage*. It's a little like PBS with many parties playing at once. There is no clear directionality. This is a world with lots of ricochet, lots of players, lots of churn. It's a perfect sneaker storm. We've got art, commerce, design, professional sports, the street, journalism, amateur sports, big business, tiny shops, and consumers with felt-tip pens. This culture is both dispersive and convergent. It is fast and it is slow. It's about producers acting like consumers and consumers acting like producers. And as usual, the corporation is the bewildered little brother, trying desperately to keep up.

Change now courses through our world on purpose. Every institution and many individuals are creating novelty as a matter of course. We have to add to this all the change that happens by accident. As change ricochets around the deck like so many cannons, other events are set in motion. Some of these are as cataclysmic as they are unforeseen. Nassim Nicholas Taleb calls these "black swans," events that are in a sense unimaginable, until, like a failure of the banking system, they are incontrovertible.[5]

And this is why there has to be a CCO in place. Only a CCO has the weather maps to keep track of all this information. Only a CCO can know those players as groups and as individuals. Only a CCO can manage a market like this. So what's a CCO to do?

"HOW'S THAT BOOK?"

If I sit beside someone in public, I usually ask a question. The results are sometimes ugly, like that cool look that says, "Mind your own business." Happy to, but my job as a student of culture is minding your business, and your personal life, and what you're watching on TV, and how your eating habits are shifting, and how you are going to vote in the next presidential election and why. If that's okay. So, how's that book?

There are lots of useful data waiting for the right question. The first rule of the CCO is: Talk to anyone who will talk to you. This was how I learned about something called "curatorial marketing." I was sitting on a plane and the guy beside me told me all about it. He worked for Nike. Now I knew. (I'll tell you about it later in the chapter.)

I get this from my father, who used to say, "Anyone will talk to you if you find the right question." And that's the second rule of the CCO: Figure out the thing that makes a person interesting. Usually people don't mind the grilling. After all, we are asking them to talk about themselves. The trick is to find the thing they know best that we know least. And then the trick is to find out what this means to them, how it looks to them, and how it feels for them. If there's lots of "found art" out there, there's lots of found anthropology, too. Be opportunistic. Seize every opportunity.

A GUY LIKE DAVE

Sometimes we know we don't know, and then it's time to go straight to the source. In the 1990s, it became clear to me that there was a gigantic hole in my knowledge of popular culture. I didn't really know anything about popular music. (Where had I been all of my youth? Not listening to music, apparently.) To make matters worse, this was the era of the Pixies, Nirvana, and "alternative" music, popular music that was deliberately unpopular and, for someone like me, especially inaccessible. I needed a crash course. As it happened, there was a little record store in my neighborhood (the Danforth in Toronto) and I just kind of threw myself at the mercy of one of the guys who worked there. Dave Dyment proved to be a superb source, giving me things to listen to, drawing me out, leading me through the history of popular music from Robert Johnson to Black Francis.

No one knows about contemporary culture because it just "comes to them." There is no such thing as "naturally hip." We have to be prepared to ask. And if that means throwing oneself at the mercy of a stranger, that's what the CCO must do. All of us need to cultivate (and incent) a guy like Dave.

EVERY EDITOR

There is a firm in New York City that listens for change in business, society, technology, and politics: Inferential Focus (IF). And IF does this by reading three hundred magazines. Apparently, that's all it takes to see the future coming. IF is famous for spotting patterns early, well before they are visible to traditional methods. Six people reading three hundred magazines.[6]

So how do they do it? It's the right six people, to be sure, highly trained, very smart. And those three hundred magazines, they are carefully chosen, too. But the secret here is the three hundred editors. Because if an editor doesn't select it, it can't get into the net. IF's data are entirely mediated by editorial choice: which topic, which treatment, which journalist, which reworking, which rewording.

This is precisely what the CCO wants to do: find the magazines that matter and take advantage of the powers of pattern recognition that editors put at their disposal. So the CCO wants to begin with three hundred magazines. But why stop there? The CCO should have several editors he or she counts as advisers and meets with regularly. Cultivate them. Befriend them. Pay them.

MONITORING POPULAR CULTURE

Sharing the labor in small collaborative groups is the only sensible way to keep track of the great blooming variety of popular culture. We need a network on Ning called "three hundred magazines" to help us find and form these groups. I think our collaborations need to be small. I would happily read *The Economist* for five other people (and rely upon them to read the

Hollywood Reporter for me). Any more than that, and I can't be relied upon to capture anything useful for anyone. If six is the magic number, who precisely are the other five people I should be collaborating with? And this suggests the value of someone who works as a kind of yenta helping put together the most productive sixsome.

As a CCO, you are now obliged to watch hours of TV. (Sorry, someone has to.) You may ask yourself questions like: What does the overwhelming success of *Two and a Half Men* tell me about how men define themselves in our culture?[7] Does the fact that *Arrested Development* topped out at 4.3 million viewers tell us that this is the natural limit of this audience in TV land, or was there some relatively simple fix that could have boosted viewership and saved the show?[8] Did the rise of Rachael Ray suggest that Martha Stewart's star was beginning to fall? Or is there room for both of them? James L. Brooks began his career writing episodes of *The Andy Griffith Show*. He now writes *The Simpsons*. It's not easy to decipher how our culture got from Andy Griffith to Homer Simpson, but that's our job. And once we've done that, we can figure out the transition from Homer Simpson to Seth MacFarlane's "Family Guy." Our culture is under constant reconstruction.

First-run movies are surprisingly hard to monitor. Going to a theater imposes a time tax that we don't have to pay when watching TV. Netflix makes access easier. *Entertainment Weekly* keeps us in touch with what's on offer in the mainstream, and the Independent Film Channel helps us pick up some of the rest. If we are not already well informed about the history of Hollywood and the European cinema, it makes sense to get to know a "Dave Dyment" who does and have him teach us. And here too we need an "exchange" that helps us find our Dyment.

See Bonus Feature B: A Tool Kit for the Rising CCO for more advice in this area.

AN EYE FOR NEW CONVERGENCES

During the early days of any movement, all we hear are weak signals. It's hard to tell whether this is just noise or the beginning of something larger, more durable, more influential. So the CCO spends a lot of time like old-time ham radio operators, headphones on, one hand on the dial, concentrating hard, trying to hear.

There is something brewing on the West Coast. It may or may not include BoingBoing, Steampunk, Make Magazine, low-tech, garage science, O'Reilly publishing, cyberpunk, technology, Nixie tubes, DIY, Whole Earth Catalog, and a deep and cranky suspicion of received wisdom. It does seem to center on impatient, smart, skeptical people looking to see what technology and "crowdsourced science" can be made to do.[9] This may be a minority opinion. It may be the first expression of the next big thing. Whatever it is, the CCO needs to have it on his or her radar.

Experiments are interesting even when they don't scale up into something large or lasting. As the great sociologist Erving Goffman taught us, every breaking of a rule *reveals* the rule, showing what is otherwise assumed and invisible.

We may not like some of the new groups that emerge. Some of them may threaten us. But that's okay. As professionals, we set our personal preferences aside. After all, it's not about us. The good news is that eventually our fear goes away. The more we know, the less we fear. For those who want a place to start, I have great admiration for Frances FitzGerald's *Cities on a Hill: A Journey Through Contemporary American Cultures.*[10] FitzGerald undertook her journey in the mid-'80s, but the book holds up well.

THE BIG PICTURE

By this time, we have identified many things we need to track. In a book called *Flock and Flow*, I proposed we build a system to do this. We want to find tiny innovations out there in the world, as early as possible. We want to place them in our "big picture" and monitor their progress as they work their way to the center of this picture, and into the mainstream of contemporary life.[11]

Some cultural shifts are heralded by tiny shifts in language, the disappearance of some terms, the rise of new phrases. With the production of blogs, status updates, and tweets, we have a great mass of language to examine. As shifts take on more material form and force, we should expect to see them expressed in clothing styles, Web design, music, filmmaking, the restaurant world, retail stores. Consider the example of the humble jalapeño chili pepper. It started as a regional enthusiasm in southern and central Mexico and rushed to the center of American cuisine very quickly indeed.

Consider the artisanal trend that changed the way Americans thought about chocolate, beer, and bread.[12] If we had been living in Los Angeles in the late 1980s we would have had a chance to glimpse this trend as it expressed itself in La Brea Bakery. Here's how the bakery tells its story.

> Back in 1989, La Brea Bakery changed the way people ate bread in Los Angeles. Those beautiful artisan loaves baked for centuries in Europe had yet to make their way to the States. The only bread available was the flavorless, squishy

> white rectangle that came presliced in a bag. Little did we know that when we began producing our crusty varieties such as olive, walnut, or rosemary that we were about to embark on an American bread revolution.[13]

Americans are beginning to deindustrialize their food. Ideally, we would have picked up the cultural impulse early and then tracked it through its many manifestations.

The idea is to have a single place to identify and track all the developments we think might matter. The next step is to make predictions. This is key because no one in cultural circles ever admits they are wrong. Everyone tends to pretend that they knew a particular trend was coming "all along." People tend to forget what they thought six months ago. (This is how we make the process of adjustment easier and less painful.) But those who work in the capital markets are often more scrupulous. They take positions and the market confirms the wisdom of their choice, or shows that they were wrong. And back they go, to scrutinize all the bad decisions and try to figure out what they missed. We need to take a page from this book.

As I argue in *Flock and Flow*, every Hollywood studio has a betting system of this kind. There are many projects in development, and each of them represents a film that might be the "next big hit." As executives read the heavens for signs of change (that is, have lunch with the competition), they will bring some projects forward and push others back. At any given moment, all those projects are their bet against the future. *Something* there is going to be right for the fall season three years hence. The studio is poised for action. Recording labels also use incremental investments of this kind to bring a band along. What I am proposing is a larger system of this kind.

The big picture will oblige us to pick up things that are surviving infancy and moving forward. We must decide where we expect them to stand in three months, six months, and a year. And then we must scrutinize our successes and our failures and see how the algorithm needs to be changed. In the case of tracking the preppy innovation, I proposed a rough sketch of the big picture that might have helped us pick it up in the late '60s and track it through to its flowering in the 1980s.

HOW TO UNDERSTAND CORPORATE CULTURE

Very well. We have our data. We have our tracking system. We have our insights. We are poised for action. But nothing can happen unless we persuade our corporation to act. Now it is time for the CCO to play the anthropologist and study his or her own corporation in a careful, thorough, dispassionate way. Almost no one does this. Most members of the corporation know it from the point of view given them by the job they have (or had). They don't survey the rest of the company.

Every corporation has a style, a characteristic way of defining processes and outcomes, problems and solutions.[14] To take the most obvious example: One kind of corporation sprang from the mind of Steve Jobs. A very different one from the mind of Bill Gates. Wall Street was famous for demonstrating how different its corporate cultures (some now vanished) could be. Differences of style made for differences of a more substantial kind. God spare the CEO who defies the internal culture. When Chuck Prince took over as CEO at Citigroup in 2003, shock waves ran through the executive suite.[15] His style was not Citigroup. It wasn't even capital markets. We might expect Citigroup to have gracefully, invisibly adjusted. After all, the CEO calls the shots. But, no. Feathers were ruffled. Waters needed calming. Culture matters but that doesn't mean we make ourselves its witting students or operators. It's up to the CCO to make it a passion that receives detailed, thoroughgoing study, and not the sort of thing that he or she captures from pithy comments by colleagues over lunch.

Within this overall culture, there are some basic principles. Theodore Levitt asked his famous question: What business are we in? The answer seemed obvious and that was the problem. Levitt's question matters because the corporation holds some assumptions so deeply that they disappear from view.[16] As we noted in the case of Mary Minnick, the Coca-Cola Company had a hard time grasping the significance of branded water and non-carbonated soft drinks, even when the evidence was piling up around it. The Coca-Cola Company was very good at making Coke. It wanted to keep making Coke. It's the CCO's job to ferret out these assumptions and release the corporation from them.

In an elegant little essay for the *Harvard Business Review*, David Gray says,

> Little attention has been paid to ignorance as a precious resource. Unlike knowledge, which is infinitely reusable, ignorance is a one-shot deal: Once it has been displaced by knowledge, it can be hard to get back. And after it's gone, we are more apt to follow well-worn paths to find answers than to exert our sense of what we don't know in order to probe new options. Knowledge can stand in the way of innovation. Solved problems tend to stay solved—sometimes disastrously so.[17]

It is the CCO's job to get back to the blank slate that shows all the strategic options, not just the local favorites.

MAKING MONEY

The office of the Chief Culture Officer is not decorative. It is not a matter of corporate due diligence. It's not to augment the intelligence of the C-suite. It exists to create value for shareholders. It exists to move product, create profit, and fatten the bottom line.

There are two ways the CCO pursues profit. The first is in the workaday business of making the C-suite's decisions better informed of the opportunities and the risks that come from culture. The second is by acting like an internal entrepreneur, an innovation agent inside the corporation.

Our hero in the second case is Geoffrey Frost and his exemplary work for Motorola on the Razr. We can say with some certainty that had it not been for Frost's intervention, the Razr would never have happened. To observe the full glory of this accomplishment, let's recall that the Razr was launched in 2004 with the expectation that it would sell 2 million units. By the end of 2005, it had sold 20 million. By the end of 2006, it had sold 50 million. One man. Fifty million handsets.

Frost's method exemplifies what a CCO can do. He had a passport to the entire corporation. He knew where the next idea might come from. But he also had a deep knowledge of the corporation. So Frost knew exactly what had to happen to get the Razr innovation out of the lab and into development. Finally, he knew the precise players and where "death by committee" was most likely to happen. Talk about a river captain. Frost singlehandedly shepherded the innovation from inception to the marketplace. It probably doesn't need saying, but I'm going to anyhow: Motorola before and after this act of administrative genius was a corporation in deep trouble that seemed somehow to specialize in getting in its own way.

The corporation cares about top-line growth. As business scholars McGovern et al. point out, this is the growth that augments shareholder value and drives investor interest.[18] (This is so because more than 50 percent of a stock's total value assumes this future growth, and because growth "purchased" through mergers and acquisitions is unreliable.) If the only thing the CCO does is help discover new ideas and promote organic growth, he or she will have justified the position. As an internal entrepreneur of the kind that Frost was for Motorola, the CCO uses executive power to give the corporation the speed and nimbleness of a start-up. In fact, the CCO is liberating good ideas from bureaucratic process and "death by committee." If *BusinessWeek* is right to say ours is an "innovation economy," the corporation needs new orders and agents of dynamism.[19]

But we must not ignore the CCO's broader role. In this case, the CCO plays an air traffic controller, surveying the three time horizons (short, middle, and distant), watching for changes that open opportunities or augur trouble.[20] As it is, the corporation attempts to adapt to these changes after they have arrived. But if we wait this long, the thing is dying even as we embrace it. Thus did Kraft "get in on" the South Beach Diet just as it was falling from fashion.[21] The CCO would have identified the great-room trend for Weyerhaeuser Forest Products, the artisanal trend for Purdue Chicken, the significance of newcomer Rachael Ray for Martha Stewart, and what the recycling trend would eventually mean for Kimberly-Clark.

PLAYING WELL WITH OTHERS: THE REST OF THE C-SUITE

The CCO works in support of the chief executive officer. And the CEO is Zeusian. Hers is the head from which the corporation springs. The CCO's job is to figure out how to insinuate cultural knowledge into the CEO's head. This can be tricky because the CEO is often a senior male, who defines and exercises his intelligence as something that cuts through noise and nonsense to get at the fact of the matter. To this man, culture often looks like noise and nonsense. This CEO thinks culture is the kind of thing that fills his daughter's head. Like that singer Lil Wayne. Covered in tattoos, master of profanity. Scary! The conventional CEO has a degree in accounting, engineering, or economics. He went to a business school where no culture was taught, and he now lives in AmericanExpressPlatinumLand, a place where culture means openings at the Met, opera in Santa Fe, Diana Krall CDs, and *Masterpiece Theatre* on Sunday nights. The CCO's job is to help this CEO understand that contemporary culture is something more than this, that it is not noise, and that it is not the enemy. Good luck.

But this is just the first problem. We should think of our CEO as a Soviet-era Moscow audience and the CCO as Radio Free Europe. The CCO is trying to penetrate an airspace constantly being "jammed" by other things. The CEO is burdened, taxed, and put upon to the very limit of human capacity. In the words of the *Harvard Business Review*,

> CEOs are being weighed down by the ever-growing complexity of doing business in a global economy. The demands and intricacies of conducting business in multiple

> cultures, time zones, and political or regulatory environments are exacting a stiff toll . . . Greater complexity on all fronts may explain why, according to one study, top management spends less than three hours a month, on average, discussing strategy issues (including mergers and acquisitions) or making strategic decisions.[22]

Everyone wants a piece of the CEO: the shareholder, Wall Street, the board, the press, and everyone in the corporation. CEOs have a very brief time to show results. What they do not want is a charming survey of contemporary culture. What they need is an elevator pitch, often delivered in an actual elevator, that establishes why *this* opportunity makes senses or *that* product will make money. Success will sound like this: "I am getting off here. Send your plan to Bill. This sounds good." Then he's gone.

CCOs will find themselves the object of suspicion and sometimes hostility. People will regard them as the spawn of the devil. Or they will dismiss them as irrelevant. The first interview I did as an anthropologist interested in contemporary culture, my respondent said, "This is a make-work project, right?" We must fight the temptation to retreat to our high horse. That's no respite. That's called sulking.

And what we must never do is play the cool card. In the early days, and perhaps indefinitely, this means no cool glasses, no hip shirts. No asking people whether they have seen the latest movie. We need to have seen that movie but no one else needs to know about it. We will find colleagues who are experts in some part of contemporary culture—action movies, soaps, and sports—and that's our opportunity to make the connection. If we make them our teachers, they will accept us as their teachers. But the first rule for the C-suite: We may never be "hipper than thou." The trick is to be open and guileless.

And here's an additional problem. If you do make contact with the CEO, and he or she does begin to pay attention to culture as an essential resource, something tricky can happen. The CEO can "go native," suddenly getting in touch with the sixteen-year-old within. Worst case, we have helped fuel a midlife crisis. How awkward! If this plays itself out, it's goodbye to your best friend in the C-suite.

But the chief problem here is open hostility. Some of our colleagues in the C-suite will say, in effect, "Listen, I don't understand culture. And it's too late to learn. If I accept that it matters, I have admitted liability and surrendered power." For some of these colleagues, it will be much easier to say, "No, you're wrong. Culture doesn't matter. And you can't make me." It can get that juvenile. Our defense: If the corporation must constantly sense and respond to the turbulence around it, if some of the opportunity and the danger of this new economy comes from culture, then the corporation needs a CCO.

There are other players in the C-suite, and we must make ourselves useful to each of them. The CIO is the gateway to the data and outreach we need to do social media. We must help him or her help us. The head of human relations (aka human capital) is dealing with new generations of workers she doesn't fully understand. CCO to the rescue. The chief marketing officer is dealing with consumer taste and preference that runs in all directions. We can help here too. The CCO can make him- or herself useful everywhere in the corporation, and the more value he or she creates, the more essential he or she becomes.

The most important rule here: Don't be partisan. Don't be cool. Treat everyone as more knowledgeable than yourself.

(Because in important matters they almost certainly are.) Trade mentorships with fellow members of the C-suite. We need them more than they need us.

BREATHING IN CULTURE

The corporation is constantly drawing from culture. A 2008 AT&T ad shows a middle-aged African American walking down the street. His phone rings. He says, "Hey, bud!"

Then in quick succession, we see a series of people answering their phones. They say:

"Hey, buddy!"

"How's it going?!"

"What's up?!"

"What's shaking?!"

"What's popping?!"

"What's crackin'?!"

"Yeah, buddy!"

"Brother!"

"Dude!"

"What's up?!" (x3)

"Hey!" (x3)

"Daddy!"

"Dog!"

"Sweetie!"

"Buddy!"

"Beautiful!"

"Ah!"

Raiding everyday life is now common in American advertising. In a 2008 Verizon ad, Dad comes storming out of his suburban home, daughter in tow.

He says, "Today I plan on not freaking out about my wireless bill."

And with this he offers a recitation of every fashionable phrase he can think of, including that he's "kickin' it," and "totally down with my boys," each with its own daffy hand gesture. Clearly, Dad has been watching too many "urban" movies. He's "straight outta Compton."

Finally, the daughter can't stand it anymore and she says, "Dad!" in a way that says, "Dad, you are embarrassing yourself beyond redemption. Worse, you are embarrassing me. Especially *me*! Stop it!"

A 2008 Bud Light ad shows us all the ways people say "dude." It turns out this one little syllable can express a lot of things, including entreaty, exclamation, accusation, exasperation, dubiety, hilarity, astonishment, and more. In one spot, two guys go to Vegas. As they make their way around town, each event is punctuated by a different, equally revealing "dude." One of the guys meets a suspiciously muscular "showgirl" and in a hasty ceremony marries her. His pal says "dude" in a voice of "I told you so" resignation, and our suspicion is confirmed. The bride is indeed a dude.[23]

In all these cases, the brand is helping itself to language that is floating around in our culture. Some of this language is from fast culture ("what's up" and "dog"), some from slow culture ("hey" and "buddy"), and some in between ("dude"). The brand is inhaling culture, drawing upon the creative commons that belongs to everyone.[24]

This is the CCO's job, to observe culture, to see language changing, to watch as "dude" travels from California through the rest of American culture, to watch as the language of hip-hop finds its way into the suburbs, to notice all the ways we greet one another, to observe the interactions of culture, fast and slow. This is our stock in trade, the kind of knowledge that defines our professional competence. It exists as general, scholarly knowledge, until someone in the corporation says, "Listen, we need to be about communication not as bits and bytes, but as actual people having real conversations." Ah, as it turns out, we do know something about culture that can prove useful here. Thus does the corporation draw upon culture. Thus does the corporation make itself part of our culture, resonating with what the CCO knows is happening "out there."

BREATHING OUT CULTURE

"Too much information!"

"Don't talk to me, talk to the hand."

"I'm not going there."

"That's why they pay me the big bucks."

"How cool is that?"

"You think?"

"It doesn't get any better than this."

"Good times."

"Did I say that out loud?"

The last was delivered by Cliff Clavin on the TV show *Cheers*. The show is long dead. The phrase lives on. Each of these phrases started in the mind of a writer, entered public life in the form of a movie or an ad, and finally found its way into everyday speech.[25] Thus does the corporation exhale.

These phrases that spring from commerce are valuable contributions to the stuff of speech. I was teaching a class at the Harvard Business School, and we were talking about unpredictable variations in supply and demand. Quixotically, a student asked about variations in the supply of cocaine. It was an odd question, just nutty enough to threaten a carefully crafted teaching plan. "I hate it when that happens," I heard myself say.

It got a laugh. The class moved on. The teaching plan re-engaged. (Whew!) It didn't matter that I hadn't made it up. It was funnier because it was prefabricated. We're happy to have our jokes ghosted by comedy writers. And why would we not be? (You've heard people tell their own jokes? How about professors?) It is, generally, a good thing to be scripted. Our audience is prepared. We are funnier.

If we were in a diminishing mood, you could say that we have been reduced to participants in that famous comedian's convention in which all the jokes are so well known they have been identified by number. You only have to say "34" to get a big laugh. This is an old argument: Culture has been flattened, creativity diminished, and we have all been turned into robots, thoughtlessly reproducing bits and pieces from the stream of popular culture that passes constantly through us.

Yes and no. And mostly no. When we appropriate the humor of a TV character, the devil is in the details. If we want the laugh (and want to avoid looking like a robot), we have to get our timing exactly right. In point of fact, we *can't* just say "34." The line has to be well chosen, timed, and delivered. What's really happening here is that commerce gives us a starter kit, and the rest is up to us.

We are availing ourselves of culture that comes from commerce. Sometimes this culture is language and sometimes it's comedy. But commerce can rework the very architecture of our culture. Starbucks created what it calls a "third space," a place between home and work.[26] It's odd to think of a commercial enterprise fashioning any part of public space. (Every bit as odd as our image of Santa being fashioned by the Coca-Cola Company.) But consider public life before Starbucks. In North America, people in public were objects of curiosity and suspicion. A man standing around on a street or in a park raised a question: "What's he doing there?" There was, in effect, a "no loitering" rule and this rule was powerful. Erving Goffman observed that people who had no reason to be "hanging around" in public were obliged to invent one. They would look at their watches ostentatiously, as if to say, "Look, I'm waiting for someone." Or they would look in a store window, "Behold, I am shopping." It was as if everyone had to create a "cover story," because in our culture standing or sitting around in public was not okay. Starbucks made a space where people could "just sit around" without attracting suspicion. Starbucks created permission, where permission was everything.

Nike helped refashion culture, too. In the early 1960s, Philip Knight was pressing his soles with a waffle iron and selling running shoes out of the trunk of his car. Fitness was for high-performance athletes and no one else. In his youth, my father was the fastest middle-distance runner in British Columbia. By middle age, he had forsaken fitness for the cargo cult of post–World War II prosperity. With millions of others, he was feasting on heroic quantities of sugar, salt, fat, sun, alcohol, nicotine, caffeine, and inactivity. Fitness in middle age? Even for this former athlete, it was manifestly for "Swedish health nuts" and other people who frequented health food stores. (We might note in passing that health food stores were once so marginal they actually seemed disreputable. Fitness and organic food—in the postwar period these were for oddball losers.)

Knight and Bill Bowerman were prime movers of a change. Teamed with Wieden + Kennedy, celebrity endorsers, and a feeling for the times, they invented a brand that helped reinvent a culture. Quite suddenly, fitness was okay. Millions of couch potatoes took to running, jogging, aerobics, step classes, mall walking, amateur sports like soccer and softball, skating, and parkour. In the place of all that inertia, all those excuses, and a culture of sloth, they "just did it." I was one of those people who ran. I am now one of the millions who walk. My life, indeed, my very body, is different for the Nike influence.

In each case—language, comedy, Starbucks, and Nike—the corporation can be seen fashioning culture, actually changing how we speak, how we interact, how we understand public life, the ideas with which we understand leisure, fitness, and our bodies. In each case, the corporation is exhaling culture. The process of creating culture will grow more intense. Corporations are beginning to reckon with their obligation to participate in culture in new ways to new degrees. As a "gift economy" emerges, the corporation will be called upon to create and share cultural capital. Watch for heavy breathing indeed.

And it won't be easy. For the gift economy is counterintuitive for the corporation. Suddenly it is required to release value into the world without any assurance of immediate return. (To use the language of the great anthropologist Marshall Sahlins, exchange is no longer direct but "generalized" and circular.)[27] This sort of thing goes against the instincts of the corporation. And it will take a CCO to call the strategic shots.[28]

A LIVING, BREATHING CORPORATION

Corporations once lived a tidy life. They made something in a factory. They sold something in a store. The transaction ended at the cash register. Value given, value got; the relationship in Adam Smith's world was crisp and fleeting.

Things are more complicated now. Now the corporation is not just an economic actor, it is also a social and a cultural one. Consumers expect it to "get down to business," to supply the world with goods and services. But they also expect the corporation to be both a good citizen and an interesting companion. The relationship, once fleeting, now endures.

What Wieden did for Nike, what Jensen did for Volkswagen, what Bogusky did for Microsoft, what Unilever did for Dove, what Glaser did for New York City—all these were contributions to our culture. What Hollywood, Nike, and Starbucks did for public life, these too rework, reform our culture. We are looking at something much more organic than Smith could ever have imagined. Instead of the interest-seeking automaton, the corporation looks more organic, like something living and breathing. A key part of its respiration now is the movement of culture in and culture out. Only a CCO in the C-suite and only a very smart person serving as CCO can manage this respiration.

CHAPTER 7

HOW-TO

NOTICING

In early 2009, I was in Chicago doing a presentation for an ad agency. I had been asked to describe how an anthropologist notices, and how he gets from noticing to insight. My talking point was something I noticed on the train that runs between New York City and Connecticut. Several guys were reading papers and magazines, and all of them seemed to be snapping each page as they went. This sort of thing is annoying and banal in equal measure, the sort of thing we notice only to dismiss. But in this case, I found myself wondering. Why snapping?

I told these young planners about the time I sat beside Marshall Sahlins, now emeritus professor at the University of Chicago, as he read one of my papers. Professor Sahlins was traveling at speed through my paper, not because it was well written but because not even bad writing could slow him down. Suddenly he stopped in his tracks and said, "Hmm, I wonder why that is."

I was noticing Sahlins notice. I was watching a very smart man acknowledge the limits of understanding. You could almost hear him thinking, "Why can't I think this?" This is the secret of noticing. Spotting things that defy expectation, that don't "compute." There is always a temptation to "fake the results" and assimilate things we don't understand to things we do. But the Sahlinsian approach says, let strange things force new ideas . . . because good noticers are fearless noticers.

Potentially, every puzzle is a stowaway with mutiny in its heart. It can overturn our existing explanations and encourage a change in the way we think. The anthropological lesson: Notice as much as you can and pay special attention to things that puzzle. Pay attention to any failure of attention. Cultivate the Sahlinsian voice within, the one that says, "Hmm, I wonder why that is?"

Why snapping? As I thought about it, the thing that came lumbering into mind was a documentary I'd seen years ago about autistic children. Some of them were shown striking themselves, or hitting their heads against walls. The documentary said these kids were "stimming." Stimming is defined as a "repetitive body movement (often done unconsciously) that self-stimulates one or more senses in a regulated manner," and it is indeed a characteristic of some autistic children.[1] Plainly, the guys on the train were not autistic. But they were engaged in patterned behavior and that's the objective of the anthropological noticing: What is the pattern? Why is the pattern?

For those guys on the train, snapping seemed like a way of marking "this page done." It could be a way of setting a pace. People seemed to be snapping at regular intervals. Money managers (most people on this train are involved in financial markets one way or another) are driven people. It even seemed possible that snapping was a way of asking us to observe how expeditiously they were dispatching the task of . . . turning a page. These guys (and they are mostly guys) are judged by results. And the issue of performance may be so pressing that they feel obliged to show efficiency even here. Yes, I know this goes a little far. But at this stage we are obliged to let an idea go wherever it wants.

We could think of stimming as a call for feedback. Banging a drum proves the existence of the drummer. It completes a task. The sound of the drum locates the drummer. For someone who lives in a soupy, indeterminate world, drumming reasserts a certain clarity. I drum, *ergo sum*.

Does *any* of this apply to money managers? Who knows! Probably not. And that's okay, because now we have something with which to think. An odd little idea that we can keep posted on the inside of our heads. It might be useful. It might not be useful. The important thing is that we noticed and noticing led to . . . something that might someday lead to . . . something we can use. Hey presto, there in the audience at the agency was a client from Wrigley's and our discussion of stimming led to a discussion of gum. (And let's be honest, for many teenagers, it's gum, *ergo sum*.)

Noticing has been taken captive by the academic set. Postmodernists celebrate the *flaneur*, a person who strolls, saunters, and loafs, noticing the city to which he or she goes.[2] The idea of a flaneur is so prized, it has become a pose. It is played out in cafés, where we see moody young men scribbling in their Moleskin notebooks (the de rigueur brand of the moment) tormented by their genius and the need to commit illumination to paper. The cost of the pose is high. Some flaneurs are so busy posturing that they don't actually notice very much. And they are so very scrupulous about what they notice, they miss a great deal. Much of the urgent work of noticing goes undone.

I much prefer the more sincere act of noticing that comes from a guy like Morgan Friedman. (No, not Morgan Freeman. You're thinking of the American film actor, the one in *The Dark Knight*.) Morgan Friedman is a guy in his thirties who has created new standards for noticing.[3] I heard him speak in New York City recently. No posturing for Friedman, no sitting in a café hoping someone will mistake him for a tortured genius.

No, when Friedman gave his talk, he was suggesting that we actually talk to people. In one of his PowerPoint points, he exhorted us to "ask old people what the city was like when they were young.

"Old people are waiting for you. They spend their days on stoops and cafés doing nothing but remembering. They're the ones at the edge between different worlds (umm, literally) connecting them together. Ask them what has changed in their everyday life the most since their childhood. Press them for details: 'The ice-man used to bring us ice once a week' or 'My husband couldn't afford my dowry!'"[4]

While the flaneur is swanning about the city in reveries of self-exaltation, the Friedmanesque observer is running the city down, seizing the opportunity it gives for investigation. In the place of the PoMoPo (the postmodern pose), Friedman wants us to chat up an ancient neighbor despite the fact that she is badly dressed and, well, old. (The CCO is interested in everything, even the banal and unattractive.)

I fell into conversation with Friedman after his talk and discovered that he's the guy who created Overheard in New York, that Web site that allows noticers to pool their observations of city life. Brilliant.

Here's a fragment of conversation overheard in an elevator in New York City at Twentieth Street and First Avenue.

TWENTYSOMETHING GIRL, hands full: Could you hit 1 for me?
MAN, pushing button: You're welcome.
TWENTYSOMETHING GIRL: Oh! Thank you.
MAN: Learn some manners.
TWENTYSOMETHING GIRL: Man, I'd tell you to fuck yourself if my mom wasn't with me.[5]

It's hard *not* to notice an exchange like this. Puzzling it out, that's another matter. Here's my brief account of the exchange. (As always, your mileage may vary.)

Things start out well enough. Passenger 1 calls for the first floor. She puts it in the form of a request, and Passenger 2 takes her at her word. When he complies, he believes he has done her a favor and that he now has a marker or a debt. He would like to see the debt discharged. A "thank you" would suffice.

But, no. Passenger 1 is not forthcoming. She just stands there. Passenger 2 reminds her of her debt by pretending that she *has* discharged it. "You're welcome," he says. Passenger 1 tries to make amends: "Oh! Thank you." But it's not enough. Passenger 2 is not mollified. The debt remains. "Learn some manners," he tells her. This is a calculated punishment. It says, in effect, what you failed to give me, I take from you.

Now it is the turn of Passenger 1 to take umbrage. As a New Yorker, she'll be damned if she is going to take criticism from a stranger. Passenger 2 has gone too far, and it's his turn for punishment.

But there's a problem. Passenger 1 is with her mom. This complicates things wonderfully, because mothers are generally the most influential source of a child's knowledge of social rules.

What to do?

Passenger 1 resorts to a strategy that is both crude and effective. She honors the constraint so that she can violate it. (The symbolic equivalent of covering her mom's ears.) Propriety is satisfied. Punishment is rendered. City life goes on.[6]

These are the two steps of noticing for the CCO. First, observe. Then explain. Noticing is a matter of having nimble eyes, and the ability to spot the telling or troublesome detail. Naturally, we want to be be discreet about it. People do not like to be observed and I don't blame them. But that's our job. The thing is not to stare. Keep the gaze moving. Periodically, it is useful to make the gaze go blank, and turn the gaze inward, to simulate distraction, absorption. But even after we have mastered the art of misdirection, someone will spot us. My one trip to Vegas was interesting in just this way. Casinos are filled with watchers, and they are trained to watch for the tiniest of details. So they picked me up as a watcher right away . . . and they didn't like it. Who was I? And what was I watching? (This was my turn to see what it's like to be watched by a watcher.)

The second step, explaining, could just as easily be called speculating. As you can see in the elevator example, I am not looking for an exact rendering of what happened there. I didn't do any ethnographic research. I didn't consult the scholarship. I merely worked up a rough sketch with no claims of veracity. This isn't inquiry. It's something more casual than an experiment. It's okay to be wrong. The thing is to engage.

The students of great Polish-English anthropologist Bronislaw Malinowski used to play a game. As functionalists, they would try to figure out the function of a custom or an institution under discussion. "If the Trobriand Islanders did it, or had it, it must be assumed to be a necessary thing for them to do or have."[7] The trick was to figure out why it was necessary. Explanation in our case is a training exercise, too. It is designed to sharpen the wits, to expand the field of explanatory possibility, to be intellectually ecumenical. It is more important to be active than accurate.

This is the job of the CCO. To notice and notice and notice some more. And propose, wrestle, reckon, and conjure with the results. A career of this and you will be a paragon.

EMPATHY

Empathy is the method that A. G. Lafley, acting as a stealth CCO, used to understand Mrs. Rios in Venezuela. As he looked at all the lotions and potions that sat before her, he grasped suddenly what they meant to her. "These are her entertainment." And in this moment of empathy, he escaped the Procter & Gamble view of things.

Empathy is the ability to feel how another person feels. As the psychologist and writer Daniel Goleman says, it "comes into play in a vast array of life's arenas, from sales to management, to romance and parenting, to compassion and political action."[8] It is an exceedingly useful way of knowing. For the CCO it is the only way out of one's own world into the world.

A. G. Lafley was born in 1948. He was raised in New Hampshire. He has a BA from Hamilton College and an MBA from Harvard.[9] He is the president and CEO of P&G, a company that generated around $83 billion in revenue in 2008. Like every CEO, he is paid handsomely. Mrs. Rios is less well known to us, but we may make a few educated guesses.[10] Chances are, she is a mother in her thirties with a high school education who raises, say, three children on a household income that is rather less handsome, and probably less than $20,000 a year.

It is hard to imagine two people more different. But empathy allows these two people to find each other across their differences. Of course, there can't be full transparency. Many of the differences between them must remain nonnegotiable. But with enough careful listening, enough thoughtful noticing, enough ethnographic due diligence, suddenly something arcs between them. Lafley escapes the P&G culture and the terrible demands that hound every CEO, and he "gets" her. It's partial. It's imperfect. It's amazing.

Empathy gives us the ability to know what someone is thinking. It feels like an effortless intuition but the mechanics of empathy are complicated. We read external signals, tone of voice, facial expression, the drift of the conversation, the details of a home in Venezuela. We observe those bottles before Mrs. Rios, how she arranges them, looks at them, handles them. We resort to the "data bank" of our own thoughts and feelings. We are searching for a match. We look for something in us that looks like something in her. Technically, it probably works like a facial recognition search, a pattern search moving at fantastic speeds, churning through vast bodies of data. And then—*ding*—a match is found. We are a little clearer. Follow-up questions narrow the possibilities, and the ding becomes a chime. A few more questions, and the chime becomes a bell-like tone, larger and truer. At the end of two hours, we have a clue. We have Mrs. Rios's world from the inside.

Part of the task is to build up the "data bank." The more diverse experiences we have of the world, the better. In Lafley's case, this meant a liberal arts education, PhD studies interrupted by the draft, five years serving in the Navy. Lafley collects comics and Vespas. He is a parent. He volunteers and sits on several boards. He reads widely, finding leadership advice in Shakespeare's *Henry V*.[11] As a thirty-two-year employee of P&G, Lafley has had assignments that take him outside the United States, including a good deal of time spent in China and Japan. We may treat these as things that make him different from Mrs. Rios, but in point of fact, used intelligently, these are the things he can use to understand her.[12]

We can learn empathy. We can improve empathy. I think some people are born or raised with a gift for empathy. Not quite like that woman on *Star Trek*, not actually hearing people's thoughts. Some people are naturals, but for the rest of us it comes from practice. We get better with experience. The more we use it, the better it becomes. Eventually, when we have logged what *New Yorker* writer Malcolm Gladwell calls our "outlier" apprenticeship, our 10,000 hours, it will serve us effortlessly.[13] We get new range, new depth. We can capture thoughts and feelings that would have been alien and irreproducible a few years before.[14]

I can imagine that some people inside the corporation will resist the idea of empathy as too "soft" and sentimental to serve the corporation. By this reckoning, what the corporation *really* wants is tough-minded decision-making. These people will complain that empathy is precisely the kind of vague and imprecise mush that gets the corporation in trouble. What we want, they argue, is numbers and a more rigorous kind of knowledge.

To refuse empathy is a kind of managerial malpractice. It costs us essential knowledge of our colleagues and our customers. It makes the world inscrutable when it doesn't have to be. And occasionally we meet someone in the C-suite who is tone-deaf when it comes to other minds. Almost always they have other analytical skills. And these skills do give them knowledge of the world that is powerful and illuminating. And we must hope it is very illuminating indeed. Without emotional sonar, there are many things he cannot know. This person is in a sense trapped in himself. And if he works for a corporation with that captivating gravitational field, he is trapped twice.

In the twentieth century, the corporation was so large, it created its own weather system. General Motors, IBM, and Coca-Cola could shape the world to their will. And in this world, it was enough to be really analytically smart. Now we have to know the world outside the corporation. We have to know worlds alien to our own. We have to know worlds that proceed according to other assumptions. Without empathy, these worlds are opaque to us.[15]

The news has reached even the Harvard Business School. When faculty members Srikant Datar and David Garvin consulted the b-school world, they were told that MBAs needed more "self-awareness and the capacity for introspection and empathy."[16] This is good news, but I am a little puzzled why they continue to call these "soft skills." In fact, empathy is frequently the blade that finds the right insight, extracts from it the real strategic and tactical opportunity, and crafts it into a final, compelling form. Is this really a "soft" skill? (And what does it say about the b-school community that it uses this patronizing language?)

The real measure of empathy's growing standing might be the success of Daniel Pink's *A Whole New Mind*. Pink shows the strengths of the "right brain": that it helps us reason holistically, recognize patterns, interpret emotions, and perceive things in a "sheet lightning" way.[17] Pink notices that it is precisely in an empathic moment that we are visited by illumination. Suddenly we "get" what it is the consumer means. Things fall into place. If these several bodies of data are true, *this* must be the way the world looks to the consumer. We assemble a world in ourselves and we experience the consumer's experience of the world.

The CEO of Delta Air Lines, Richard Anderson, was recently asked how business school should change. He gave a very Pinkian answer. As he told the *New York Times*, "We measure, study, quantify, analyze every single piece of our business. Business schools in the United States have done a phenomenal job of creating that capability. But then you've got to be able to take all that data and information and transform it into change in the organization and improvement in the organization and the formulation of the business strategy."[18]

We may think of empathy as the ability to see the bigger picture that will transform the corporation inside and out.

NOTICING + EMPATHY = ETHNOGRAPHY

When I started doing ethnographic interviews for corporations in the mid-1980s, the method was still quite rare. My first project was for Chrysler. Their question was: "Why are we selling more Jeeps in New York City than we are in Colorado?" My first respondent was a guy who lived outside of Boston. He was so nervous about inviting me into his home to do the interview, he insisted that I stand on a traffic island in his small town in Massachusetts and drove around me several times before deciding that I was okay.

Put noticing and empathy together, and add the opportunity to talk to people closely, and we have the ethnographic method. The ethnographic interview takes us into someone's home, where we sit listening ever so carefully to them talk about the product, themselves, their families, their lives, until eventually we begin to see where the logic of the product intersects (or may be made to intersect) with the product or communication.

Ethnography has come a long way. Indeed, it is now in danger of being killed by its success. It is practiced by many people and several companies without the benefit of formal training or a disciplined approach. It's become a way for companies to do due diligence, to check the "ethnography" box. For many people, "ethnographic research" is merely research conducted in the home. Surely this is better, sometimes, than the sterility of the focus-group facility. More information is bound to leak into the interview, and because we are interviewing one person instead of twelve, we can concentrate a little more carefully. But too often ethnographic research practiced by the corporation does not deliver the full value of which it is capable.

Take, for instance, the story of a new chain of stores in the United States. Tesco's Fresh & Easy grocery stores have been in the United States for about fifteen months. Tesco appears to have done its ethnographic due diligence, according to an anonymous writer for *The Economist*.

The company has spent years gathering detailed information on every aspect of American life. Most retailers would think they had done their homework after the usual focus groups and surveys, but Tesco went much further. Researchers, including a small cohort of top executives, spent two weeks living with sixty American families. They poked around in their kitchen cupboards, watched them cook, and followed them as they shopped.[19]

That does sound as if the ethnographic boxes have been checked off. But there is a distressing habit these days to think the ethnographic due diligence has been satisfied if interviews are done in-home and in-store. In fact, an in-home interview is not necessarily ethnographic. It may be merely an interview done in-home.

The ethnographic interview creates an opportunity for noticing. It's good at discovering the telling detail, the one that makes a larger life make sense. Why, for instance, the fridge has all those photos on it. Or, as in the case of Chapter 4, why no one goes in the living room. IDEO, the design and strategy firm, specializes in the cunning observation, the one that says, "Wait a second, if you look at the way they turn the handle on that thing, it's clear that . . . " And when we devote ourselves to a single interview over a couple of hours, our noticing can be systematic and not merely opportunistic.

This can give the interview all the charm of watching paint dry. We want to examine all the possibilities. And this takes a certain patience. We will let the respondent run awhile and then ask him or her to narrow down. "Do you serve this dinner because of X, Y, or Z?" An answer is forthcoming. A choice is made. "Ah, is it X^1, X^2, or X^3?" "Ah, is that $X^{2.1}$ or $X^{2.2}$?" And so it goes, a little like optometry. Clients sometimes like to come to the interview. After a while, they say, "Okay, that's fine, carry on," and they leave.

The CCO must be prepared to admit ignorance and ask naive questions. And this takes a certain humility. There are no fixed questions in an ethnographic interview. This is because the method is designed to proceed opportunistically, to capture the unknown unknowns. Quantitative work keeps the instrument absolutely uniform, the better to control data quality. But this qualitative approach is designed to rebuild questions over the course of the interview. As new intelligence is forthcoming, it is clear that certain questions are wrong, the new topics are now urgent. The ethnographic interview is adaptive.[20]

The method depends on an intellectually mobile interviewer. He or she has to be able to shift frame to see the significance of what the consumer is saying. This is especially difficult when we have to do it in real time, under pressure, on schedule. What does this mean? What can she mean? What's the best way to think about this? What is she really saying? We keep ransacking the intellectual and empathic resources at our disposal. What is the theory, the notion, the memory that could help us make this remark make sense?

In all of this we are constantly hearing new remarks and having to decide: Is this something or is it nothing? If it's something, how do I pry it open? How much time do I give to it? Are we going someplace vital, or will this dead-end up ahead? In the meantime, we are keeping track of the questions we must ask, the things we want to come back to, the hunches that look promising. It's exhausting stuff, and I remember sitting in the lobby of a hotel in Kansas City. I wanted to go up to my room, but I was so tired after a week of interviews, I wasn't sure I had the mental wherewithal to operate the elevator. I know that sounds improbable, but believe me when I say there is no fatigue like ethnographic fatigue.

And the ethnographic interview creates the opportunity for empathy, to glimpse family life from the inside. It's not just about, in this case, groceries, but about how the householder sees and thinks about groceries in the kitchen, in the home, in the meal, in the life of the householder, in the family. Constantly, as the data comes in, we are asking ourselves, I wonder if it's like this, or this, or this. We have turned our brain into a little laboratory. We are hoping to re-create some part of the respondent here. And eventually we will capture how this consumer thinks and feels. Eventually we will anticipate answers. I remember doing an interview on the street in Austin, Texas, with kids coming out of bars. This was in the early 1990s and everyone was in a band. One of the respondents was telling me about his band with a certain drunken enthusiasm, and then he said, "There's one problem, though." And now that I was beginning to grasp the music scene and the impulse from which this style of music sprang, I could say, "Don't tell me. I think I know. You're getting too good." "Yes," he said with a little resentment, implying "you were supposed to be surprised."[21]

When practicing ethnography, we want to see how all the pieces go together.[22] Americans' lives are riddled with discontinuities and contradictions, but there remains an embracing conceptual and emotional logic that helps make them make sense. Indeed, most of the time our lives feel irresistibly sensible, obvious, and inevitable. It's the ethnographic jobs of capturing how and why the assumptions in this life go together, or feel they do. It is this embracing context that goods and services must honor, enter, and resonate with. And it is this embracing context that is so often atomized and broken down by traditional research methods. The embracing context, the bigger picture, lets us say, "Yes, this innovation makes sense for the consumer." Or, "No, this makes sense in the lab. It won't make sense in the home."

Thus does ethnography take advantage of a minute examination of the consumer's world. Thus does it "helicopter" up to see the life of the consumer from a very great height. Eventually we must see this consumer's life in a still larger strategic and quantitative context. We want to see how it is shaped by internal forces. We want to see where it stands against all the other households in this market, city, region, class, or gender. Too often ethnography is treated like a cottage industry, an artisanal activity, a purely person-to-person enterprise. Too often the ethnographer puts on airs about being the only one who can "feel" what is happening. Too often ethnography is taken captive by people who despise the corporation. But this is the usual "culture war" nonsense with which we set up mutual exclusion where something more collaborative is both possible and desirable. Finally, the ethnographic interview needs access to the data and intelligence that matter to big management consulting houses like Monitor and McKinsey. Now ethnography is looking at the life of the consumer from the outside in. When we put these two together, real insight becomes possible.

The Tesco case has all the outward signs of ethnography. Executives left the corporate citadel. They visited the consumer in her home. But what was missing, apparently, was the close-order engagement on which the method relies. It's not clear that real noticing took place. It's not clear empathy was activated. It's not clear that careful questions elicited interesting answers and more questions until "ah, this is who this consumer is." There is something intimated and deeply engaged about ethnography. This is not the place to be going through the motions.

BRAINSTORMING AND OTHER ACTS OF INTELLECTUAL IMPROV

I got my first training in the corporate approach from Denise Fonseca, now director of global business and consumer insights at the Coca-Cola Company. She was running a brainstorming session in New York City. I don't remember the topic. I do remember the training and especially the M&M's.

Fonseca had assembled people with various kinds of expertise. Most were from the academic world. They do not play well with others. They object, cavil, quibble, carp, and niggle.

Fonseca gave us fair warning. She said something like,

> There is one rule in this room: No no's. You may *not* contradict, dispute, or disagree with the things you hear here. I am going to enforce the "no no's" rule with my M&M's. When I hear you contradict, dispute, or disagree, I am going to pelt you with an M&M. Or several M&M's, depending on the severity of your offense.

I listened with interest. And I tried my best. But years of academic training got the better of me. I caviled, quibbled, and disputed several times. The first M&M struck me in the lapel. The second bounced off the notes in front of me. The last one was a direct hit, caroming off my noggin. (Nice shot, Fonseca!)

The "no no's" rule comes as a surprise to a lot of people. It seems like a recipe for chaos. Isn't caviling the very method of quality control? Actually, it isn't always. Too often it's the way academics jam the airwaves against new ideas. But the point of this undertaking is *not* quality control, it's idea generation. When what we are looking for is a sheer profusion of possibilities, no no's is the path to riches.

Good brainstorming is an act of intellectual improv. A group of people agree to break the normal rules and reservations of interaction and "go for it." Their objective: to go places they could not get on their own. To go places no corporation has gone before. To go places the corporation needs to go if it is to have any hope of anticipating the future.[23]

But how are we to separate the good from the bad ideas? The good news is that, in good groups, bad ideas go away by themselves. No one picks them up. No one remains their champion. Groups flock, and they always move in the direction of the good ideas. What James Surowiecki calls the "wisdom of crowds" appears to operate even when we are not drawing from a decision market, but a roomful of creative types.[24]

One of the conditions of brainstorming is a "nonproprietary" approach from the participants. The moment an idea escapes our lips, it belongs to the group, and, if it's a good one, to the corporation. We have to learn to say goodbye. We will get credit in general for our performance and might get a high five from a fellow participant when we have distinguished ourselves, but otherwise ideas end up belonging to everyone. This is sometimes the hardest lesson for academics to learn.

The reward is this: Few things are more exciting than thinking in a group. A group mind emerges. We are now thinking with everyone's ideas. The momentum is remarkable and the moment of discovery is thrilling. We can almost feel a rising drama. The group knows it's "on to something." It will issue from someone's mouth (and of course we hope it's our own) but it will in fact issue from everyone's mind. Suddenly all the disparate pieces, all the hunches, the false leads, the failed experiments clarify and out of the mist emerges Newfoundland.

I saw a wonderful demonstration of how this process can go wrong. I saw a person so monstrously unsuited to idea generation that he was an object lesson, a "how not to do it." Here are several rules I extracted from his example.

- Offer a facial expression that suggests boredom or disdain.
- Offer a body posture that suggests reluctance or disengagement.
- Never look at anyone else in the group.
- Use a slightly peevish tone when speaking.
- When someone offers affirmation of what we say (sometimes the group offers the urgings of a Baptist service: "That's right. Say it!"), never accept his or her acceptance.
- Never acknowledge anyone else's contributions.
- Refer often and with affection to your own contributions.
- Say "but," "I don't think so," "oh, come on," "oh, please," and, yes, "no" as often as possible.

If we want to wither the proceedings, this should do it.

Once we learn to say no to no, we have to learn to say yes to yes. Even when I have my MIT students committed to generating ideas, they sometimes act like snipers, working from afar, picking things off from a great, disengaged distance. What is missing is that all-in intensity that characterizes a good working session inside the corporation. They are not blocking the process. They are just doing what academics always seem to do: phoning it in. Brainstorming works best when we commit heart and soul. It works best when we engage in a kind of improv. The first *positive* rule of brainstorming is just what it is in improv: Take up every pretext and run with it. Get as many ideas onto the table as possible. Happily, good ideas multiply and the bad ideas go away on their own.

Good ideas should get tagged with a word or phrase. This makes it easy to evoke the idea in the discussion that follows. We can say something like, "This [new] idea is like the network idea we were talking about before . . . " And in this case I like to look at the person who came up with the "network" idea as a way of acknowledging his or her contribution.

We are building a kind of airspace. Ideas are tagged but kept ill-defined. The airspace is porous. New ideas are welcome. Old ideas are free to leave. And this airspace is dynamic. No necessary relationships between ideas are specified. We are being deliberately vague because this "problem set" will be reconfigured several times before our work is done. Ideas move in this airspace. The good ones ascend, growing in power and complexity as they go. Ascent is consent. The group likes this configuration. Eyes shine, bodies gesticulate, people lean forward. The idea is taking shape. We can tell it's in transit before it actually arrives. All those fractious people, herded by M&M's, drawn out of their "zero-sum" individualism, are now acting like a group and thinking like one. They are one, brainstorming.[25]

BRANDING

Could it be? I think it is. Tentatively I approach the Coke machine. Gingerly I press the fat plastic rectangle. There's a rumbling sound and a can appears. It's true. This Coke machine doesn't take quarters. This Coke is free!

The temptation to press again is strong. I do. Another can tumbles into view. I am here at the headquarters of the Coca-Cola Company as a consultant, but maybe not for long. There's a good chance I am now stuck in the "refreshment center." I can imagine someone popping into the boardroom down the hall and asking, "Who's the guy in the refreshment center? He's got, like, twelve cans in his pockets."

The Atlanta headquarters of the Coca-Cola Company is magnificent. We approach by a circular driveway that runs around a reflecting pool. Water leaves this pool in a gentle, controlled pour. It looks as if the water could brim at any moment and hold. But there's always just enough water to break the surface tension.

Inside there is another circle, a rotunda of buttery marble. As I wait for security to confirm my credentials and print out a badge, I can't help noticing "The Coca-Cola Company" carved into the marble. Running letters on running marble. Spencerian script, high serif, you might say. It's a virtuoso demonstration of the sculptor's art. So simple, so elegant, so perfect. A corporation is sending us a message: "Ain't nothing to it."

But of course there is something to it. Inside, this corporation may be the very image of Southern grace and charm, all blond wood, subdued colors, a charmed circle. But outside the corporation, it's another story altogether.

The world of the carbonated soft drink, as we have seen, is not well.

Consumers are flocking to a new breed of coffees, juices, and teas—all categories where Coke has historically been weak. For the longest time, Coke seemed in denial, more fixated on reversing the stagnation in soda than investing in the alternative beverages that consumers were clamoring for.[26]

Coke is the most valuable brand in history, but its value has declined 20 percent since 1999. The company stands accused of being unresponsive. Oh, the shame of it. The company that helped create American culture is falling out of touch with it.

In the early days, the Coke brand was a potent bundle of meanings. It stood for the sociality of the drugstore soda fountain we see in the opening scene of *It's a Wonderful Life*. It stood for the inspired "loafing" of the general store described by Harvard anthropologist Evon Vogt.[27] It stood for the America visible to Europeans yearning to breathe free. It stood for the generous man of plenty called Santa Claus. It was charged with Southern grace, and the mystery of its early ingredients. Coke was deeply embedded in the way Americans thought of themselves.[28]

The brand was created by the commercial art of Thomas Nast and Norman Rockwell, the advertising of D'Arcy and McCann-Erickson and then a flood of agencies, the Spencerian script of the brand name, the contour bottle, the many slogans by which Coke has been known ("Coke is it"), the Coke machines, that ubiquitous presence in the American garage.[29] Out of these instruments, the brand was made.

The American verities began to disappear one by one. That rural American disappeared. So did the drugstore. So did anything resembling the general store. So did some American ideas of sociality. So did the white picket fence communities. The culprits are youth culture, the counterculture of the 1960s and 1970s, the fragmentation of consumer taste and preference, the end of the "fun in the sun" concept of adolescence, the arrival of the big-box store and the twenty-four-hour supermarket, and the rise of new beverages: water, sports, and energy drinks, and new-age concoctions. American culture marched away from Coke.

A 2006 ad for Diet Coke shows promise. A young woman enters an old-fashioned barbershop. She asks to have her hair cut off. She emerges triumphant. The risk has paid off. She went into the shop a great beauty. She emerges a great beauty who has claimed her beauty with an act of daring and imagination.[30]

With this spot, the Coca-Cola Company laid claim to some of the more interesting cultural experiments at work in our world. It lays claim to self-ownership, self-construction, self-transformation, blurred boundaries, the playfulness of self-presentation. All of these were previously "no fly" zones for Coke. With the Coca-Cola Company's fastidious reluctance to treat these themes, PepsiCo has enjoyed a free run of the most dynamic and vital parts of contemporary culture. In the 1990s, Snapple and other little brands took up the opportunity.

What is gone forever are the monolithic meanings out of which Coke once built its magnificent brand. What there is, instead, are all the many thousands of meanings into which American culture has fragmented. The good thing about the Diet Coke spot is precisely that it takes up one of the new larger themes, self-transformation. Coke can find a way to get back in touch with culture. It can find a way of creating a brand out of what is happening in America to Americans.

Coke will always use the old arts of advertising but now there are many more instruments: new media, Twitter, Facebook, cell phones, and Web sites. Coke can now be present in all that sociality, not just as a beverage but as a brand. It can make itself a conduit for sociality, not just as the pause that refreshes, but as the brand medium through which people find one another. But it's probably going to take a CCO to make this possible.

New meanings, messages, and instruments can help the corporation solve the real problem: to escape that perfect citadel in Atlanta. For the danger is that this statement of corporate mastery will become a kind of museum for its pretentions, and a fortress so formidable it lets little out and still less in.

There are signs of new life, as brands begin to awaken from their slumber. Brand builders are experimenting with new acts of "meaning manufacture."[31] Brands are joining the rest of culture as a creature of new subtlety, complexity, and sophistication. There are lots of models that describe what branding is and how it works. There are also many intellectual subroutines within the branding world. At your leisure, you will want to master experiential marketing, transmedia, curatorial marketing, and new ideas of multiplicity, cocreation, charisma, mystery, and theater. These represent a tool kit, on which you will draw as the problem at hand demands.[32]

As you can see, I think of brands as bundles of meaning and branding as a process of meaning manufacture and management.[33] Branders find meaning in our culture and invest this meaning in brands. They *build* the brand. When they have done intelligent and vivid work, consumers respond. They find these brands interesting and navigational. They draw meanings from the brand and deploy these meanings for their own purposes, in the construction of the self, as content to distribute to networks, as resources for creative activities of their own. But listen, there are many approaches to branding and I do not wish to commandeer your attention.[34]

For many years, brands were the backward little brother of the cultural world, not as extravagant as film, not as experimental as art, not as forceful as fiction. Brands had a simple task, to bang the drum on behalf of a product or service, to play carney barker for the corporation. Brands were predictable. They were tedious. They subordinated intelligence and creativity for marketing's favorite rhetorical devices: repetition, good humor, simplicity, and of course repetition. But if we scrutinize the work of the stealth CCOs above, it's clear that creative standards are rising.

Branding practice was not much better. Bad ideas were allowed to flourish. Anyone could hang up a shingle and offer advice on branding. There are a slew of books on branding that are appallingly bad. A CCO will have to make smart choices and embrace better, more powerful ideas. The presence of the CCO in the corporate world should have a galvanizing effect on both theory and practice.

DESIGN

The world of design is a little bit mysterious to me. I notice how things are designed. And because I am married to a designer, I am the beneficiary of lots of conversation at the dinner table about design. But as my wife, Pam, will tell you, my feeling for design is merely an amateur's appreciation. I have struggled to come up with a definition of design. Here's my epigram. Design may once have existed to make the world attractive to the eye. Now it exists to make the world attractive to the mind.

Let's triangulate. Consider three designers: Michael Bierut, Brian Collins, and Bruce Mau. I heard Bierut talk recently. He was just getting started and the projector wouldn't cooperate. Someone fiddled with it, and finally the screen lit up. But only three words appeared there: "searching for signal." Bierut paused for a moment in a courtly way and said, "What do I mean when I say 'searching for signal,'" and proceeded to treat this alert from a faulty machine as his one and only slide. Brian Collins recently did some work for an enterprise called wecansolveit.com. They asked him for an icon, and Collins's idea was to make it the word "we." The clever thing: The "w" is actually an upside-down "m." Bruce Mau recently did an exhibit in the museum world called "Massive Change." His idea was roughly this: There are lots of problems in the world, social, technical, ecological. Someone has got to fix them. Why not designers?[35]

I find this dazzling stuff. It is alert, vivid, interesting, playful, brainy, ambitious, and effective. Some part of capitalism may be dour, penny-pinching, and grinding. This isn't it. If we are now a knowledge economy, an innovation economy, a weightless economy, an economy that runs on new and imaginative ideas, designers are precisely the ones we want to work with.[36]

If you talk to the old-timers in the design world, you understand how far design has come. Business was a hardheaded undertaking, a rock 'em, sock 'em Roller Derby. There wasn't much room for designers. And the best the usual C-suite could say in defense of the design budget item was, "How come it costs this much to make things look nice?" And that was the idea. The company was there to identify a need and build a product, and just as it was about to go into production, someone would say, "Geez, shouldn't we get someone to fix it up a little?" The designer would be summoned and in these fleeting last moments asked to do the best he or she could.

Compare this to the present day. Designers are now there at the creation. Often they are called upon to find the "big idea" so the lab can have something to work on. And they are then party to all the processes that see the product, service, or experience out of the corporation into the world. In effect, the designer is now charged with finding the idea and revealing the idea. As A. G. Lafley puts it,

> There are instances where we had great technology, great chemistry, but we did not get the product design or package design or the design of the delivery system right, and the consumer couldn't appreciate what the product had to offer.[37]

Design now has friends in high places. It is routinely featured in the pages of *Wired* and *Fast Company*. It has found a champion in *BusinessWeek*'s Bruce Nussbaum, IDEO's Tom Kelley, Roger Martin at the Rotman School at the University of Toronto, and David Kelley at the Hasso Plattner Institute of Design at Stanford.[38] Once an afterthought, now design's claims to usefulness are truly imperial. As Stanford professor Bob Sutton puts it, "In some parts of American business, every problem can be solved by design." Marissa Mayer at Google is said to see everything as a design problem.[39]

Designers are interested in culture. But sometimes they treat it the way the corporation used to treat design: something consulted too little, too late. It is rare for me to talk to designers who have a deep and thoroughgoing knowledge of American culture. This always strikes me as especially odd when we consider how often designers have shaped this culture.[40] The CCO has to speak design . . . and work with designers who speak culture.[41]

NEW MEDIA

Engineers call Twitter messages "exhaust data." For them these messages are just so much noise in the system, stuff that gets "thrown off" when we attend to more important things. But the CCO has to do better than the engineer's point of view.

Here's another view. I went to Korea a couple years ago to see how kids were using the 3G networks already installed there. It turned out they were using the new electronic networks to build social networks. They would gather friends on their e-mail lists and on Cyworld (the Korean equivalent of MySpace). And they would send them clouds of pictures. The effect was amazing. If you and I had gone to high school together, we were still sending pictures to each other several years later. Even if we went on to separate colleges and lived in separate cities, the bond endured. Photos from a friend in junior high would follow them into college, graduate school, adulthood, and beyond.

For these kids there was relatively little friendship attrition. They were now able to keep almost every friend they ever made. Take your own example, dear reader. How many of the people you knew in elementary school are you still in touch with? How about high school and college? (Me, I'm in touch with about two people from high school and two from college.) Before the advent of 3G, the conventional pattern in Korea was what it was here: ferocious attrition. People lost friends as quickly as they made them. Within a couple years, the link was dead. After a decade or so, even a "dear" friend was a memory. In a moment of nostalgia, we might wish to get in touch. But this was usually difficult. Phone numbers had changed. People had moved. Getting back in touch was an exercise in frustration. We would have to find the guy who knew that girl who might have the number . . .

Korean kids were *keeping* their friends as they went through life. And the trick was that stream of photographs. We might not have seen each other for a couple years, but, ping, I get a photo of you graduating from college. Ping, a wedding photo. Ping, baby picture. The network kept us in touch. Actually, it was a network in a network in a network. That photograph of your wedding activated the memory node I have in my neural network, which in a sense duplicates my social network, which in a sense duplicates on the communications network. We stay connected.

And that's what "tweets" are for. They beam a little message to everyone in our network.[42] The message says, I exist, I am active, I am thinking, feeling, busy, up to stuff. These messages are not exhaust data. They do not empty out of our lives as so much vapor from a pipe. They do not fall upon deaf ears. I may not especially care that you just fed the cat. But you continue to live in memory and in networks when you tell me that you have. And after a while if you have your wits about you and value my attention, your tweets will get wittier and more interesting. (When people are tedious tweeters, we sometimes decommission them.)

All this frantic activity online has a purpose. People are using the networks to build networks. They are keeping all the friends they ever met. And this is something more than a sentimental or trivial activity. Having a robust network, staying in touch will actually change what sociologists like to call our "life chances." For Generation Y, the possession of a network is already making a difference in where they work, whom they marry, what those "life chances" actually are. For my boomer generation, networks are the outcome of accident and attrition. For Generation Y, they are an opportunity to live in a sorted, filtered world. They are opportunity machines.

People my age sometimes ask me, "What's the deal with Generation Y? Why are they so casual about working at this company! They don't seem to think they owe us anything. They're spoiled, right?" And I have to say, as diplomatically as

I can, "It's the network, stupid." My generation treated the corporation as a source of security. This generation has another source of security. As long as they have their social network, the place they work matters much less. And this is where I'm asked, "Okay, tell me the difference between Facebook and MySpace again."[43] Networks have changed the very axis of loyalty in the career lives of Generation Y. The corporation was once a monarch that could demand our fealty. Now it is just another player in our social world.

Those who live by the network may also die by it. For networks do not sustain themselves. If we want our network to sustain us, we must maintain it. And this means feeding it. In this sense, networks have a hydraulic quality. They're a little like mushrooms. Unless they are fed with content, they wither and die. That's one reason 24 million photos are lodged with Facebook each day. In the manner of those Korean kids, these are people "pinging the hive." They are reminding their networks that they exist. And it's not just photos.

There is a hierarchy of content. In the first tier, we let the network know what we're doing, with tweets, texts, Facebook updates, and photographs. In the second tier, we distribute things we have found: articles, images, clips of music and movies, photographs. In the third tier, we say what we think, often about the things distributed in the second tier. We are adding value to content by offering opinion, comment, and criticism. In the last tier, we are saying, "Here's what I made." We are offering blog posts, YouTube video, music on MySpace, art, text, and photographs.

This content becomes capital. As we distribute it around the 'Net, our friends repay us with acknowledgment, respect, regard, admiration. And this becomes profile, cultural capital, and perhaps in the longer term profit of a more tangible kind. But even lesser outcomes are valuable. Our network is sustained, our "life chances" augmented.

The movement of content through networks and the world has been misreckoned in several ways. Richard Dawkins has suggested that we think of these things as memes. "Just as we have found it convenient to think of genes as active agents, working purposefully for their own survival, perhaps it might to be convenient to think of memes in the same way."[44] The trouble with this argument is precisely that content has no intelligence, no motive power of its own. It moves only as and when someone else, the network owner, sees the value in seeing to its transmission through the network. "Cultural ideas do not have agency. They cannot conspire to replicate themselves or to leap from brain to brain. They are not in the business of ensuring their own survival. In fact, the only thing a meme explains is itself."[45]

Douglas Rushkoff has it wrong as well. As my colleague Henry Jenkins has pointed out, things moving online and in-game are not "viral."[46] They do not move by infection. They move because we see value in augmenting and communicating them. A great industry, variously called viral marketing, etc., is founded on a bad metaphor. People trade this stuff in exact proportion that it has value as content and it creates value as capital.

This is where the CCO comes in. The corporation is dealing with consumers who don't just want a can of Coke, bar of soap, TV show, or Vespa. Well, they still want each of these, but there is now something much more precious than their stocks of possessions. It's their network, and what they want from the corporation is content with which to sustain this network. The corporation, the brand, the product, or the experience that can deliver this added value delivers something very precious indeed.

Consumers (aka multipliers) will embrace our inventions when those inventions can add value. They will embrace our inventions when they can distribute them. They will see the point of the value we make available, when they can appropriate and augment this value. It is precisely here that the CCO helps the corporation address itself to people at the end of a long process of production and marketing, as copartners who engage in cocreation in the pursuit of mutual advantage and indeed a richer culture. If what the CCO cares about is helping the corporation participate in a living, breathing culture, new media is key.

PLANNING

Adrian Gunn Wilson is standing onstage at London's Conway Hall. He's the first speaker. His topic: splitting wood.

The event has been created by Russell Davies. He had studied the usual conference and found himself looking at something very like an instrument of medieval torture. In the usual conference, we are as if strapped to a chair in a large hotel room unable to look away or shut our ears against the ramblings of someone offering thinly concealed self-advertisement that threatens to drone on into the evening, quite a lot like this sentence, just going on and on . . . and on. I expect Davies said, "Wouldn't it be more interesting to listen to someone talk about splitting wood?"

The room was filled with three hundred people, many of them planners, virtually all of them "cultural creatives," as

Richard Florida calls them.[47] Most of them, that is to say, make their living by working with, inventing, combining, and assigning cultural meanings. And for this group, splitting wood was flat-out interesting. The room fell into a state of silent absorption.

Wilson told us about axes, technique, and how to know when wood was ready for splitting and when it was too green. Good, metaphorical stuff, all of this was, but what really caught the room's attention was Wilson's description of the big piece of wood that serves as the splitting platform. It's huge and well scored. It stabilizes the wood being split and catches the ax, especially important when it misses its mark. You could almost hear three hundred people go, "You know, this is a pretty good metaphor for an ad agency." Wilson emphasized that this piece of wood was strange and horrible to look at. Yes, very like an agency.

As a planner, Davies is a student of our culture. He's watched the tectonic plates of the conference presentation shift for some time. Davies knows our world has become steadily decentered, flattened, destabilized, distributed, participative, anarchical, and self-organizing. The last thing anyone wants to do is listen to an "expert" ramble on. And that's why Davies created Interesting2007. Why not use the creative intelligence of the audience to make the talk work? Give them a starter, and let them do the rest. They'll be happier and the conference will be much more interesting.

This is just the sort of ingenuity we can expect from planners. CCOs may treat these professionals as particular partners in crime. Planners have a deep knowledge of culture. This is their stock in trade. After all, planners are the people in an ad agency who are charged with representing the consumer.[48]

Years of careful study, constant observation, probing questions, and the planner knows all about culture.

Davies has a good blog post on "How to Be Interesting." His Rule 7 is worth repeating.

> Once a week sit in a coffee-shop or cafe for an hour and listen to other people's conversations. Take notes. Blog about it. (Carefully) Take little dips in other people's lives. Listen to their speech patterns and their concerns. Try and get them down on paper. (Don't let them see. Try not to get beaten up.) Don't force it, don't hop from table to table in search of better eavesdropping, just bask in the conversations that come your way.[49]

This is another way of saying that planners are good at noticing, empathy, and ethnography. Davies is also very good at brainstorming, which he does with great discretion. When he worked for Nike, someone said, "Have you noticed that when the best ideas turn up, Davies is always in the room?"

Planning was created in England by Stephen King at JWT and Stanley Pollitt.[50] It was popularized in the United States by Jay Chiat and widely adopted in the 1990s. It is now a fixture of the ad world. And it serves to give this part of the marketing world a deep well of knowledge. It is staffed by people who make substantial contributions to our knowledge of contemporary culture. Some of this is kept under lock and key. But other work is there for the asking.[51]

The CCO should treat the planner as a gifted partner in the study of culture, the person to ask to do the "deep dive" for which the CCO hasn't the time. Planners can answer the kind of question Davies addressed with Interesting2007: What is the present state of the "conference" and what can we do to fix it? They can answer questions like, "What is the artisanal trend?" "What is the state of breakfast in America?" "How do people think about leisure time?" They are, in short, fantastically useful as a source of data and intelligence. As it stands, planners exist almost exclusively in the agency world. But someday every CCO will want to have one or two of their own.

CHAPTER 8

PHILISTINES

IF YOU'VE READ THIS FAR, YOU COULD BE FORGIVEN FOR thinking the case for culture is irresistible and that it's only a matter of time before every C-suite has a CCO. I wish this were so. In fact, there are several parties who refuse or distort the idea of culture. I like to think of them as Philistines, the name traditionally given to enemies of culture.

ENEMIES IN THE C-SUITE

Michael Eisner was for many years the head of Disney. *Ad Age*'s Claude Brodesser-Akner asked him a very good question.

> One of the ironies of spending two decades as the head of a big media conglomerate is that you're paid to have your finger on the pulse of what's cool and where popular culture is going, but the job almost makes you the most isolated person on the planet. How does a sixty-five-year-old multimillionaire stay connected to what's cool these days so he knows he's headed in the right direction?
>
> Eisner replied:
>
> Well, we're all much more connected now by new media, so you'd have to be pretty much brain-dead not to be

> connected. I have the benefit of being in the baby-boom generation, which was always the largest part of the population. I never spent any time thinking about popular entertainment: I just lived it. And I don't think about it now. You're informed by the very nature of being alive. A good story is still a good story.[1]

Really? I think it's fair to say that Eisner knows about boomer culture, an increasingly small subsection of our culture. But if that's all we know about contemporary culture, we are badly out of touch. And yes, Eisner's life is soaked, as most lives are, with media of many kinds. But media is now so finely segmented and in the case of mainstream radio so repetitive, consuming media does not guarantee broad acquaintance. No doubt, Eisner avails himself of new media. This tells us only that he drinks from a fire hose, not that he's well informed.

Many CEOs insist that they do know contemporary culture. They share Eisner's convention, "I don't think about [culture] now. You're informed by the very nature of being alive." Or, more chillingly, they admit that they don't know contemporary culture and that's okay, because it's all just noise. Sometimes this sort of thing is said as a badge of courage, to show how tough-minded the speaker is, how surely he bats aside what doesn't matter to zero in on what does. Yes, but if culture is where opportunity and danger come from, this sort of thing is just self-indulgent, and indeed the very thing that should draw the attention of the board member and the stock analyst and provoke the question, "Is this man fit for office?"

Let's dig a little deeper into the curious case of Michael Eisner. Yes, he is a boomer. Does this mean he knows about culture? Well, I guess it means he knows about boomer culture. But are we not obliged to acknowledge that boomers are moving away from contemporary culture at speed? Symptoms? They don't quite get *The Simpsons*, not to mention *Family Guy* or *American Dad*. Which is to say, they don't get Seth MacFarlane, one of the most influential comedians working in television and new media. In sum, being a boomer means a person is out of touch with contemporary culture. Chances are, the counterculture of the '90s was a mystery. Chances are, the social networking and new media are a bit of a blur.

And, yes, everyone's life is soaked through with media content. But when I turn on the radio when driving to the store here in Connecticut, what I hear is Van Halen and Kenny Loggins. "Soaked through," yes. "In touch with," no. Now, as Disney CEO, Eisner had a seat at a very interesting window, to say nothing of access to the best consulting advice money can buy. And this no doubt gives him a deeper knowledge than most of us. But, notice, he is not claiming this as his defense.

And, fair enough, the new media give us extraordinary opportunities to stay in touch, from YouTube as the raw feed of contemporary culture, to the many critics and commentators who work these turbulent waters.

On his retirement in February 2009, Robert Lutz was the vice chairman in charge of product development for GM. Lutz was routinely referred to as the "design czar" at GM. And indeed it's clear he cared about design. He was responsible for the development of the Buick Enclave and the Chevy Malibu.

The trouble is Lutz knew relatively little about our culture. What Lutz knew was cars, and what he liked about cars, by all accounts, was speed. A former pilot in the Marine Corps, he never got over his love of fast planes. In later life, he purchased and flew an Aero L-39 ex-Soviet jet fighter. And Lutz loved muscle cars.

But if we know anything about contemporary culture, it is that General Motors was out of step. The Japanese owned quality and used it to take away the sedan market. The Germans owned engineering and used it to take away the upper end of the boomer car market. Detroit struggled to improve on both counts, but it was clear that it would never catch up to Japanese quality or German luxury.

There was a competitive opportunity remaining, a place where Americans could beat the challengers. The real chance for Detroit was design, to make cars that vibrate with the cultural moment as deeply and profoundly as they had in the 1950s. Harley Earl was that man. It is impossible to overestimate the skill with which he spoke to (and for) the culture of the postwar period. It is impossible to calculate how much money he made for General Motors.[2]

What Detroit needed was a man or a woman in every C-suite who understood what was happening in culture. It needed someone who understood what was happening in the minds of boomers (and why they were so deeply wedded to German cars), in youth culture (when the muscle car culture was back with new and strange differences, and why cars like the funny, boxy little Scion were flourishing), and in the life, the heart, and the mind of the soccer mom (for many of whom the minivan felt like the end of everything and especially their youth and their joy). Detroit needed a senior executive who understood the consumer, and the American feeling for mobility in every sense of the word.

And what they had was Robert Lutz. He loved cars for his own deeply personal reasons. He loved muscle cars because they went fast. Lutz was worse than average as a "river captain." I think it's fairly safe to say that Lutz did not ever grasp the muscle car revival (the one portrayed by Hollywood in *XXX*, *The Fast and the Furious*, and now *Fast and Furious*). He must have gloried in the power and the glory and all that sound. Just as surely, he must have been mystified by the fact that it was being produced in some cases by tiny, winged Hondas.

But, you might well say, Lutz is retiring. Clearly Detroit got the message. It is reaching out to another kind of manager, another order of CCO. Correct? Here's what the *Wall Street Journal* has to say on the matter:

> Mr. Lutz will be succeeded as head of global product development in April by Tom Stephens, who runs the company's powertrain unit, which develops engines and transmissions. In a cost-saving move, the product development and powertrain operations will be merged, GM said . . . Mr. Stephens has little input into sharing the design and aesthetic appeal of GM's vehicles.[3]

I rest my case.

THE COOL-HUNTER

There are people who engaged in what Malcolm Gladwell called the cool hunt. Cool-hunters will, for a substantial fee, come into the corporation and help put us in touch with contemporary culture.[4] The trouble is that cool-hunters frequently confuse being informed with being hip. They often show up dressed in black, wearing incredibly cool glasses.

Cool-hunting is under challenge. A couple years ago we were treated to this recantation in *Time* magazine: "The trouble was, it turned out that cool hunting didn't work. 'As hip as it was, as exciting as it was, very few people were able to monetize anything that came out of that,' [Irma] Zandl explains. 'People were fed this line that if the cool hunter found it, then six months from now you would have a rip-roaring business. And I think a lot of people got burned by that.'"[5]

Cool-hunters are the natural enemy of the CCO. They know only what suits them. They don't ever know about slow culture. After all, what's hip about slow culture? They frequently give off a "hipper than thou" and "too cool for school" attitude, and leave a trail of resentment in their wake.

My advice to you as a CCO is this: The moment someone wants to sell you consulting advice and he shows up wearing Prada and really cool glasses, put a hand on your wallet and run for your life. At some point in the conversation, ask him about some aspect of culture that is not fashionable, and see how he handles it. Ask him, say, about swap meets, NASCAR, or gardening. If he doesn't know, that's okay. No one can know everything. But listen carefully what happens next. Does he dis or dismiss the topic? Does he offer hipster's answers, that swap meets are great because they have so many vinyl records (and vinyl is so much truer than digital, blah, blah, blah)? The moment a consultant starts demonstrating this fatal confusion about culture and cool, we have to signal our assistant to fake an urgent phone call. It's time to go.

THE GURU

Sometime in 2008, PepsiCo Americas CEO Massimo d'Amore decided to rebrand the Pepsi brands, including Pepsi, Gatorade, Tropicana, and Mountain Dew.

D'Amore turned to Peter Arnell. Wise choice. Arnell is a brilliant designer, famous for his work for DKNY, Tommy Hilfiger, The Home Depot, Samsung, Hanes, Chanel, and Anne Klein. He is the man who designed the Peapod, the automobile that might just set the pace for the future of the automotive industry.

But things went badly on the Tropicana part of the assignment. The new package was launched in January 2009. Consumers reacted with fury. Sales fell 20 percent. The package was withdrawn in late February.[6]

Arnell's idea for the redesign was laudatory. "We needed to rejuvenate, reengineer, rethink, reparticipate in popular culture."[7] But Arnell's first act of office, apparently, was to embark upon what *BusinessWeek* calls a "five-week world tour of trendy design houses."

This is where he went searching for culture? Design houses? Dude! This is the trouble with gurus. They don't much care about American culture. What they care about is what other incredibly hip people think about culture. We don't find American culture well represented in the design house. Indeed, the rest of American culture is, I would argue, sometimes systematically excluded from the design house.

The America Arnell should have paid attention to is the one that is struggling to survive three storms. First, Americans are working to raise a couple kids, running a home, and struggling to achieve sufficiency for the family. This is always tough, but no sooner do they work things out than Dr. Phil starts beaming them new instructions on how to be a better "parent," "child," or "family." Second, they are wondering if the present downturn will cost one or perhaps all of the incomes on which the family relies. The anxiety is palpable. It's audible. It's there all the time. Third, they are trapped in a new health regime, one that forces them to give up the sugar, salt, fat, richness, and gusto that makes a meal rich and satisfying.

The old Tropicana package was a welcome presence in this household. It was familiar, cheerful, good-hearted. Sitting on the breakfast table, it was a little like a lighthouse, a symbol of some of the things that are a good way to break the fast and prepare for the day. But Arnell felt it wasn't hip enough. He decided to "evolve it into a more current or modern state."[8] How would this play for the American consumer? Who cares! In this case, design is about what the guru wants, not the consumer, not the family. Arnell's response? Almost completely unrepentant. "Can you imagine such *mishegoss* over a freaking box of juice? I can't believe that for the rest of my life I'm going to be known as Peter 'Tropicana' Arnell. I have my own perspective on it. But it's not my brand. It's not my company. So what the hell? I got paid a lot of money, and I have 30 other projects. You move on."[9]

Yes, the guru gets to move on. And the CEO and the rest of her C-suite are obliged to stay on. In a more perfect world, gurus would be chosen with great care and not before the CCO had vetted them for their cultural credentials. CCOs need to work with gurus from time to time. But we will want to watch them like a hawk.

ENGINEERS

"If I leave them alone for a moment in that room, they start building a machine!"

So spoke a client of mine who was growing tired of working with her product development team. I expected to sympathize with her, and it's customary for anthropologists to dislike engineers. But I like working with engineers. They think clearly. They exclude all noise from the problem set. And they start building machines! (This book is a machine for thinking.)

Still, the engineer is inclined to see the world as a place without culture. In the case of Twittering, they see chat online. It looks content free. So it must be content free. It must be what they call "exhaust data." But when we see things through another set of eyes, we can see what's happening here. This exhaust data can be seen as "phatic communication." In spoken language, phatic communication consists of sighs, murmurs, grunts, shouts. It is designed to show people how we feel. It doesn't have much informational content, but lots of emotional and social content. Phatic communication doesn't get much said, but it has social effects so powerful, it gets lots done.[10]

Phatic communication sends a series of messages. These stack rather nicely, each presupposing and building on its predecessor. These messages are, roughly:

1. I exist.
2. I'm okay.
3. You exist.
4. You're okay.
5. The channel is open.
6. The network exists.

7. The network is active.
8. The network is flowing.

This type of communication helps sustain networks. After all, these networks often have many weak links and no hierarchy. They require a steady stream of small messages to sustain themselves. Our networks need phatic communication.

So I'm okay and you're okay. How banal this looks to the engineer. But then cultural meanings and social effects are often invisible to the engineer. This may be one of the reasons that marketing expert Paul Otellini was recently appointed CEO of Intel. Through most of Intel's history, every new product followed a simple pattern: The engineers figured out what was possible and then told the marketing department what to sell. When Otellini took charge of the chip-making division, he "turned the process on its head."[11]

But for every Otellini, there remains Howard Stringer, CEO of Sony. When he was appointed in 2005 as Sony's first non-Japanese CEO, he pledged to make the company "cool again." The revolution has failed. It is not clear that Stringer has any gift for understanding the consumer. And it is not clear that he has appointed anyone who would perform this role for him. The results are yet another large, dopey corporation badly out of touch with its consumers . . . and a CEO for whom the world seems unfair. "[Stringer now] bristles every time he gets the question: Why can't the Japanese electronics giant be more like Apple?"[12]

ECONOMISTS

In *Freakonomics*, Steven Levitt contemplates an important puzzle: In the 1990s, violent crime in the United States fell suddenly and steeply.

He reviews, and finds wanting, the usual explanations. He says the drop in violent crime cannot be exhaustively explained by any one, or combination, of the following factors: innovative policing strategies, increased reliance on prisons, changes in crack and other drug markets, aging of the population, tougher gun control laws, a strong economy, increased number of police, increased use of capital punishment, concealed-weapons laws, gun buybacks, to name most of them.

Levitt prefers his own, now famous, account: legalized abortion diminished the population most likely to commit crime, specifically teens brought into the world by reluctant mothers.[13] This may very well be. But there is a simpler, I think, more obvious explanation. And it comes straight out of culture.

As Levitt points out, we are talking not about crime but violent crime.[14] Lesser crimes—burglary, robbery, and auto theft, for instance—have a "direct financial motivation." Violent crimes (assault, rape, homicide) appear to have an extra-economic motivation. They damage not only the material interests of the victim, but something more. Victims of assault and rape say they feel diminished and even humiliated, and that this immaterial loss creates injury every bit as grievous as the loss of money and possessions.

Violent crime is a crime against esteem, as much as it is a crime against property. (By "esteem," I mean the value attached to the individual by the individual and by others. We could also call this "face," as Erving Goffman did.) And it is as a crime against esteem that violent crime is sometimes committed. The diminishment and humiliation the victim feels is no mere accident of the crime, but an outcome the criminal intends.[15]

If violent crime began to fall in the 1990s, the cultural question is: Why was the need to commit crimes against esteem felt less urgently? What had changed?

To answer this question, we must answer several smaller questions. First, we must ask who would commit a crime against esteem. The answer: those who have suffered attacks upon their own esteem. And who has suffered attacks upon their esteem? Those who endure poverty, stigma, and stereotype.

The criminal commits violent crimes as an act of revenge. He or she is punishing the victim for having so much esteem when the criminal has so little. The criminal may even hope for redistribution. The criminal doesn't get to "keep" the esteem he/she "takes" from a victim. But something like redress has been accomplished. The criminal might not have more esteem, but the victim does have less.

So what happened? What changed the world of the urban criminal? Hip-hop happened. The world of the criminal was transformed by the rise of the single most important development in popular musical taste of the past thirty years.

Rap is seen to be the creation, the voice, of the urban teen. And its rise in popular culture and its domination of taste in matters of music, clothing, and speech had a very interesting outcome. It bestowed new esteem upon impoverished urban teens. As long as it remained the possession of impoverished teens, black and white, rap did not change the esteem equation. But sometime in the late 1980s, it crossed over into the mainstream, black and white. Beastie Boys and Run-DMC were calculated to have crossover appeal, and the former's "Fight for Your Right" entered the top ten in 1986. In 1988, Public Enemy released *It Takes a Nation of Millions to Hold Us Back* and NWA released *Straight Outta Compton*. Rap was now headed for the suburbs. And once this diffusion of musical form had taken place, the position of the impoverished teen went from scorned loser to a creature of standing, status, and credibility. So utterly did rap win the day that, with a brief but interesting interruption in the form of "alternative music," suburban children now wanted very much to walk, talk, and otherwise conduct themselves as if they came from very different socioeconomic origins.

The rise of rap represented a massive transfer of esteem from the teens of the middle-class suburb to those of the impoverished city. There was in short an abrupt and thoroughgoing reversing of the asymmetries. Those who once suffered esteem shortages now enjoyed whacking great surpluses. Violent crime? To protest what exactly? To exact revenge? To appropriate esteem? Violent crime was now an antique of another age, the dangerous preoccupation of another generation, an activity that was now just odd. I believe this is why violent crime began to drop in the early 1990s. As the suburbs began to absorb rap, the esteem economy began to tip in a new direction. Violent crime has become an increasingly pointless enterprise.

True, this treatment of violent crime takes the economist beyond his or her comfort zone. But given the urgency that Levitt addresses in *Freakonomics*, this is perhaps a good idea. We know *why* culture is missing from capitalism. Adam Smith removed it. He said in effect, "To understand this thing called a market, we need two parties, engaged by interest, in an act of exchange . . . and that's all. The social and cultural context we can leave aside."[16] It was a liberating idea, but a partial one. We have been trying to recover from its partialness ever since.

Smith's ideas, sufficient in the eighteenth century, seemed to lose their candlepower as markets shifted their focus from producer to consumer, from supplying "needs" to supplying "wants." Economic actors appeared driven by something larger than self-interest.[17] Furthermore, it was capitalists who addressed the culture deficit, smuggling it back into the pursuit of markets and profits. The newspaperman Alfred Harmsworth (later Lord Northcliffe) talked not about interest but interests. The president of CBS, William S. Paley, talked about taste. Charles Revson of Revlon wasn't interested in "interest" at all. Something more was animating markets, he thought. "In the factory, we make cosmetics; in the store we sell hope."[18]

These capitalists were quietly, unofficially restoring what Smith had excised. After all, to talk about taste is to talk about culture. It is culture that informs the eye, supplies the imagination, and shapes desire. It is culture that says what a "person" is and provides the ideas of gender, age, status, ethnicity, beauty, personality, and emotion we use to classify any particular person.[19] Culture is the Platonic cave containing the "originals" from which our thoughts and feelings spring. In the practice of capitalism, merchants cultivated an idea of culture and a way around Smith.

This rehabilitation of Smith's ideas continues by fits and starts. We dolly back from interest to taste, and from taste to intellectual stopgaps of every kind: demographics, status, psychographics, lifestyle, personality, motivation, decision-making, information processing, and attitudes. All have been proposed as ways to understand the secrets of the economy. The business literature of the twentieth century is littered with "eureka!" proposals, but from an anthropological point of view, all swap one partial view for another.

Culture is missing from the work of most economists. There are glorious exceptions like Tyler Cowen, and I salute them.[20] But most of the professional world embraces Smithian assumptions, insisting that taste and culture are fixed and removed from the explanation. (*De gustibus non est disputandum*!)

THE BUSINESS SCHOOL PROFESSOR

A couple years ago, in an article in the *Wall Street Journal*, Clayton Christensen, Scott Cook, and Taddy Hall endeavored to set the field of marketing back a hundred years. If they were merely three cranks in a coffee shop, this wouldn't matter. But Christensen is a vastly and deservedly influential professor at the Harvard Business School, Cook the cofounder of Intuit software, and Hall the chief strategy officer for the Advertising Research Foundation.

The three wise men assert,

> A simple rule has been forgotten. To build a product that people want, you need to help them do a job that they are trying to get done. The marketer's fundamental task is not so much to understand the customer as it is to understand what jobs customers need to do—and build products that serve those specific purposes.[21]

I had a philosophy professor who, when confronted by nonsense he regarded as especially egregious, would put down his book, look away, and close his eyes. Think of me so.

The "purpose brand" proposition is egregious nonsense. Brands, at their best, and among other things, are bundles of meanings, some of them robust, some of them delicate, all of them poised to speak to one or more segments and to deliver unto them an understanding of not just what the product does but what it stands for, how it may be used, for whom it may stand, and where it is located in the larger scheme of things, commercial and cultural. (These values are not functions. They are values that create value.)

To reduce the brand to "purpose" is to dumb down the enterprise, diminish the art and science of marketing, beggar the consumer, and so displace the marketer that our three wise men must be seen to conduct themselves as proverbial bulls in the china shop of marketing concept, method, and action, destroying advances made over the past hundred years.

Shakespeare was clear on this. When Lear objects to being stripped of the markers of his standing, he is told that he doesn't really need them. He replies,

> Allow not nature more than nature needs,
> Man's life is cheap as beast's.[22]

But not just Shakespeare takes umbrage. The social sciences once embraced and then quite emphatically repudiated the "purpose" approach to things. They called it "functionalism" and came to regard it as a violent act of reduction. Functionalism reduced complicated human artifacts to purposes they served. Thus did theory make us stupid. Functionalism obliged us to ignore much of what we knew to be true about the object of study.

Some costs of the Purpose Brand proposition: Puccini becomes entertainment, indistinguishable from Disney. There is no difference between timekeeping devices called Patek Philippe and Timex. Ford makes the same thing as Volkswagen. All business schools (mark you, Dr. Christensen) are pretty much the same. Intuit is only a couple of features different from Microsoft Money. Most of all, Mr. Hall, there is no longer any such thing as advertising strategy. Now, it's sell the function all day long.

The three wise men are a wrecking crew. They would have us forget the advances made by Professors Jack Trout, Al Ries, Sidney J. Levy, Philip Kotler, Theodore Levitt, to name a few.[23]

They would commit the marketing professional to the cultural illiteracy now installed in the business school world. They restore to usefulness a theory that is scorned in the rest of the academic world. But most of all they would will away some of the most interesting, most difficult, and, yes, most useful elements of the marketer's responsibility.

Join with me now. Let us look away and close our eyes.

CODE-CRACKERS

Every time I hear the name Clotaire Rapaille, I remember a marketing conference a couple years ago.

We were sitting around a table, four or five of us. It was late. We were deep into our cups. The evening was over. Rapaille's name came up. Someone said, "Oh, yeah, that guy. We hired him. He told us our ATM machine was 'mother.'"

Heads shot up around the table, and almost simultaneously, several voices protested, "That's what he said our product was!"

"Hmm," I thought, "that's the trouble with Jungian archetypes. There are only a few of them, and eventually you have to start recycling."

This is unkind. Rapaille and I are in the same business. And he's a big success. According to a recent story in *Fast Company*, Rapaille has a mansion in Tuxedo Park, a ninth-century castle in France, his own helicopter, and millions of dollars.[24] Until recently, I lived in a rickety condo in Montreal without a car, a chateau, a helicopter, or much in the way of a bank account. (I take my profits and pour them straight down the hole marked "deservedly obscure books." Clearly I need a new investment adviser.)

But this is not the only provocative thing about the guy. Rapaille claims to have understood Japanese, Chinese, German,

American, and Indian culture by "cracking the code." Rapaille says, "The code is like an access code: How do you punch the buttons to open the door? Suddenly, once you get the code, you understand everything. It's like getting new glasses."[25]

When I listen to this kind of thing I think of Milton Singer, the great anthropologist, now deceased, at the University of Chicago, who devoted his life to studying India. "Did Professor Singer discover a code?" I ask myself. "Did he break through the South Asian security system?" The head spins.

I know enough about India to know that it encompasses an almost limitless diversity. And this was true *before* it embraced the postmodernism that has reshaped global and local cultures. The idea that there is a code is ludicrous. That someone can crack this code with a simple proposition, a lively phrase, a striking image! I think it's just possible even the infinitely gentle Professor Singer might have strangled you for suggesting as much.

There is no code. There is just good listening. There are not twelve "answers" as we try to understand culture. There are as many answers as there are problems. Research has to be bespoke. It has to come from the interviews in a particular way. It has to speak to the problem in a particular way. It has to be custom made. No prefab archetypes. No Jungian dartboards.

Despite the protestations of Jerry Zaltman, professor emeritus of the Harvard Business School, there are no deep metaphors that stretch across cultures. To suggest otherwise is to engage in junk science. The point of the exercise is to go and talk to the consumer, in the manner of an A.G. Lafley. There is no single set of meanings from which the CCO may choose. Culture is a many-splendored thing. It may not be stuffed into a few categories or extracted therefrom.[26] When Zaltman and company presume to give us culture as simplified into a few metaphors, what they really give us is culture lite. To be sure, it is better than nothing. But the corporation that cannot do better than this is courting accusations of malpractice.

Cultural knowledge should not be parading around in grand declamations and charismatic presentation. We are not branding an idea. We are reporting our findings. Good research is thoughtful, grounded, nuanced, and precise. It is not theater of any kind.

Fast Company records Rapaille's eagerness to claim the success of the PT Cruiser as his own. "I discover the code, and—bingo!—the car sells like crazy." The article also notes the unhappiness of Chrysler employees when they hear of this. Good research delivers new insight, but this insight will come from the corporation as much as it does the researcher. The research is working collaboratively with the consumer and the client.

But, hey, I'm keen on anything that works. And evidently, Rapaille has created lots of value for lots of clients. *Fast Company* suggests that up to 25 percent of his utterances may have substance. And let's be fair. Sometimes it takes a P. T. Barnum to create a PT Cruiser.[27]

ANTHROPOLOGISTS

Stephen Tyler is Hubert S. Autrey Professor of Anthropology at Rice University. About fifteen years ago, he won an award for this passage.[28] Go ahead and read it. I dare you.

> Though post-modern ethnography privileges discourse, it does not locate itself exclusively within the problematic of a single tradition of discourse, and seeks, in particular,

> to avoid grounding itself in the theoretical and commonsense categories of the hegemonic Western tradition. It thus relativizes discourse not just to form—that familiar perversion of the modernist; nor to authorial intention—that conceit of the romantics; nor to a foundational world beyond discourse—that desperate grasping for a separate reality of the mystic and scientist alike; nor even to history and ideology—those refuges of the hermeneuticist; nor even less to language—that hypostasized abstraction of the linguist; nor, ultimately, even to discourse—that Nietzschean playground of world-lost signifiers of the structuralist and grammatologist, but to all or none of these, for it is anarchic, though not for the sake of anarchy but because it refuses to become a fetishized object among objects—to be dismantled, compared, classified, and neutered in that parody of scientific scrutiny known as criticism.[29]

Ah, yes. "All or none of these" sums up postmodernism in anthropology. It is rhetorical pudding. And now that this is the language of anthropology, it's pretty hard to know what anthropologists are saying.

But the problem went deeper than obtuse language. For anthropologists had fallen under the dark spell of the continental philosophers Foucault, Derrida, and Lacan. They ceased to believe in their ability to study culture, in the possibility of an anthropology, in the existence of a thing called culture. Surely what looked like culture was really a figment of the social scientific imagination, a master narrative now discredited, an exercise in the hegemony with which the West imposed its will and ideas on the world, and most simply a bad idea. Generalizing was now impossible. What's more, it was politically monstrous. What's still more, it was morally wrong. Anthropologists now believed their anthropology to be unlawful and unclean.[30]

I don't doubt the motives of these scholars. They mean to be intellectually scrupulous. Still, one detects an ambivalence. As Donald Levine notes, there was something eager about this attack on the verities of the Western tradition, as if these scholars were in a rush to close their discipline down.[31] Whether their motives were scrupulous or mischievous, this was the outcome. Anthropology, the cultural part of the anthropology, fell increasingly silent. As the publisher of one of the great university presses said to me the other day, "It's pretty hard to get you guys to write anything." There is some evidence that anthropology's epistemological panic is lifting. Perhaps anthropology will someday return to usefulness.

This would be a good thing. Because as it stands, anthropology is the best instrument for solving key problems of the C-suite. Here's what it's for. It can "see into" the cultural thing (a movie, a celebrity, a brand, a trend, for instance) and say what it is. For instance, anthropology can give a cultural account of who John Cusack is as an actor. This account should allow us to say how Cusack differs from, say, any of the actors who starred in *The Usual Suspects* (Kevin Spacey, Kevin Pollack, Stephen Baldwin, Gabriel Byrne, and Benicio Del Toro). Is this useful? If we are betting $100 million on a Hollywood movie, it is very useful. If we are looking for a celebrity endorser, it is very useful. If someone says, "Look, this city needs to be to the world of tourism what Cusack is to the world of filmmaking," it is very useful. Cusack is a cultural invention, fantastically successful in the 1990s, perhaps the best brand of his industry. To know what he is (and was) is to navigate the high waters of contemporary culture.

It would be grand if the anthropology that serves in this way could be reflexive and poetical, but it can't. An anthropology of this kind must be rough and ready. It is intellectually opportunistic, slapping together concepts and insights like a Thor Heyerdahl hoping for landfall soon, because, let's face it, this implausible floating machine isn't floating much longer. That's in the nature of the exercise. We are not seeking perfection. We are seeking to construct an idea just robust enough to get us from confusion to clarity. Once we get there, it can gracefully decay on the beach for all we care.

Were my account more learned, elegant, sophisticated, it would look exactly like the classic liberal arts notion of the "argument." And it is, I think, entirely astonishing that anyone should now be called upon to describe what an "argument" is. To walk away from the intellectual machinery (if you will) that brought us the magnificent ideas *that make us possible*, it's really, well, just bizarre. I picture Watson and Crick sitting at the Eagle pub in Cambridge. One of them reaches into the envelope that contains the grainy X-ray and, potentially, our first glimpse of DNA. The question: "So what do we have?" The reply, "Oh, geez. It's hard to say, really. You know, it almost looks like . . . Couldn't be. Fuck it. Let's have another pint." For all of its vaunted philosophy, the postmodernists' repudiation of clarity was as cavalier as this. They took one of the great thinking instruments ever created by any culture, and broke it over their knees like willful children.

The point of every formal intellectual exercise is to decide what the question is, to survey the answer "options," to refine or reform the questions where necessary, to collect data and other kinds of evidence, to refine and reform our proposition and venture conclusions that upon exposure to public scrutiny will undergo still more refinement and reformation. This is what Western thinkers are so very good at. This is precisely why Western thought managed, in the notion of Claude Lévi-Strauss, to escape circularities and insularities of "wild thought" and find its way to ideas that were evermore transparent to a reality.[32] It is of course the first principle of postmodernism that there is no real real, everything is constructed, idea is everything. It is impossible to become evermore transparent to reality, for there is no reality. To think that the postmodernist's "discourse" is typically composed on a computer that is, if nothing else, a demonstration of the ability of IBM labs to make electrical charges dance with unfailing precision on the head of a pin, well, it's sad and strange. Laptops are an extraordinary engagement with reality. It does make you wonder about the intellectuals' "fitness for office." These creatures of the humanities and the interpretive social sciences, should we not take the university away from them? Pay them off if need be. But for God's sake, send them home. They have wrecked the liberal arts. They have made it nearly impossible to study contemporary culture. This is to say they have created opacity at two of the places we hope for light.[33]

There was a time when anthropologists were ferocious problem solvers. Lewis Henry Morgan, Franz Boas, and Émile Durkheim took on the largest issues of their day.[34] Evon Vogt and W. Lloyd Warner prepared to study America in illuminating ways.[35] Warner and others made themselves useful at home.[36] Fredrik Barth and Ulf Hannerz have prepared us to deal with variation and complexity.[37] We must hope for a renaissance. In the meantime, the best anthropology is happening outside the field performed by journalists, essayists, filmmakers, sociologists, musicologists, and novelists.[38]

THE CORPORATION

The corporation has deeply anticultural instincts operating within. It wishes to believe that it is a fully rational enterprise speaking to fully rational consumers. And I haven't any objection to this approach, except to say that the notion of rationality is always defined too narrowly.

Take the case of Doug Ivester, once CEO at the Coca-Cola Company. A brilliant tactician with a deep understanding of mechanics of the company, Ivester nevertheless managed to offend several parties at Coke, from kingmakers on the board to the bottlers on Coke's perimeter. He was asked to resign in December 1999, a brief two years after taking office.[39]

There were several incidents that suggested Ivester was the wrong man for the job, that he was perhaps tone-deaf when it came to culture. But the clearest case was his proposed reinvention of the vending machine. The boys in the lab came to Ivester with what they thought was good news. It was possible to reengineer the Coke machine so that it could raise prices in warm weather. Ivester was interested. Surely, he speculated, a cold Coke should be worth more on a hot day.[40]

Well, yes, a reinvented Coke machine *could* raise prices on a hot day. And, yes, this would speak to the economic forces of supply and demand that organize every marketplace. But culturally speaking, would this make any sense? Actually, no, it wouldn't make any sense at all.

This is not hard to reckon. Imagine a consumer on a dusty Alabama roadside in deep summer, thrilled to find a Coke machine. Relief! But as he reaches for his wallet, the consumer notices that the price is ten cents more than he paid yesterday in Birmingham. He's *heard* about this machine, but he can't believe it. "Coke is going to charge me more because it's hot out?" And in that instant, more than a hundred years of marketing and millions of dollars of advertising vanish without trace. In its attempt to capture ten cents of value, Ivester's machine would destroy much of the brand . . . at least for this consumer.

But it's actually worse than this. Ivester had talked about selling pricier Coke to legions of fans as they poured from a sporting event. And if the team had won? Wouldn't it look like Coke didn't care about the victory? And what if the team had lost? Wouldn't it look like Coke was piling on? The vending machine might be a technological wonder. It might be sound economics. It might be a great profit opportunity. But it was a bad idea because it was inevitably going to make Coke look clueless or cruel.

There is an opportunity here. If Ivester had some cultural training, he might have seen it. If Ivester had a CCO, surely she would have seen it. Coke could use the new vending machine not to charge more, but to charge less. Charge less when it's really hot outside . . . as an act of sympathy. Charge less when the team does badly . . . to share defeat. Charge less when the team does well . . . to celebrate the win. The vending machine was a marketing opportunity, not a revenue opportunity. It gave Coke the opportunity to make the brand more responsive, animated, and companionable. But we can see this opportunity only if we see the vending machine from a cultural point of view. Of course, an economics perspective is always well advised. Without it, the corporation would surely parish. But we also need to see that supply and demand always play themselves out in a social world shaped by cultural meanings. And that's what the CCO is for.

CHAPTER 9

CONCLUSION

CHRIS HUGHES HELPED FOUND FACEBOOK AND ELECT THE forty-fourth president of the United States, Barack Obama, both before he was twenty-five years old. As one of three founders of Facebook, he had his own responsibilities. While Mark Zuckerberg and Dustin Moskovitz were writing code and building the infrastructure, Hughes was trying to figure out what Facebook was *for*. How would people use it? Hughes had CCO-like abilities to call upon. Insiders called him "the empath," and he emerged as the "official Facebook explainer: part anthropologist, part customer-service rep, part media spokesperson."[1]

Hughes didn't think Facebook users wanted a virtual Rolodex. (This seemed to be the LinkedIn idea.) He believed the big idea here, the killer app, was *sharing content*. People would use Facebook to distribute knowledge and photographs. And he was right, to the tune of 24 million photos a day. Without Hughes acting as unofficial CCO, Facebook might be yet another online experiment, an Orkut or a LinkedIn. Certainly, if Hughes were still at Facebook, it would never have declared itself the owner of all the content on the network. The idea was to *share* content, not give it to Facebook. (You didn't have to be an empath to see this, but being an empath made it easy.)

Hughes helped build MyBarackObama (MyBO), a Web site that put enthusiasts in touch with the campaign and the campaign in touch with them. The party fund-raiser wanted to use the network to raise cash.[2] But here too Hughes had a better idea. He suggested supporters be deputized as spokespeople. He gave power to supporters on the ground and decentralized the campaign. It was daring, to be sure, but it made the campaign responsive to local conditions. Who better than a local to speak to locals?

Then Hughes turned the MyBO into a great tributary system. Meg Galipault started an Obama volunteer group in rural Ohio. As Galipault told *Fast Company*, "Instead of reciting a list of why we wanted people to vote for Barack, like we did for Kerry, we were told to ask what was important to people and listen to them."[3]

Galipault and her group gave the Obama campaign eyes and ears in place, an unrivaled source of information about what local Ohioans were thinking. MyBO could have been the usual electronic outreach campaign device, patronizing, laborious, a virtual newsletter. Hughes helped the Obama campaign master the challenge that confronts every organization. He made MyBO a way for the campaign to breathe . . . in and out.

Chris Hughes served both Facebook and the Obama campaign as a Chief Culture Officer. He had a feeling for the moment, for the opportunity, and he drew these from his knowledge of who the "consumer" was and what the consumer wanted. It would be wrong to think that these accomplishments came effortlessly. The seas did not part for Boy Wonder. The guys at Facebook thought their network was manifestly useful, no empathy required. The head of the Obama campaign wanted votes and money *now*.

Acting as a first-generation CCO is never easy. The first order of business is humility. Many people in the C-suite will not get what we do. They will think we mean "culture" with a capital C, as in high culture, museums, art, and orchestras. Or they will think we mean "corporate culture." Or they will ask why the corporation will have to care about something as manifestly unimportant as "popular culture." It will be up to us to explain what culture is, why it matters, what we do, and how we create value.

Here's what we cannot do. We cannot be the hippest person in the room. We cannot ever sneer at those who don't know as much about culture as we do. We can't ever pull rank. We cannot imagine ourselves as the only ones who "get it." We cannot complain that everyone is clueless and insensitive. We cannot cultivate a sense of grievance. This is precisely what everyone in the C-suite thinks of everyone else. Capitalism has excluded cultural knowledge since Adam Smith. We are rewiring the system.

Here's what we are looking for. We want to help someone in the C-suite solve a problem. Their problem. We want to show how knowing about culture makes them more strategic and more tactical. We want to make ourselves indispensable, the person who really "gets" the problems that human resources (human capital) is wrestling with. We want to be at the right hand of the CEO when he or she looks into the middle future and asks, "Okay, what's our best play?"

The corporation has been keeping culture at bay for a very long time. Our job is to manage its new spirit of openness. The best way to do this is to demonstrate the value of what we do, as when we supply critical intelligence, help answer the big question (what business are we in?), see the significance of shifting technologies, read sudden changes in consumer taste and preference, sift the perfect storm of the economy for opportunity and danger, and perform pattern recognition now that pattern recognition is the first order of business.

In sum, we are the first generation, and we have to act like one.

BONUS FEATURE A

Ten Candidates for CCO

1. JUSTIN IS SEVENTEEN. He's lived in California, Germany, and Florida. This was his first visit to New York City and his parents charged Pam and me with keeping him safe over the weekend.

It turns out Justin has three passions: film, history in general, and military history in particular. Well, there's a fourth: popular culture. But everyone his age has a passion for popular culture.

When I hear that Justin loves military history, I tell him about the image of Napoleon's Russian campaign of 1812, the one by Charles Joseph Minard made famous by Edward Tufte.[1] We haul down a copy of Tufte's reproduction. It shows Napoleon's army, 422,000 strong, as it enters Russia, smaller by 412,000 soldiers as it leaves. Tufte calls it perhaps the "best statistical graphic ever drawn." Justin is captivated.

It's hard to know where Justin's career will take him. With a little luck, he'll end up working at the History Channel or making documentaries with the Burns brothers. But as I listened to him talk about the things he cares about, I thought, "This kid could be a CCO." He has the first quality of the CCO: a kind of hyperalertness. And he has the second, a questing quality. What's out there? How do I find it? The follow-up questions (What's it for? How will it employ me?) come later and distantly.

Justin expects the world to submit to his scrutiny. And he's intellectually ecumenical. He doesn't much care what the explanation is, just so long as it helps him make the world make sense. And he likes "big pictures," a view of the world that brings order to complexity. (This is why he loves Minard's map.) He will probably take a BA in history, and this will be good training. Of all the humanities, history is best at weaving diverse data sets. And if Justin is lucky enough to find a program that believes in doing history until the historian "can hear people talking," he will learn the empathy, the insider's view, that is the CCO's most important skill.[2]

Justin is already halfway to mastering the rhetorical skills he is going to need to talk about culture, to make it live in the corporation culture and especially the C-suite. But most of all, he knows popular culture. He has a deep and detailed knowledge even as he honors its ability to entertain. What is especially good is that Justin isn't fooled by popular culture, as some people are. He knows the fact that it looks easy, that it comes to us effortlessly, doesn't mean that it is easy. Justin knows to look for the grammar, the generative devices, that create the things he loves.

There are many career paths to becoming a CCO. I thought I would examine people who seemed right for the job. I talked to people who are engaged in the world around them, curious, lively, shaped by popular culture. They seem comfortable working with rich and complicated data sets. They're good at finding patterns. They are equally at home casting the net wide to capture lots of data, and drilling down to work on very particular topics. And as I say, some of them have a certain earthling-Martian hybrid quality. (They are good at seeing things from the inside and the outside.) Plus, they are good at improv, both intellectual and emotional. We can throw them into a situation and they will find their way home, often with a systematic understanding in tow.

As in Justin's case, there was something questing about these people. They are interested in everything: bowling tournaments, NASA conventions, tea parties convened by eight-year-olds, the unofficial exchange networks that spring up in the business-to-business relationship, why Germans are changing their cuisine at such a furious pace, how Facebook is changing. It's all grist for the mill. They are happy when they can find an academic treatment but happier still when they can participate. They like actually having been to SxSW, and not merely knowing it by the coverage, the blogging, and the tweets.

2. RICK LIEBLING was raised in the Valley near Los Angeles. He was born in 1970, which puts him, as he says, "at the crossroads of so many things: VCRs, cable TV, video games, Dungeons & Dragons, and personal computers all were being created or reaching mainstream around the time I was seven to twelve years old." He took a broad major, "liberal studies," and this gave him the chance to take classes in religion, science fiction, art history, astronomy, spring wildflowers, philosophy, Penrose tiles, and Fibonacci numbers.

I asked Rick a tough question: Why do you think I think you'd be such a good CCO? The correct answer is, "How would I know what you're thinking?" But Rick kindly said,

> The CFO knows a lot about a little. The CMO knows a little about a lot. The CCO knows a lot about a lot. My

> greatest strength is my ability to take a deep dive, really get immersed in something, retain a ton of knowledge, then move on to something else and repeat the process. I've been a comic book nerd, a sci-fi nerd, a baseball nerd, I know more about movies, TV shows, and music than anybody who isn't a real expert in one of those subjects. I know international soccer better than anyone you'll ever meet . . . The real key is the ability to dive deep, come up for air, swim a mile down shore, and dive deep again.[3]

3. DEBBIE MILLMAN grew up in challenging circumstances. She feels the world intensely; she shares her reactions openly. She wears her heart on her sleeve. (The slogan of her blog is "What would you do if you weren't afraid?") She knows a lot about contemporary culture because like all CCOs she's paying attention. When she's not running Sterling Brands, she is board member of the National American Institute of Graphic Arts, teaching at the School of Visual Arts and Fashion Institute of Technology, writing for the design blog *Speak Up*, contributing to *Print Magazine*, and hosting a weekly Internet radio talk show on the VoiceAmerica Business Network called *Design Matters*. She has written three books: *How to Think Like a Great Graphic Designer*, *Essential Principles of Graphic Design*, and *Look Both Ways*. In her spare time, she works as a DJ. This is what happens, I guess, when we are both vulnerable and fearless.

4. ERIC NEHRLICH went to MIT as an undergrad and to Stanford to study physics. Schools like this can turn some people into one-dimensional drones. Not Eric. He sang in choirs, played volleyball, went to lots of talks, and ran the alt.tv.buffy-v-slayer FAQ. Eric now writes a blog called the *Unrepentant Generalist*. After Stanford, he worked at an interdisciplinary science start-up. He found himself figuring out the dynamics of the organization, the interactions of engineers, testers, biologists, physicists, and managers. "I began to see my value . . . was not my specialized software expertise—it was my ability as a generalist to meld different viewpoints into a coherent synthesis that happened to be expressed in software." Next step: management. Eric now works for Google as an analyst developing revenue forecasting models to help the company's executives make decisions. "I get to use my quantitative skills in building the models and my generalist skills in that the models are built on understanding everything from the technical product decisions being made, to sales and marketing strategies, to what customers and competitors are doing, to the larger economic and business environment."

5. AND 6. BETH COLEMAN AND HOWARD GOLDKRAND. Talk about a power couple. Beth teaches new media at MIT. She writes for *Artform*, *Artbyte*, and *Nka*. As an artist, she specializes in sound, art, and architecture. Howard works at Modernista. His art has been displayed from Marfa, Texas, to the Bronx Museum to the Tribeca Film Festival. Beth and Howard founded the Cultural Alchemy's SoundLab. They call it an "electrotectural nomadic happening," and they stage it opportunistically in places someone has forgotten to board up.

What I particularly like about Beth and Howard is that they operate well off the map of mainstream culture even as they have "day jobs" at MIT and Modernista that locate them in the mainstream. They are great to talk to. They spot someone like me as clueless when it comes to the kind of art they do, but they are perfectly happy to talk about "electrotectural nomadic happenings" until I begin to get it. So many people who occupy the avant-garde are "too cool for school" and implicitly committed to the notion "if you have to ask, you can't come in." But Beth and Howard are prepared to share. I think this is probably one of the marks of CCOs, that they are creatures of many worlds, captives of none. They are prepared to learn, and to teach even when this means dismantling their claim to cool.

7. ROCHELLE GRAYSON. Rochelle and I fell into conversation at a conference in Vancouver, and I remember thinking, "Wow, the woman had an all-access pass to, well, just about everything." She grew up in Germany. Her dad was an African American professor of nineteenth-century German philosophy and her Puerto Rican mother was an opera singer. Rochelle has an MBA in finance and business strategy from the University of Chicago. She started an early mobile social networking company for young urban women. She has worked in the film industry and held several positions in the C-suite. She and her husband, Geoff, live in Vancouver, where she is COO of the Donat Group, a social media company. If I were a CEO looking for a CCO right now, I would pick up the phone and call her.

What I particularly like about Rochelle is that she understands business in a formal and a practical way. The CCO needs to understand both culture and commerce. Some people disqualify themselves because they know only half the proposition.

8. SAM FORD grew up in rural Kentucky. His grandmother Beulah Hillard wrote a "society column" in McHenry, population four hundred or so. With his grandmother's illness, Sam (then twelve) took over the column, and he's been writing ever since. He went to Western Kentucky University to study journalism. At this point he was writing 6,000 words for the *Ohio County Messenger* each week, covering police news, politics, Little League games, local businesses, and town characters, and writing a weekly column on pro wrestling. Almost perfect training for a CCO.

Sam's interest in pro wrestling became the focus of his academic research. He taught a course on pro wrestling's place in American culture as an undergraduate. And when he moved to MIT's Comparative Media Studies master's program, he taught a course as a graduate student. When home for the holidays, Sam occasionally makes appearances at Universal Championship Wrestling in Hartford, Kentucky, where he plays an evil version of himself, the hometown boy who left to seek greener pastures on the East Coast.

Sam has several gifts. He is superbly accumulative. As he moves from world to world, he takes things with him. I think every CCO needs to resist the modernist inclination to forget and forgo. Furthermore, Sam is versatile. He has a way of acting like an adult when he is supposed to be a child, a teacher when he is supposed to be a student, a participant when he is supposed to be an observer. He even helps found the things he is supposed to belong to. He helped found the Convergence Culture Consortium (C3) at MIT. His particular interest is in popular culture and media products. Sam says, "[I look at] television studies and 'immersive story worlds' like the massive volume of pro wrestling texts, soap opera texts, comic books, episodes of shows like *The Colbert Report*—in order to understand how these processes of meaning-making work."

9. BOB MCBARTON AND HIS FRIENDS created something miraculous: proof that access is possible, that good, stout conversation is there for the asking. McBarton and friends created something called the Luncheon Society. They invite interesting people like Abu Ghraib military prison commander Janis Karpinski, physicist Brian Greene, former Secretary of State Warren Christopher, writer Christopher Hitchens, and Melba Pattillo Beals and Terrence Roberts, who were members of the Little Rock Nine, a group of African American teenagers who were sent to the all-white Little Rock Central High School during the civil rights movement. Some years ago McBarton staged a luncheon in which movie critic Roger Ebert told stories for four and a half hours at Michael's restaurant in Santa Monica. "Think of the Luncheon Society like a college survey course," McBarton said. "But there are no tests, the food is a lot better, and you've learned something at the end."

10. NOW I SEE THEM EVERYWHERE. A planner like Lesley Bielby, a woman who has served as a planner for fifteen years and now has a remarkable knowledge of American culture; Bill T. Jones, founder of a dance troupe, explorer of the complexities of American culture; Bill Buford, editor of a literary magazine, student of British soccer hooligans and the world of the American chef; comedian Chris Rock, who just sees things the rest of us can't. There are many paths to becoming a CCO.

BONUS FEATURE B

A Tool Kit for the Rising CCO

CCOs have a lot of waterfront to cover. They must know slow culture. And this means doing ethnographic interviews in the field and mastering the work of academics and journalists. They must know fast culture. This means doing ethnographic interviews in the field and mastering media feeds to follow the constant churn of fad and fashion. Whew! Here's a tool kit that will help. You are encouraged to build your own.

MAGAZINES ON- AND OFFLINE

Good editors are geniuses, gifted with sight, and, with the exception of people like David Remnick, Graydon Carter, and Tina Brown, mostly unsung. They canvass the world and work down to a relatively few choices, some of them predictable, some of them exquisite, all of them useful. The idea is to find the magazines that supply current knowledge for our strengths and supplement those areas in which we are weak. (I am assuming you are looking through *Newsweek, Atlantic, The Economist, Slate, Salon, Mother Jones,* and *Utne Reader* for general coverage.) What follows is a partial list given for "starter" purposes. There are lots of options and plenty of room for disagreement. In a more perfect world, we would get together and craft top-ten lists like the guys at Championship Vinyl in John Cusack's *High Fidelity*.

The *Hollywood Reporter* is filled with early intelligence. After all, every film is a cultural artifact on which fans will someday vote with their tickets. Who's doing deals with whom? Which stars are flourishing? We could have charted Judd Apatow's rise this way and with him an interesting genre of comedy, a cultural sensibility, no less. *Entertainment Weekly* is good for general coverage and the movie review work of Lisa Schwarzbaum and Owen Gleiberman. James Poniewozik reviews TV for *Time*, and Nancy Franklin does so at the *New Yorker*. For music, see *Pitchfork, Q, Mojo, Paste Magazine, The Fader*, and Kelefa Sanneh at the *New Yorker*.[1] For treatments of commerce and culture, see *Fast Company*, *Wired* magazine, *BusinessWeek* (especially Jon Fine), and *Fortune* (especially Pattie Sellers). For design, *I.D., Design Matters, Logic + Emotion*, and *Core 77*. Betsy Sussler's magazine, *Bomb*, is good for art; see also *Esopus*. Each subculture and lifestyle is served by a magazine; see, for instance, *Thrasher*. The Web site http://issuu.com/ gives access to hundreds of small magazines. For me, the best periodical coverage of the intellectual world is the *Times Literary Supplement*. Again, these are all personal favorites. I recite them here as a starting point.

OTHER MEDIA

Many aggregators work well for culture. See, for instance, Kottke.org, PSFK, the Huffington Post, the Daily Beast, and Popcultures.com. We can create our own aggregations using RSS feeds, and feed readers like FeedDemon or Google Reader. Bookmarking sites are useful for keeping track of what comes pouring in: Del.icio.us, Diigo, Digg, Friendfeed, and StumbleUpon.

Very Short List and Flavorpill don't aggregate. They choose very carefully. The Arts and Letters Daily offers a dazzling glimpse of the intellectual world. Ning is a vast catalog of social networks, many of which will serve as good listening posts. There are topic-specific sites: glamour from Virginia Postrel and plastic surgery from Joan Kron, for instance. There are now a host of "mommy blogs." (See momversation.com.) I can't stress too much how important it is to drop by *This Blog Sits at the Intersection of Anthropology and Economics* (www.cultureby.com) at least once a day.

We will want to blog, to post status updates on Facebook, and to tweet on Twitter. Four reasons: (1) In the new "gift economy," we have to give to get; (2) to understand these media, we have to use them; (3) to appreciate how these media are changing, we need to use them constantly; (4) these are, in any case, useful conduits for knowledge of the contemporary world. (There is indeed so much "on tap" here that a great deal of anthropology can be done from home. "Armchair anthropology" gets a new lease on life.) For blogging, WordPress is the reigning champ. For managing outgoing and incoming messages in Twitter, Seesmic and Tweetdeck are recommended. To keep track of the diverse materials that exist online and off, Evernote is ever useful.

TV

Reality television can be an ethnographic treasure trove. Some shows, like *Survivor*, take people out of the world. These are interesting for psychological purposes, but less so for anthropological ones. Shows like *Real Housewives of New Jersey/Orange County*, on the other hand, take us into the participants' worlds and sometimes deliver riches. (Yes, people are showing off for the camera and otherwise distorting the data, but with enough time on camera, certain things leak through.) With the profusion of cable shows, there is a niche impulse that makes TV culturally responsive in ways it never was before.

The talk show world of late night (Conan O'Brien, Jimmy Fallon, Jon Stewart, Craig Ferguson, Jimmy Kimmel, and David Letterman) offers a reading of fast culture. The producers of these shows have their ears to the ground and it is useful to know what they hear. If only the hosts of these shows were better interviewers! Very often, interesting guests leave without sharing any of the things that make them interesting. (George Stephanopoulos should go into late night. He's becoming an increasingly skillful interviewer.) At this reading, MTV's *It's On with Alexa Chung* has just started, and so far, so good. (Yes, sometimes it can seem like a slumber party for big girls, but that's sometimes better than the frat-house atmosphere we get from the guys.)

All TV programming reflects someone's idea of the current state of American culture, of what we will find funny, engaging, moving, or informative. TV has a way of shaping American culture, which is to say it is creative when made and when seen. But the fun of this exercise is to play the game that says, "If I were a Martian, what would this show tell me about this culture?" I watch a lot of TV and not just for anthropological purposes. I like it. But the game has a way of sneaking up on me and before I know it, I have a blog post. Like the one that began like this:

> I watched heroic quantities of TV over the holidays. And I was struck by how much comedy now comes from

> characters who are self interested, self serving, self aggrandizing. I'm thinking of Charlie Harper, played by Charlie Sheen on *Two and a Half Men,* and Barney Stinson, played by Neil Patrick Harris on *How I Met Your Mother*. Both Charlie and Barney are in it for themselves. They have no empathy. They have no principles. They have no shame. They are serene in the knowledge that they are without moral reflex of any kind . . . and that that's ok. The rest of us are struggling to live a good life (more or less, give or take) and these guys just couldn't care less.[2]

I titled this post "The Charlie and Barney Show: The Birth of a New American Male?" The post is not a revelation, I know that. I wrote it in a few minutes. But it was fun to think, and fun to write. Is this a larger trend in American culture? Have we seen the rise of a newly unapologetic male? It would take more investigation and data to say. But the point of the exercise is to keep looking for early signals. Early detection puts us in a position to see the larger trend, if and when it emerges, more quickly. We supplied our own early warning.

The idea here is to ask, "In what way is this show interesting? What might it tell me about the state and direction of contemporary culture?" Much of the art of the CCO is finding (or inventing) the frame that helps show us the significance of what we're looking at.

There are several useful tools: subscribe to TVbythenumbers.com, the Programming Insider, and the Live Feed, James Hibberd's daily news site covering the television industry. Hulu.com makes anytime, anywhere viewing easier, and Boxee.com makes it more social.

COMEDY CLUBS

In *Comedy at the Edge*, Richard Zoglin describes the rise of the comedy club and its influence on TV and film.[3] Many Hollywood stars began in comedy (Richard Pryor, Jim Carrey, Whoopi Goldberg, Catherine O'Hara, Drew Carey, Lily Tomlin, Jerry Seinfeld, Tina Fey, Ellen DeGeneres, Steve Martin, Robin Williams, Sarah Silverman, Chris Rock, Larry David, Amy Poehler, Amy Sedaris), and many shows go from the comedian's club persona straight to the screen (*Roseanne, Home Improvement, Everyone Loves Raymond, The Drew Carey Show, Curb Your Enthusiasm*, etc.). We could have seen all of these people very early on at their local comedy club. These clubs are a place to watch for culture "in the works."

EVENTS

The Coca-Cola Company once sent me to a food fair in Cologne, Germany. It was one of those "far as the eye can see" trade shows, three buildings each the size of a football field, where every player in every food industry seemed to have a booth, and every new idea, however nutty, found a place: Wine in a bag! Camembert meets Roquefort! And my favorite, "Adventure Gum." (This was a plastic cylinder, with a whistle at one end, a little compass at the other, and in between, well, lots of gum. Just the thing for an anthropologist lost at a food fair.)

Comic-Con brings together more than 100,000 people for four days in San Diego to talk about comics and science fiction, film and television. Comic-book writers may look like a minority presence in our culture, but as an anonymous graphic novel (aka comic book) artist said recently, "We like to think of ourselves as the people who do the R&D for Hollywood." So Comic-Con is an excellent place to see the future.

Conferences, trade shows, boat shows, craft fairs—all of these have something to teach us. Feel free to wander and wonder.

FIELD TRIPS

Or we can make our own event. These are sometimes called field trips. I saw Andrew Zolli do one on behalf of the Global Business Network, and it was pretty interesting. We moved around New York City, visiting places like the Campbell Apartments, retail experiments by Hershey's and Disney, new hotels like the Soho Grand, and restaurants like WB 50. These are a useful way of introducing other members of the C-suite to the realities of the world. There is nothing like eyes-on exposure.

What this event needed was some time in the classroom working on readings and case studies, a kind of Harvard Business School classroom. Except this one would be dedicated to helping people master the knowledge they need to be better CCOs. It's this combination of lectures and discussion in the seminar, and investigation in the city that promises the opportunity for the fastest acquisition of cultural knowledge.

CITY-STATES AND THE INTELLECTUAL IMPRESARIOS WHO MAKE THEM

Call it the conference that really isn't a conference. Often it centers on one person, someone with sufficient credibility to make him- or herself the center of affairs social and intellectual. I have come to think of these people as "city-states." They resemble those centers of medieval Europe, sustaining trade and government while other institutions (read: universities) fail us.

They have these things in common. They are relatively egalitarian, more interested in expressive individualism than instrumental individualism, more concerned with intrinsic than extrinsic rewards, suspicious of power and rank asymmetries, playful, dramatic, less interested in due process and more interested in the counter-expectational, the ad hoc and the improvisational. We have to be nimble-witted to take advantage of these things. And we come away more nimbly witted still.

There are now a lot of these unconferences: the Foo Camp invented by Sara Winge and Tim O'Reilly, Andrew Zolli's PopTech, TED founded by Richard Saul Wurman and now reformed by Chris Anderson. There is Jay Meyers's SxSW and Larry Harvey's Burning Man.[4] We may choose between Bob McBarton's The Luncheon Society, Cecily Sommers's Push Institute, Henry Jenkins's C3, Russell Davies's Interesting200x, John Kearnon and Susan Casserly Griffin's xFest, Walter Isaacson's Aspen Institute, Ric Grefe's AIGA conferences, Dave Isenberg's F2C, Jerry Michalski's retreats, and Pip Coburn's dinners in New York City and San Francisco, and Piers Fawkes's PSFK conferences.

THE LUNCH LIST

Here's a list of twenty people who would be excellent expert advisers. The opening question over appetizers: "So tell me what's happening in your part of the world, and what you think it means for culture." Unless this is the beginning of some enduring connection, we are obliged to pay these people. Handsomely. That will make it an expensive lunch, but if this intelligence is an "early warning" of things to come, it's money well spent. (What should we pay them? $1,000 is a nice round figure.)

More particular things to ask: (1) What's the status quo in your world? (2) What are you noticing lately, who's doing something new, what's happening that strikes you as odd? (3) How does this suggest a new pattern in your world? (4) If we generalize most broadly, how does this possible development work with (or against) other things that are happening in the world?

1. Lisa Schwarzbaum, *Entertainment Weekly*
2. Danielle Sacks, *Fast Company*
3. David Brooks, *New York Times*
4. Sarah Zupko, PopCulture.com
5. Drake Bennett, *Boston Globe*
6. Patricia Sellers, *Fortune*
7. Tim Sullivan, Basic Books
8. Steven Johnson, stevenberlinjohnson.com
9. Marian Goodman, Goodman Galleries
10. Eric Nehrlich, Google
11. Pip Coburn, Coburn Associates
12. Jerry Michalski, Sociate.com
13. Klaus Schwab, founder of Davos
14. Kelefa Sanneth, *New Yorker*
15. Kevin Slavin, Area/Code
16. Russell Davies, Open Intelligence Agency
17. Ed Greenspon, *Globe and Mail*
18. Henry Jenkins, MIT
19. Greil Marcus, Berkeley
20. Michael Bierut, Pentagram

This is a starter list. Craft your own. (And send me a copy, please.)

METRICS

There are not enough metrics for culture. And American capitalism runs on numbers. Our contribution to the corporation, our ability to win arguments in the C-suite—these will turn on whether we have numbers and how intelligently we use them.[5] Because there are no direct measures, the trick is to find numbers that can serve as indirect measures of something else. Take the best-seller list. If we know the author and what she stands for, we can use sales figures as a very rough metric of other things. Thus, the book by author "x" might be taken, especially in conjunction with other things, as a measure of cultural development "y."

It is possible to scrape numbers from Amazon, and a useful intermediary is TitleZ.com, which allows us to monitor the titles of our choice. TV shows are monitored by Robert Seidman and Bill Gorman at TVbythenumbers.com and by Marc Berman at ProgrammingInsider.com. The Media Cloud from the Berkman Center for Internet and Society at Harvard gives us a chance to track the flow of media and the incidence of news stories. Google Trends help as well. All are powerful instruments to analyze and visualize changes in something close to real time.

The *Hollywood Reporter* has a list of current movies with box office numbers. The important column here is the one called "% changed." All movies have some hope of success. A lot of producers, agents, and actors have made a calculated bet. And it is not uncommon for movies to spend $30 million on marketing. What really matters is what happens once the movie must rely on word of mouth. This is when it becomes a measure of popular sentiment. The website HSX.com is a Hollywood "stock exchange" (aka "decision market").[6] This is going to be an exercise in ingenuity.

But let's be honest. There are rarely any "hard" numbers, so our best efforts will be impressionistic. We will not be "number crunchers" so much as "number whisperers." We will have to exercise a little ingenuity, perhaps even a little creativity. In the section on "cool" in Chapter 4, I offered a picture of the hippie trend in the United States in the 1960s. For scholarly purposes, these numbers are impressionistic at best. But if this were 1971 and we were sitting in the boardroom of PepsiCo, even this statistical "impression" would be quite useful. If nothing else, it would oblige the anticulture crew (the CIO and CFO, perhaps) to respond with something more than airy dismissal.

WAR ROOMS

Some companies monitor culture by creating a "war room," and we may want to make one of these for ourselves. A "war room" is a room at headquarters devoted to a topic of interest, say, Generation Z, the future of food, or what Detroit will look like in twenty years. Usually it is decorated with hundreds of images and articles ripped from magazines and pinned to the wall. Plus those broadsheets left over from brainstorms. In the corporate case, this is an attempt to capture culture and bring it "indoors." More dramatically, it is sometimes an attempt to smuggle intelligence past security and into the corporate culture. Now some part of culture outside the corporation lives in a modest way inside the corporation. Still, sometimes these rooms can be a little forlorn. We know how robust this stuff is in the world, and can't help feeling that it looks a little vulnerable and unconvincing on the wall.

There are firms that can build war rooms for us. Toniq is one example. This consultancy ventures out into the world, to talk in a careful way to people there, translates what it hears into a set of images, and brings those back to us. This is an excellent way to help get a deeper, more systematic feeling for what is happening outside the corporation to come inside the corporation.

DATA AIR-TRAFFIC CONTROL

We need companies that can help us find and sort through the great volumes of data out there. They don't exist yet, but surely this will change. I imagine a group of superbly well-informed people working together in a kind of conning tower, watching the streams of data emerging from the work and directing them to clients at the appropriate time in the appropriate form. Some people think that information robots will do this sorting for us, but consider the books Amazon thinks might interest you. These "infobots" have a long way to go. It will take awhile to figure out the business model of a group like this (how many clients at what fee, etc.), but surely there are several start-ups, a small industry, waiting to happen, and a new profession waiting to rise. I like to think of a group of people in an old warehouse space in Baltimore, with access to every imaginable information source, and blocking, tagging, and directing this data to subscribers for whom competitive advantage depends on being fully informed. In a sense this is a Bloomberg system that delivers data not on markets but culture, and it does so at the direction of professionals who create value by directing data streams as appropriate and customizing where necessary. (This too is a start-up opportunity. Entrepreneurs, start your engines.)[7]

I HAVE A DREAM (TEAM): THE NEW MCKINSEY

What the CCO needs is a consultancy that keeps track of culture as assiduously and skillfully as McKinsey and the big consulting companies that now map and track the business world. It is a thing of joy to see McKinsey address a problem. They bring a very high order of intelligence and professionalism to bear upon it. The client corporation is now dramatically better informed. It can't be long before the CCO has access to a McKinsey for cultural consulting. This group would create bespoke research and managerial advice on a project-by-project basis. (This is another entrepreneurial opportunity waiting to happen.)[8]

STRATEGIC OUTSOURCING

The CCO who does not have the advantage of a full staff or deep pockets may in the short term want to access a team on a strategic outsourcing (SO) basis. (Strategic outsourcing places what is normally an internal corporate function on the outside of the corporation. It now comes from an external supplier.) And here too it shouldn't be long before CCO-SO groups spring up to supply the need. Here too it's a small team of gifted analysts who will visit the corporation, scrutinize its corporate culture, examine its industry and competitive context, visit the product development people, and perform the research necessary to spot the cultural opportunity and assess the culture threats. We could take any five names from the lunch list and have a pretty good consultancy. (Call me.)

DEPUTIZING EVERYONE IN THE CORPORATION

The CCO can't cover all the waterfront. It makes sense to ask members of the corporation to help out. When every member of the corporation has a natural enthusiasm (jazz for one person, fusion cooking for another, vampire novels for a third), we should ask them to pay attention from time to time on behalf of the corporation and report back. It's not enough that people merely read more "foodie" magazines. We need to train them so that they are prepared to spot patterns. The CCO could encourage "brown bag" lunches so that the person following jazz can compare findings with the person following fusion cooking. (What happens in one cultural domain often has resonances in another.) The stock guru Peter Lynch likes to present himself as a guy who can spot investment opportunities while walking through a hardware store. Appropriately trained, every member of the corporation could exercise this alertness all the time. The trick is to turn members of corporations into more active, thoughtful, observant observers. As the founder of Vloggerheads, Tom Guarriello, likes to say, "Corporations that don't take advantage of all the things their employees know are leaving money on the table."

ACADEMICS

A few of my favorites: Greil Marcus at Berkeley, Michael Wesch at Kansas, Henry Jenkins at USC, Tyler Cowen at George Mason, William Uricchio at MIT, Steve Postrel at UCLA, Richard Florida at the University of Toronto, Robert Thompson at Syracuse, and Clay Shirky at New York University. I know I am missing hundreds of people here. There are several programs: the Berkman Center at Harvard, the C3 program at MIT, the Humanities Lab at Stanford, the Interactive Telecommunications Program at New York University, Michael Wesch's digital ethnography program at the University of Kansas. The best business school for CCO training is probably the Rotman School at the University of Toronto. The best design school may be the one at Stanford. There is a little movement called the applied humanities that is particularly promising. I would keep a Google search going with these as my search terms.[9]

BUILDING A LIBRARY (FOR SLOW CULTURE)

These are old and new classics, a foundation on which to build. I have avoided books on theory and method, however useful. All these books are about some part of American culture. Just a few to get the library started.

1. Brooks, David. 2001. *Bobos in Paradise: The New Upper Class and How They Got There*. New York: Simon & Schuster.
2. Dickstein, Morris. 2002. *Leopards in the Temple: The Transformation of American Fiction, 1945–1970*. Cambridge, MA: Harvard University Press.
3. FitzGerald, Frances. 1986. *Cities on a Hill: A Journey Through Contemporary American Cultures*. New York: Simon & Schuster.
4. Florida, Richard. 2003. *The Rise of the Creative Class: And How It's Transforming Work, Leisure, Community and Everyday Life*. New York: Basic Books.
5. Fox, Kate. 2008. *Watching the English: The Hidden Rules of English Behaviour*. London: Nicholas Brealey Publishing.
6. Goffman, Erving. 1959. *The Presentation of Self in Everyday Life*. New York: Anchor.
7. Jenkins, Henry. 2008. *Convergence Culture: Where Old and New Media Collide*. Revised. New York: New York University Press.
8. Johnson, Steven. 2005. *Everything Bad Is Good for You: How Today's Popular Culture Is Actually Making Us Smarter*. New York: Riverhead Books.
9. Kamp, David. 2006. *The United States of Arugula: How We Became a Gourmet Nation*. New York: Broadway.
10. Katz, Donald R. 1993. *Home Fires: An Intimate Portrait of One Middle-Class Family in Postwar America*. New York: Perennial.

11. Klein, Richard. 1993. *Cigarettes Are Sublime*. Durham, NC: Duke University Press.
12. Long, Elizabeth. 1985. *The American Dream and the Popular Novel*. London: Routledge & Kegan Paul.
13. McCracken, Grant. 2008. *Transformations: Identity Construction in Contemporary Culture*. Bloomington: Indiana University Press.
14. Shirky, Clay. 2009. *Here Comes Everybody: The Power of Organizing Without Organizations*. New York: Penguin.
15. Thornton, Sarah. 1996. *Club Cultures: Music, Media, and Subcultural Capital*. Middletown, CT: Wesleyan University Press.
16. Warner, W. Lloyd, J. O. Low, Paul S. Lunt, and Leo Srole. 1963. *Yankee City*. New Haven, CT: Yale University Press.
17. Waters, Mary C. 1990. *Ethnic Options: Choosing Identities in America*. Berkeley and Los Angeles: University of California Press.
18. Weinberger, David. 2003. *Small Pieces Loosely Joined: A Unified Theory of the Web*. New York: Basic Books.
19. Wolfe, Tom. 2001. *A Man in Full*. New York: Dial Press Trade Paperback.
20. Zerubavel, Eviatar. 1993. *The Fine Line*. Chicago: University of Chicago Press.

PATTERN RECOGNITION

As this appendix demonstrates, we will need to consult a lot of information sources to stay in touch with contemporary culture. But the real problem comes after we make contact. How to sort and make sense of all these stimuli? What is called for now is someone or ones with formidable powers of pattern recognition. And this comes from those who have the benefit of good, sometimes classical educations, in the liberal arts *or* engineering, who have mastered many versatile interpretive frames, who possess very assimilative powers of survey, and rapid and penetrating powers of thought and action.

The bad news is that there is no simple set of understandings. In the American and increasingly the global case, there is no single, simple culture, no easy answer, no pat recommendations to be produced by rote and delivered as boilerplate. It's not as bad as the academic anthropologists will tell you. These poor unfortunates took their great intellectual patrimony, the field's most powerful notion and valuable asset, the idea of culture, and, at the bidding of French postmodernists, bet it at the epistemology table. In a couple of rolls, they lost the whole thing, rendering themselves penniless, provincial, and now pretty much the poor cousins of the social sciences. (Oh, those French croupiers. Never trust them!) Fortunately, the culture concept was spirited away by other disciplines and certain anthropologists just in time. Now it's up to you.

ACKNOWLEDGMENTS

This book was written with the help, near or distant, of many people and especially George Anastaplo, John Deighton, Susan Fournier, Jim Gough, Tom Guarriello, Henry Jenkins, Leora Kornfeld, Guy Lanoue, Kate Lee, Kay Lemon, Bill O'Connor, Steve and Virginia Postrel, Montrose Sommers, and Marshall Sahlins. Special thanks are due to my editor, Tim Sullivan, for his sterling intellectual partnership.

I am also grateful to the following people for support and inspiration of many kinds: Susan Abbott, Andrew Amesbury, Ken Anderson, Kevin Anderson, Will Anderson, David Armano, David Armour, Celestine Arnold, Tom Asacker, Ivan Askwith, Alec Austin, Jack Avery, Eleanor Baird, Laurie Baird, Darren Barefoot, Pippin Barr, Jonathan Salem Baskin, Ed Batista, David Bausola, Chris Baylis, Nancy Baym, Angele Beausoleil, John Bell, Brad Berens, Scott Berkun, Russell Bernard, J. Duncan Berry, Ralf Beuker, Stephanie Betz, Lesley Bielby, Gloria Bishop, Martin Bishop, Michael Blankenship, Danah Boyd, Mark Brady, Noah Brier, Amanda Briggs, David Bujnowski, Jeremy Bullmore, Timothy Burke, David Burn, Kenelm Burridge, Larry Buttress, Bud Caddell, Jim Carfrae, Ray Cha, Suw Charman-Anderson, Jeremy Cherfas, James Chatto, Allan Chochinov, Carol Cioppa,

Kevin Clark, Patricia Cleary, Marni Zea Clippinger, Don Coffin, Chris Commins, Colby Cosh, Ed Cotton, Tyler Cowen, Steven Crandall, Pat Crane, Andrew Creighton, Gary Cruse, Simone Cruickshank, Rob Curedale, Tom Daly, Russell Davies, Guy Davies, Patrick Davis, Abigail De Kosnik, Leslie and Faith Dektor, Dino Demopoulos, Stephen Denny, Paul Dervan, John Dodds, Ana Domb, Amy Domini, Judith Donath, Colin Drummond, Dave Dyment, German Dziebel, Mark Earls, David Edery, Scott Ellington, Sean Embury, Peter England, Jim Ericson, Mike Everett-Lane, Francis Farrelly, Piers Fawkes, Rob Fields, Charles Firth, Sandy Fleischer, Jeff Flemings, Richard Florida, Denise Fonseca, Sam Ford, Nicolai Frank, Morgan Friedman, Nancy Friedman, Charles Frith, Bruce Fryer, Jed Feuer, John Galvin, Barbara Garfield, Marc Garnaut, Carol Gee, Larry Gies, Morgan Gerard, Vesna Gerintes, Nick Gillespie, Jamie Gordon, Francois Gossieaux, Jim Gough, Guy Gould-Davies, Dan Gould, Katarina Graffman, Stephen and Gillian Graham, Liz Grandillo, John Grant, Jonathan Gray, Rochelle Grayson, Lee Green, Edward Greenspon, Ric Grefe, Susan Griffin, Tom and Karen Guarriello, John and Janice Gundy, Nick Hahn, Scott Haile, Monica Hamburg, Tom Harle, C. V. Harquail, C. Lee Harrington, Stephen Hicks, Jens Hilgenstock, Leigh Himel, Ryan Holiday, Adrienne Hood, Ted Hovet, Kerry Howley, Christine Huang, Andy Hunter, Matthew Ingram, Leon Jacobs, Joseph Jaffe, Lance Jensen, Derek Johnson, Hylton Jolliffe, Matt Jones, Phil Jones, Shaista Justin, Max Kalehoff, A.J. Kandy, Anik Karimjee, Garth Kay, John Kearon, Tom Kelley, Paul Kemp-Robertson, Lynne Kiesling, Peter Kim, Rob Kleine, Nancy Koehn, Rob Kozinets, Holly Kretschmar, Joan Kron, Polly LaBarre, Vince LaConte, Johanne Lamoureux, Alain Lapointe, Joe Lassiter, Jon Leach, Anthony Leung, Curtis Lew, Mark

Lewis, Xiaochang Li, Josh Liberson, Rick Liebling, Jeppe Trolle Linnet, Victor Lombardi, Geoffrey Long, Amanda Lotz, Ted Lowitz, Zbigniew Lukasiak, Tom Luke, Michael Madison, Eamon Mahony, Thomas Malaby, Beatriz Mallory, Brett Marchand, Margaret Mark, Roger Martin, Mary, Steve, Zack and Lee Mazur, Megan McArdle, Peter McBurney, Karen McCauley, Jake McCall, Andy McCauley, Seamus McCauley, Emmet McCusker, John McGarr, Joe and Christine Melchione, Bud Melman, Paul Melton, Jerry Michalski, Alan Middleton, Debbie Millman, Mary Mills, Candy Minx, Prashant Mishra, Jason Mittell, Sean Moffitt, Johnnie Moore, Karl Moore, Kim Moses, Roop Mukhopadhyay, Mark Murray, Eric Nehrlich, Matt Nolan, Bruce Nussbaum, Bill O'Connor, Charlotte Odes, Richard Oliver, Gian Pangaro, Clay Parker Jones, Lisa Parrish, Jan and Lauren Parsons, Chee Pearlman, Daniel Pereira, Martin Perelmuter, Neil Perkin, Mary Pisarkiewicz, Barbara Pomorska, Faith Popcorn, Steve Portigal, Michael Powell, Tony Princisvalle, Brandon Proia, Aswin Punathambekar, Mike Rao, Shaka Rashid, Rita Rayman, Adam Richardson, Rodrigo M. S. dos Reis, Diego Rodriguez, Daniel Rosenblatt, Mike Ronkoske, John Roscoe, Susan Royer, Monica Ruffo, Doris Rusch, Juri Saar, Danielle Sacks, Kevin Sandler, Gladys Santiago, Fredrik Sarnblad, Sean Sauber, Mary Schmidt, Nick Schultz, Yasha Sekhavat, Matt Semansky, Parmesh Shahani, Richard and Pam Shear, Brent Shelkey, James Sherrett, John Sherry, Al Silk, Simon Sinek, Naunihal Singh, Kevin Slavin, Tina Slavin, Alix Sleight, Drew Smith, Paul Snyderman, Ruth Soenius, Evan Solomon, Sir Martin Sorrell, Peter Spear, Daria Steigman, Rick Sterling, Diana Stinson, Will Straw, Rory Sutherland, Bob Sutton, Craig and Cheryl Swanson, Ashley Swartz, Wodek Szemberg, Ed Tam, Rodney Tanner, Andrew Taylor, Earl Taylor, Clive

Thompson, Anne Thompson, Amelia Torode, Scott Underwood, William Uricchio, Shenja van der Graaf, Ilya Vedrashko, Carlos Veraza, Kelly Verchere, Greg Verdino, Michel Verdon, Colleen Wainwright, Jimmy Wales, Mark Warshaw, Mary Walker, Rob Walker, William Ward, Reiko Waisglass, Chris and Nancy Weaver, Henri Weijo, David Weinberger, Scott Weisbrod, Stefan Werning, Elvi Whitaker, Martin Wiegel, Sara Winge, John Winsor, David Wolfe, Stacy Wood, Bob Woodard, Michelle Yagoda, Faris Yakob, Khalil Younes, Andrew Zolli, and Edward Zuber.

NOTES

INTRODUCTION

1. Espen, Hal. 1999. "Levi's Blues." *New York Times Magazine*, March 21: 56.

2. Deighton, John. 2002. "How Snapple Got Its Juice Back." *Harvard Business Review*, January: 47–53. Deighton, John. 1999. "Snapple." *Harvard Business School Case Study*, N9–599–126, July 8: 1–17. Bailey, Steve, and Steven Syre. 1997. "A Billion-Dollar Snapple Bath." *Boston Globe*, March 28.

3. Zuckerberg, Mark. 2009. "Update on Terms." *Facebook Blog*, February 18. http://blog.facebook.com/blog.php?post=54746167130. Source for number of photos: Smith, Justin. 2008. "How Facebook Stores Billions of Photos." *Inside Facebook*, June 27. At this writing, the number of photos on Facebook was 6.5 billion. www.insidefacebook.com/2008/06/27/how-facebook-stores-billions-of-photos/.

4. "As hip as it was, as exciting as it was, very few people were able to monetize anything that came out of that [cool hunting]," [Irma] Zandl explains. "People were fed this line that if the cool hunter found it, then six months from now you would have a rip-roaring business. And I think a lot of people got burned by that." In Grossman, Lev. 2003. "The Quest for Cool." *Time*, September 8. www.time.com/time/covers/1101030908/xopener.html.

5. "C-suite" means the suite of offices occupied by senior managers. Drucker, Peter. 1954. *The Principles of Management*. New York: HarperCollins. Deming, Edwards. 1982. *Out of the Crisis*. Cambridge, MA: MIT Press. Hammer, Michael, and James Champy. 1993. *Reengineering the Corporation: A Manifesto for Business Revolution*. New York: Harper. Peters, Tom, and Robert Waterman. 1982. *In Search of Excellence*. New York: Harper Business. Porter, Michael. 1998. *Competitive Strategy: Techniques for Analyzing Industries and Competitors*. New York: The Free Press.

CHAPTER 1: GETTING PAST GURU: BEING STEVE JOBS

1. Derbyshire, David. 2006. "Apple Bites Back." *My Telegraph Blog*, September 13. http://my.telegraph.co.uk/david_derbyshire/go/tag/view/blog_post/consumer%2Belectronics.

2. Harvey Pitt in Slater, Don. 2009. "Harvey Pitt, Former SEC Chairman, Discusses 'Steve Jobs' Health' Factor." *Wall Street Journal Law Blog*, January 23. http://blogs.wsj.com/law/2009/01/23/harvey-pitt-former-sec-chairman-discusses-steve-jobs-health-factor/.

3. Reisinger, Don. 2008. "Why Steve Jobs' Health Matters More than Apple Says." *Digital Home at CNET*, July 23. http://news.cnet.com/8301–13506_3–9997315–17.html.

4. Hill, Brad. 2006. "Howard Stringer's Push and Pull Generation." *DigitalMusic*, January 11. http://digitalmusic.weblogsinc.com/2006/01/11/howard-stringers-push-and-pull-generation/. Siklos, Richard, and Martin Fackler. 2006. "Sony's Road Warrior." *New York Times*, May 28.

5. Anonymous. 2008. Form 10-K Martha Stewart Living Omnimedia Inc. MSO. Filed March 17 (period December 31, 2007), pp. 12–13.

6. Jobs, Steve. 2005. "'You've Got to Find What You Love,' Jobs Says." *Stanford Report*, June 14. http://news-service.stanford.edu/news/2005/june15/jobs-061505.html.

7. "Prior to the Sundblom illustrations [for Coca-Cola], the Christmas saint had been variously illustrated wearing blue, yellow, green, or red. In European art, he was usually tall and gaunt, whereas Clement Moore had depicted him as an elf in 'A Visit from St. Nicholas.' After the soft drink ads, Santa would forever more be a huge, fat, relentlessly happy man with broad belt and black hip boots—and he would wear Coca-Cola red." Pendergrast, Mark. 1993. *For God, Country and Coca-Cola*. New York: Collier Books, p. 181.

8. Foust, Dean. 2006. "Queen of Pop: Meet Mary Minnick." *BusinessWeek*, August 7. www.businessweek.com/magazine/content/06_32/b3996401.htm?chan=search.

9. Ibid.

10. This campaign was started in 1996. For more detail, see the press release on the campaign here: www.thecoca-colacompany.com/presscenter/nr_20060330_coke_side_of_life.html.

11. Foust, Dean. 2006. "Queen of Pop." *BusinessWeek*, August 7. www.businessweek.com/magazine/content/06_32/b3996401.htm?chan=search.

12. Tynan, Dan. 2005. "The 50 Greatest Gadgets of the Past 50 Years." *PC World*, December 24. www.pcworld.com/article/123950/the_50_greatest_gadgets_of_the_past_50_years.html.

13. Anthony, Scott D. 2005. "Making the Most of a Slim Chance." *Strategy and Innovation* 3, no. 4 (July/August). Reproduced in the *Harvard Business School*

Working Knowledge under the title "Motorola's Bet on the Razr's Edge," September 12, 2005. http://hbswk.hbs.edu/archive/4992.html.

14. Roger Jellicoe quoted in Anthony, Scott D. 2005. "Making the Most of a Slim Chance." *Strategy and Innovation* 3, no. 4 (July/August). Reproduced in the *Harvard Business School Working Knowledge* under the title "Motorola's Bet on the Razr's Edge," September 12, 2005. http://hbswk.hbs.edu/archive/4992.html.

15. Frost's exact words were retrospective: "We made a determination that we didn't care how many we sell. It was decided we were going to do it for the learning and the brand building. That enabled it to bypass a lot of the internal hurdles." Anthony, Scott D. 2005. "Making the Most of a Slim Chance." *Strategy and Innovation* 3, no. 4 (July/August). Reproduced in the *Harvard Business School Working Knowledge* under the title "Motorola's Bet on the Razr's Edge," September 12, 2005. http://hbswk.hbs.edu/archive/4992.html.

16. Murph, Darren. 2007. "50-percent of Your iPhone Purchase to Pad Apple's Wallet?" *Engadget*, January 18. www.engadget.com/2007/01/18/50-percent-of-your-iphone-purchase-to-pad-apples-wallet/.

17. Miller, Paul. 2008. "Motorola Officially Considering Dropping Its Phone Unit. *Engadget*, January 31. www.engadget.com/2008/01/31/motorola-officially-considering-dropping-its-phone-unit/.

18. Block, Ryan. 2008. "Motorola Insider Tells All About the Fall of Technology Icon." *Engadget*, March 26. www.engadget.com/2008/03/26/motorola-insider-tells-all-about-the-fall-of-a-technology-icon/. McCracken, Grant. 2005. "The Malamud Effect: Ideas and the Corporation." *This Blog Sits at the Intersection of Anthropology and Economics*, September 23. www.cultureby.com/trilogy/2005/09/the_malamud_eff.html. Sampey, Kathy. 2005. "Motorola CMO Geoffrey Frost Dies." *BrandWeek*, November 17. www.brandweek.com/bw/esearch/article_display.jsp?vnu_content_id=1001524081.

19. Sutherland, Rory. 2005. "The Campaign Essay: Adland's Hidden Talent." *Brand Republic*, January 14. www.brandrepublic.com/News/232515/.

20. Husband, Stuart. 2008. "An Interview with Anne Rice." *Telegraph*, October 2. www.telegraph.co.uk/arts/main.jhtml?xml=/arts/2008/11/02.

CHAPTER 2: STEALTH CCOS

1. Katz, Donald. 1994. *Just Do It*. New York: Random House, p. 138. Marshall, Caroline. 2001. "I've Only Done Great Work for Nike." *Brand Republic*, June 22. www.brandrepublic.com/Campaign/News/46980/.

2. Hunsberger, Brent. 2008. "Nike Celebrates 'Just Do It' 20th Anniversary with New Ads." *Playbooks and Profits* blog, July 17. http://blog.oregonlive.com/playbooksandprofits/2008/07/nike_celebrates_just_do_it_20t.html.

3. See "Tag" on YouTube here: www.youtube.com/watch?v=YOzIZwRiN-I.

4. Director is Frank Budgen; creative directors, Dan Wieden, Hal Curtis; art directors, Andy Fackrell, Monica Taylor; agency producer, Andrew Loevenguth;

copywriter, Mike Byrne; production company, Anonymous, Gorgeous Films; executive producers, Paul Rothwell, Shelly Townsend; producer, Alicia Bernard; editorial company, Lookinglass Editorial; editor, Russell Icke; telecine company, Company 3.

5. See the work of Improv Everywhere at YouTube: www.youtube.com/user/ImprovEverywhere and at www.improveverywhere.com.

6. Some students of culture will see the influence of the Fluxus art movement, which sought to make art out of accident.

7. Kauffman, Stuart A. 1995. *At Home in the Universe: The Search for Laws of Self-Organization and Complexity*. New York: Oxford University Press.

8. Culp, Kristine. 2003. "*Paradise Lost* Found in a Phone Booth in Edmonton," *National Post*, January 4.

9. See www.geocaching.com and www.wheresgeorge.com. The Web site at www.phototagging.com is now defunct.

10. Rheingold, Howard. 2002. *Smart Mobs*. New York: Basic Books. See ImprovEverywhere on YouTube and its own Web site, www.improveverywhere.com.

11. Weber, Max. 1946. "Science as Vocation." In H. H. Gerth and C. Wright Mills, trans. and ed., *From Max Weber: Essays in Sociology*. New York: Oxford University Press, pp. 129–156.

12. Levitt, Theodore. 1986. "The Marketing Imagination." In *The Marketing Imagination*. New York: Free Press, p. 128. For more on Levitt, see Hanna, Julia. 2008. "Ted Levitt Changed My Life." *Working Knowledge from the Harvard Business School*, December 17. http://hbswk.hbs.edu/item/6054.html.

13. See "Pink Moon" on YouTube: www.youtube.com/watch?v=8lSKUL_n6c0. I believe this ad appeared in late 1999. One recent convert was Shane Hutton, senior copywriter at the Boston ad agency Arnold Communications, who flashed upon the song while helping conceive the Cabrio ad. "We went through a bunch of songs, but that one kept sticking to the wall," he says. "It transports you, and it's difficult to forget once you hear it." VW director of marketing Liz Vanzura says no one at her company had heard of Drake, but she thought the track's "warm-hearted, free-spirited feeling" was a perfect fit. The creative team for "Pink Moon": Arnold, Boston, chief creative officer, Ron Lawner; creative directors, Lance Jensen, Alan Pafenbach; art director, Tim Vaccarino; copywriter, Shane Hutton; agency producer, Bill Goodell; production company, Bob Industries, Venice, California; directors, Jonathan Dayton, Valerie Faris.

14. See "Synchronicity" on YouTube: www.youtube.com/watch?v=8hgrFExRReI.

15. Kiley, David. 2002. *Getting the Bugs Out: The Rise, Fall, and Comeback of Volkswagen in America*. New York: John Wiley and Sons, p. 245. For more on "reviewing" as an occasional and unexpected requirement of popular culture, see McCracken, Grant. 2007. "Chinatown: Noir Pour Nous." *This Blog Sits at the Intersection of Anthropology and Economics*, April 24.

16. So spoke F. R. Leavis, E.M. Forster, Evelyn Waugh, and T. S. Eliot. Carey, John. 1992. *The Intellectuals and the Masses: Pride and Prejudice Among the Literary Intelligentsia, 1880–1939*. London: Faber and Faber.

17. As LeMahieu observed, "Intellectuals believed that low, vulgar, common culture played upon the baser instincts, whereas superior culture emanated, in its creation and appreciation, from the higher, more subtle, complex, and integrative faculties." LeMahieu, D. L. 1988. *A Culture for Democracy: Mass Communication and the Cultivated Mind in Britain Between the Wars*. Oxford, UK: Clarendon Press, p. 136.

18. Mumford, L. 1961. *The City in History: Its Origins, Its Transformations, and Its Prospects*. London: Secker and Warburg, p. 486.

19. Yates, Richard. 1961. *Revolutionary Road*. New York: Greenwood Press. MacDonald, John D. 1964. *The Quick Red Fox*. New York: Ballantine, pp. 167–168. Galbraith, John Kenneth. 1958. *The Affluent Society*. Boston: Houghton Mifflin, p. 223. In 1963 Pete Seeger sang "Little Boxes," a song composed by Malvina Reynolds in 1962. Minow, Newton. 1961. "Television and the Public Interest." An address delivered May 9, 1961, Washington, DC.

20. Baritz, Loren. 1990. *The Good Life: The Meaning of Success for the American Middle Class*. New York: HarperCollins. Ewen, Stuart. 1976. *Captains of Consciousness: Advertising and the Social Roots of the Consumer Culture*. New York: McGraw-Hill. Ewen, Stuart. 1988. *All Consuming Images: The Politics of Style in Contemporary Culture*. New York: Basic Books, pp. 217–232. Frank, Thomas. 1997. *The Conquest of Cool: Business Culture, Counterculture, and the Rise of Hip Consumerism*. Chicago: University of Chicago Press. Klein, Naomi. 2000. *No Logo: No Space, No Choice, No Jobs, Taking Aim at the Brand Bullies*. Toronto: Alfred A. Knopf. Kunstler, James Howard. 1994. *Geography of Nowhere*. New York: Free Press. Holt, Douglas B. 2002. "Why Do Brands Cause Trouble?" *Journal of Consumer Research* 29 (June): 82. Lehmann, Chris. 2003. *Revolt of the Masscult*. Chicago: Prickly Paradigm Press. Marcuse, Herbert. 1964. *One-Dimensional Man*. Boston: Beacon Press. Postman, Neil. 1985. *Amusing Ourselves to Death: Public Discourse in the Age of Show Business*. New York: Penguin. Riesman, David. 1964. *Abundance for What?* Garden City, NY: Doubleday. Benjamin Barber, for instance, refers to "the numbing and neutering uniformity of industrial modernization and the colonizing culture of McWorld," and to the "trivialization and homogenization of values [which are] an affront to cultural diversity and spiritual and moral seriousness" (Barber, Benjamin R. 1995. *Jihad vs. McWorld*. New York: Random House, pp. 9, xii). This interpretation of popular culture is now a theme of popular culture. See the play *Suburbia* by Eric Bogosian and movies by Richard Linklater (*SubUrbia*), Ang Lee (*The Ice Storm*), Sam Mendes (*American Beauty*), Gary Ross (*Pleasantville*), Todd Solondz (*Happiness*), Peter Weir (*The Truman Show*), and Lars von Trier (*Dogville*).

21. Jenkins, Henry. 1992. *Textual Poachers: Television Fans and Participatory Culture*. New York: Routledge, p. 55. Caughey, John L. 1984. *Imaginary Social*

Worlds: A Cultural Approach. Lincoln: University of Nebraska Press. See also Ellis, John. 1982. *Visible Fictions: Cinema, Television, Video*. London: Routledge & Kegan Paul. Long, Elizabeth. 1987. "Reading Groups and the Postmodern Crisis of Cultural Authority." *Cultural Studies* 1, no. 3 (October): 306–327. Radway, Janice A. 1984. *Reading the Romance: Women, Patriarchy and Popular Literature*. Chapel Hill: University of North Carolina Press.

22. Johnson, Steven. 2005. *Everything Bad Is Good for You: How Today's Popular Culture Is Actually Making Us Smarter*. New York: Riverhead Books.

23. The Fox series *The Sarah Connor Chronicles* is described by Wired.com as "a deeply felt and artfully imagined drama with so many unexpected gifts that it's often hard to believe you're watching broadcast television." Poulsen, Kevin. 2009. "Urgent: Save *Sarah Connor Chronicles* from Termination." Wired.com, May 4. www.wired.com/underwire/2009/05/sarah-connor-chronicles/.

24. Itzkoff, Dave. 2008. "Complexity Without Commitment." *New York Times*, August 24.

25. Brantlinger, Patrick. 1983. *Bread and Circuses: Theories of Mass Culture as Social Decay*. Ithaca, NY: Cornell University Press. Cowen, Tyler. 1998. *In Praise of Commercial Culture*. Cambridge, MA: Harvard University Press. Docker, John. 1994. *Postmodernism and Popular Culture: A Cultural History*. Cambridge, UK: Cambridge University Press. Dickstein, Morris. 1999. *Leopards in the Temple: The Transformation of American Fiction, 1945–1970*. Cambridge, MA: Harvard University Press. LeMahieu, D. L. 1988. *A Culture for Democracy: Mass Communication and the Cultivated Mind in Britain Between the Wars*. Oxford, UK: Clarendon Press. Pells, Richard H. 1989. *The Liberal Mind in a Conservative Age: American Intellectuals in the 1940s and 1950s*. Middletown, CT: Wesleyan University Press. Susman, Warren I. 1984. "Introduction: Toward a History of the Culture of Abundance: Some Hypotheses." In *Culture as History: The Transformation of American Society in the Twentieth Century*. New York: Pantheon Books, pp. xix–xxx. This new view of contemporary culture was aided by historians who began to look at the origins of the consumer culture. Braudel, Fernand. 1973. *Capitalism and Material Life, 1400–1800*. Miriam Kochan, trans. London: Weidenfeld and Nicolson. (I am treating the geographer Braudel as a historian for the purposes of this argument.) Brewer, John, and Roy Porter, eds. 1993. *Consumption and the World of Goods*. London: Routledge. Bushman, Richard L. 1992. *The Refinement of America: Persons, Houses, Cities*. New York: Alfred A. Knopf. Carson, Cary, Ronald Hoffman, and Peter J. Albert, eds. 1994. *Of Consuming Interests: The Style of Life in the Eighteenth Century*. Charlottesville: University Press of Virginia. McKendrick, Neil, John Brewer, and J. H. Plumb. 1982. *The Birth of a Consumer Society: The Commercialization of Eighteenth-Century England*. Bloomington: Indiana University Press.

26. The reaction to "Pink Moon" and "Synchronicity" was immediate. Older viewers were threatened. David Letterman led the mainstream reaction by making fun of Volkswagen. This was the very thing advertisers had traditionally feared: confusion and ridicule that spelled the end of clients, the end of careers.

But Arnold was thrilled. "More buzz. Our stuff just kept getting more buzz and that's how we knew it was right." (Kiley, David. 2001. *Getting the Bugs Out: The Rise, Fall, and Comeback of Volkswagen in America*. New York: John Wiley and Sons, p. 245.) When you were released from the rules of mass marketing, bearding the lion of conventional taste was not the end of everything. It was the inevitable consequences of speaking more powerfully to a smaller audience. In the language of Levine et al., it was the way you "started a conversation." Levine, Rick, Christopher Locke, Doc Searls, and David Weinberger. 2000. *The Cluetrain Manifesto*. New York: Basic Books.

27. I evoke the AMC TV show by Matthew Weiner because it is so very bad at capturing the finesse and intelligence with which good ads interact with culture. *Mad Men* is too busy sensationalizing the story of three-martini lunches and 1950s' infidelity to reflect the realities of this creative business. The TNT series *Trust Me* managed the story in a more sophisticated way, but it did not survive. Clearly, Weiner is the better CCO.

28. *Macworld* Staff. 2005. "'I'll Kill Google,' Threatens Ballmer." www.PCadvisor.co.uk, September 5. www.pcadvisor.co.uk/news/index.cfm?newsid=5030. For more on Microsoft's reputation, see Chapter 6, "Trusting Microsoft," in Spar, Debora. 2001. *Ruling the Waves*. New York: Harcourt.

29. McCracken, Grant. 2007. "The World According to Microsoft." *This Blog Sits at the Intersection of Anthropology and Economics*, August 23. www.cultureby.com/trilogy/2007/08/todays-post.html.

30. Sacks, Danielle. 2008. "Can Alex Bogusky Help Microsoft Beat Apple?" *Fast Company*, June. www.fastcompany.com/magazine/126/believe-it-or-not-hes-a-pc.html.

31. "'Crispin probably has one chance to do something big with Microsoft, and if it fails, I think all bets are off for the agency,' says Gartner analyst [Andrew] Frank." Quoted in Sacks, Danielle. 2008. "Can Alex Bogusky Help Microsoft Beat Apple?" *Fast Company*, June. www.fastcompany.com/magazine/126/believe-it-or-not-hes-a-pc.html.

32. See the Kylie "I'm a PC" ad at YouTube here: www.youtube.com/watch?v=DtilWL4mnhI.

33. Trilling, Lionel. 1965. Preface. *Beyond Culture: Essays on Literature and Learning*. New York: Penguin Books.

34. McCracken, Grant. 1998. *Plenitude*. Toronto: Periph.:Fluide. We will develop this point later in the section on status.

35. Of course, advertising can merely change the terms of reference. It cannot change the brand's history or the reputation. This is up to Microsoft. Bogusky had made a start. And again, what a start. The rest was up to Microsoft, but now the company had movement where before it had stasis.

36. Berner, Robert. 2003. "P&G: New and Improved." *BusinessWeek*, July 7. www.businessweek.com/magazine/content/03_27/b3840001_mz001.htm. Lafley, A. G., and Ram Charan. 2008. *The Game-Changer*. New York: Crown.

37. Ellison, Sarah. 2005. "P&G Chief's Turnaround Recipe: Find Out What Women Want." *Wall Street Journal*, June 1, p. 1.

38. Levitt said of Detroit that it "never really researched the customer's wants. It only researched . . . [what] it had already decided to offer him." Levitt, Theodore. 1960/1986. "Marketing Myopia." In *The Marketing Imagination*. New York: Free Press, p. 154. This resonated with another telling moment in the history of American capitalism. Some fifty years before, Levitt quizzed the people who ran the American railroad. "What business are you in?" he asked them. "Why," came the surprised reply, "we're in the railroad business." Levitt shook his head at this dismal case of marketing myopia. "No," he explained patiently. "Unless you want to be eclipsed by change, you're in the transportation business." The gurus, Lafley and Levitt, were saying it's not about who we think we are.

39. Lafley, A. G., and Ram Charan. 2008. *The Game-Changer*. New York: Crown, p. 36.

40. Ibid.

41. Deighton, John. 2008. "Dove: Evolution of a Brand." *Harvard Business School Case Study,* No. 9–508–047, March 24, p. 3.

42. Ibid.

43. Ibid., p. 4.

44. Kim, W. Chan, and Renee Mauborgne. 2005. *Blue Ocean Strategy*. Boston: Harvard Business School Press. How disappointing then that Chan and Mauborgne talk about culture not at all.

45. Research results from Landor Associates as reported in Deighton, John. 2008. "Dove: Evolution of a Brand." *Harvard Business School Case Study*, No. 9–508–047, March 24, p. 7.

46. *Fast Company* writers William Taylor and Polly LaBarre call 2004 the "high point of HBO's hold on pop culture." Taylor, William C., and Polly LaBarre. 2006. *Mavericks at Work*. New York: HarperCollins, p. 23. I am indebted to Taylor and LaBarre for their account of HBO. Chris Albrecht declined to be interviewed for this project.

47. Ibid., p. 25. Emphasis in the original.

48. Cawelti, John G. 1976. *Adventure, Mystery, and Romance: Formula Stories as Art and Popular Culture*. Chicago: University of Chicago Press. Mittell, Jason. 2004. *Genre and Television*. New York: Routledge.

49. Let me emphasize: This is surmise on my part. I am imagining, not reporting, what Albrecht said.

50. Perhaps coincidentally, this was one of the devices feminists used in the 1970s as a sexism detector. What if you took a phrase and an action and moved it from women to men? (To those who argued that there is nothing sexist about women covering their mouths while they laughed, the test was to see if a man ever did it. The answer of course was no.)

51. Taylor, William C., and Polly LaBarre. 2006. *Mavericks at Work*. New York: HarperCollins, p. 26.

52. Ibid., p. 29.

53. Sutton, Bob. 2009. "Esther Dyson's Refrigerator Magnet: Always Make New Mistakes." *Work Matters Blog*, April 29. http://bobsutton.typepad.com/my_weblog/2009/04/esther-dysons-refrigerator-magnet.html. Sutton and Diego Rodriguez, both faculty members in the Hasso Plattner Institute of Design, have invented what we might call the Stanford variation of this wisdom: "Failure Sucks But Instructs." Rodriguez, Diego. 2009. "Failure Sucks But Instructs." *Metacool Blog*, May 20. http://metacool.typepad.com/metacool/2009/05/14-failure-sucks-but-instructs.html.

54. Albrecht in Taylor, William C., and Polly LaBarre. 2006. *Mavericks at Work*. New York: HarperCollins, p. 25. Here is Albrecht elaborating on this second point: "You learn to trust the talent. We are the network and we don't always agree with the final product of the things that we put on the air. But everybody can walk away feeling a little bit better because we haven't screwed up somebody's good idea. They have had a chance to deliver their vision and I think, more often than not, that is how you get the best stuff." In Johnson, Ted. 2003. "Risks and Rewards: Albrecht's Visceral, Hands-Off Approach a Magnet for Talent." *Variety*, August 24. www.variety.com/article/VR1117891249.html?categoryid=1675&cs=1.

55. Minow, Newton. 1961. "Television and the Public Interest." An address delivered May 9, 1961, Washington, DC.

56. See the Wikipedia entry "History of New York City (1946–1977)" for more details and the phrase given here: http://en.wikipedia.org/wiki/History_of_New_York_City_(1946–1977).

57. Glaser, Milton. 2000. *Art Is Work*. New York: Overlook Press, p. 206.

58. Glaser is a fan of Lewis Hyde's *The Gift*. He believes, as Hyde does, that designers (and other artists) help build communities by gifting them with beauty and design. But one can't help noticing that a lot of these gifts appear to be keeping something for the designer. "I ♥ New York" was, by contrast, the freest of gifts. It kept nothing for Glaser. Hyde, Lewis. 2007. *The Gift*. New York: Viking.

59. Stohr, Kate. 2003. "I Sell New York." *Gotham Gazette*, March 17. www.gothamgazette.com/article/issueoftheweek/20030315/200/312.

60. Glaser, Milton. 2000. *Art Is Work*. New York: Overlook Press, p. 206.

61. See Sir John's remarks on YouTube: www.youtube.com/watch?v=INQnoeYawao.

CHAPTER 3: CULTURE FAST AND SLOW

1. McCracken, Grant. 2005. "Homeyness." In *Culture and Consumption II*. Bloomington: Indiana University Press. For a fuller account of my Oprah experience, see

McCracken, Grant. 2005. "On Oprah." In *Culture and Consumption II*. Bloomington: Indiana University Press. I have borrowed heavily from this account.

2. All of the quotes from the designer are recalled from memory and appear here as paraphrase.

3. See the results of my ethnographic investigation here: McCracken, Grant. 2005. "Homeyness." In *Culture and Consumption II*. Bloomington: Indiana University Press, pp. 22–47.

4. When Marcus Felson studied homes in Detroit, he was mystified by what he called the "bric-a-brac factor." He confessed to things in these homes "beyond the reach of this writer's sociological imagination." Edward Laumann and James House acknowledged "distinctions beyond the untutored grasp of our interviewers." Felson, Marcus. 1976. "The Differentiation of Material Life Styles: 1925 to 1966." *Social Indicators Research* 3: 414. Laumann, Edward O., and James S. House. 1970. "Living Room Styles and Social Attributes: The Patterning of Material Artifacts in a Modern Urban Community." *Sociology and Social Research* 54 (April 3): 338.

5. Spears, Richard A. 2002. *Common American Phrases in Everyday Contexts: A Detailed Guide to Real-Life Conversation and Small Talk*. 2nd ed. New York: McGraw-Hill.

6. Goffman, Erving. 1959. *The Presentation of Self in Everyday Life*. Harmondsworth, UK: Penguin. Huber, Richard M. 1987. *The American Idea of Success*. New York: Pushcart Press. Klein, Richard. 1993. *Cigarettes Are Sublime*. Durham, NC: Duke University Press. Lakoff, George, and Mark Johnson. 1980. *Metaphors We Live By*. Chicago: University of Chicago Press. Zerubavel, Eviatar. 1993. *The Fine Line*. Chicago: University of Chicago Press. I recommend Fox's treatment of English culture: Fox, Kate. 2008. *Watching the English: The Hidden Rules of English Behaviour*. London: Nicholas Brealey Publishing. It is useful for insight into American culture and useful as an opportunity of contrast.

7. Toffler, Alvin. 1970. *Future Shock*. New York: Bantam, p. 17.

8. Harris, Mark. 2008. *Pictures at a Revolution: Five Movies and the Birth of the New Hollywood*. New York: Penguin. Marc, David. 1997. *Comic Visions: Television Comedy and American Culture*, 2nd ed. Malden, MA: Blackwell Publishing. Zoglin, Richard. 2009. *Comedy at the Edge: How Stand-Up in the 1970s Changed America*. New York: Bloomsbury.

9. World Intellectual Property Organization. 2003. "10% Increase in International Patent Applications Filings in 2002." Press release, Geneva, Switzerland, February 18.

10. This 2002 figure combines the surface Web and the deep Web. This is roughly the equivalent of ten Libraries of Congress. www2.sims.berkeley.edu/research/projects/how-much-info-2003/internet.htm.

11. Collingwood, Harris. 2003. "The Sink-or-Swim Economy." *New York Times*, June 8.

12. In Salamon, Julie. 2001. "When It Comes to TV, Coveted Adolescents Prove to Be Unpredictable." *New York Times*, March 13.

13. "My mind would run down a ledger of slights: the first boy, in seventh grade, who called me a coon; his tears of surprise—'Why'dya do that?'—when I gave him a bloody nose. The tennis pro who told me that I shouldn't touch the schedule of matches pinned to the bulletin board because my color might rub off; his thin-lipped, red-faced smile—'Can't you take a joke?'—when I threatened to report him." Obama, Barack. 1995. *Dreams from My Father*. New York: Times Books, p. 80.

14. Ariely, Dan. 2008. *Predictably Irrational: The Hidden Forces That Shape Our Decisions*. New York: HarperCollins. Brown, Shona L., and Kathleen M. Eisenhardt. 1998. *Competing on the Edge: Strategy as Structured Chaos*. Boston: Harvard Business School Press. Davis, Stanley M., and Christopher Meyer. 1998. *Blur: The Speed of Change in the Connected Economy*. Reading, MA: Addison-Wesley. Evans, Philip, and Thomas S. Wurster. 2000. *Blown to Bits: How the New Economics of Information Transforms Strategy*. Boston: Harvard Business School Press. Gates, Bill. 2000. *Business @ the Speed of Thought*. New York: Warner Books. Gleick, James. 1999. *Faster: The Acceleration of Just About Everything*. New York: Pantheon Books. Hamel, Gary, and C. K. Prahalad. 1994. *Competing for the Future*. Boston: Harvard Business School Press. Handy, Charles. 1990. *The Age of Paradox*. Boston: Harvard Business School Press. Kelly, Kevin. 1995. *Out of Control: The New Biology of Machines, Social Systems, and the Economic World*. New York: Basic Books.

15. Hagel III, John, John Seely Brown, and Lang Davison. 2008. "Shaping Strategy in a World of Constant Disruption." *Harvard Business Review*, October. Taleb, Nassim Nicholas. 2007. *The Black Swan: The Impact of the Highly Improbable*. New York: Random House. Schwartz, Peter. 1996. *The Art of the Long View: Planning for the Future in an Uncertain World*. New York: Currency Doubleday. Christensen, Clayton M. 1997. *The Innovator's Dilemma: When New Technologies Cause Great Firms to Fail*. Boston: Harvard Business School Press. LaBarre, Polly. 2003. "The Industrialized Revolution." *Fast Company*, November. www.fastcompany.com/magazine/76/revolution.html.

16. Mandel, Michael. 2004. "This Way to the Future." *BusinessWeek*, October 11. www.businessweek.com/magazine/content/04_41/b3903402.htm.

17. Schumpeter, Joseph A. 1942/1975. *Capitalism, Socialism and Democracy*. New York: Harper, pp. 82–85. Foster, Richard and Sarah Kaplan. 2001. *Creative Destruction*. New York: Currency.

18. "Gillette Company is accelerating the pace at which new products are unveiled globally from three years to two. Chrysler Corporation is compressing the new-car development process, from 4 years to 33 months. The next car will take 2 years. International Business Machines Corp. now takes an order for a personal computer over the phone, and builds and ships the PC within 24 hours. At Bell Helicopter, the lead time for building helicopters has been reduced to 12 months

from 24 months since 1991." Bulkeley, William M. 1994. "Pushing the Pace: The Latest Big Thing at Many Companies Is Speed, Speed, Speed." *Wall Street Journal*, December 23, pp. A1, A5.

19. Powell, Walter W. 2001. "The Capitalist Firm in the Twenty-First Century." In Paul DiMaggio, ed., *The Twenty-First Century Firm*, p. 39. Princeton, NJ: Princeton University Press. Davenport, Thomas H. 1996. "The Fad That Forgot People." *Fast Company*. Reproduced at the University of Toronto's Rotman School of Management, www.rotman.utoronto.ca/~evans/teach363/fastco/reengin.htm. Hammer, Michael, and James Champy. 2004. *Reengineering the Corporation: A Manifesto for Business Revolution*. Rev. ed. New York: Collins Business, p. 144. Chesbrough, Henry. 2003. *Open Innovation: The New Imperative for Creating and Profiting from Technology*. Boston: Harvard Business Press. Foster, Richard J. 1986. *Innovation: The Attacker's Advantage*. New York: Summit Books.

20. A new order of problem solving is now called for in the C-suite, with Roger Martin leading the charge. Martin, Roger L. 2009. *Opposable Mind: How Successful Leaders Win Through Integrative Thinking*. Boston: Harvard Business School Press.

21. See www.sherwin-williams.com/search/white+paint&section=pro-products. See also Anonymous. 2007. "Why Are There So Many Shades of White?" *Crooked Eyebrow*, October 4. www.crookedeyebrow.com/2007/10/why-are-there-so-many-shades-of-white.html.

22. Sam McKnight, in Healy, Kathy. 1992. "Behind the Scenes with a Virtuoso Stylist." *Allure*, September 9, p. 140.

23. Anonymous. 2003. "Company News; Best Buy Sheds Musicland in No-Cash Deal." *New York Times*, June 17.

24. Kim, W. Chan, and Renee Mauborgne. 2005. *Blue Ocean Strategy*. Boston: Harvard Business School Press.

25. Lafley, A. G., and Ram Charan. 2008. *The Game-Changer: How You Can Drive Revenue and Profit Growth with Innovation*. New York: Crown Business.

26. Hein, Kenneth. 2009. "The Winners and Losers of the Digital Transition." *Brandweek*, January 3. www.brandweek.com/bw/content_display/special reports/features/e3i7a4b4ca5771c6f2d5e0c63c69931210a.

27. This research was done at the Institute of Contemporary Culture at the Royal Ontario Museum, and it resulted in an exhibit there titled "Toronto Teenagers: Coming of Age in the 1990s."

28. *Family Ties* was a situation comedy that ran on NBC from September 1982 to September 1989. Unexpectedly, it proved an ideological beachhead of the neoconservative movement of the decade, converting teens to Reaganesque and Republican values. Alex Keaton (the seventeen-year-old played by Michael J. Fox) slept with a picture of William F. Buckley over his bed. Designed as an object of mockery, this character surprised everyone by becoming a champion of the "preppy" era. Was he influential? Here's a passage from a Web diary, part of some-

one's very interesting Pepys-like experiment on the 'Net (www.widomaker.com/~xiled/journal/121497.html):

> I was an 80s over-achiever. I rooted for Alex Keaton. I wanted to be Alex Keaton. It was during the 80s that I learned that enough money could iron out any problem and make you happy. Any job was tolerable if it paid well enough. I decided to become a lawyer in the 80s. I espoused a Darwinian winner-take-all philosophy because I always won. I would do anything to win. I wore preppy clothes: topsiders, khaki pants, the whole deal.

This web writer is documenting his transformation from "slacker guy to working stiff."

29. This speciation in the teen world has not been well documented. "Toronto Teenagers" documented five categories: punks, preps, heavy metal, b-boys/girls, and hippies. Polhemus documents the stylistic signatures of many more: Polhemus, Ted. 1994. *Street Style: From Sidewalk to Catwalk*. London: Thames and Hudson.

30. From a white, middle-class, professional woman in her late forties in Toronto, Ontario, October 1990. For a very useful study, see Palladino, Grace. 1996. *Teenagers: An American History*. New York: Basic Books. Palladino notes that the term "teenager" was first used in 1941 and took shape in America, especially in the 1930s–1960s. For a more scholarly view, see Kett, Joseph F. 1977. *Rites of Passage: Adolescence in America, 1790 to the Present*. New York: Basic Books. For a collection of essays, including an excerpt showing G. Stanley Hall's turn-of-the-twentieth-century promotion of the term and concept "adolescence," see Rapson, Richard L., ed. 1971. *The Cult of Youth in Middle-Class America*. Lexington, MA: Heath.

31. "The worlds in which different societies live are distinct worlds, not merely the same world with different labels attached." Edward Sapir in Shweder, Richard A., and Edmund J. Bourne. 1984. "Does the Concept of the Person Vary Cross-Culturally?" In LeVine, Robert A., and Richard A. Shweder, eds. *Culture Theory: Essays on Mind, Self, and Emotion*. New York: Cambridge University Press, p. 195.

32. This was brought home for me by comments on my blog. Ben K. remarked, "We have such fine control over our own identities that we don't need to resort to big, poorly-defined memes like generational labels." Noah Brier said, "Generations are dead. Thanks mainly to technology, the people I know . . . range in age from 18–60, but they all feel like my generation inasmuch as we share similar beliefs, interests and ideas. The idea of being associated with a group of people because we happen to be the same age seems more ridiculous than ever." See the first and second comments on this post: McCracken, Grant. 2008. "Millennials: Who Gets to Define and Design This Generation?" *This Blog Sits at the Intersection of Anthropology and Economics*, December 8. www.cultureby.com/trilogy/2008/12/millenials-who-gets-to-define-and-design-this-generation.html.

33. On this phenomenon, see Keith, Jennie. 1982. *Old People as People: Social and Cultural Influences on Aging and Old Age*. Boston: Little, Brown and Company; and Kaufman, Sharon R. 1986. *The Ageless Self: Sources of Meaning in Late Life*. Madison: University of Wisconsin Press. For the popular literature that picks up this theme, see Chopra, Deepak. 1993. *Ageless Body, Timeless Mind*. New York: Harmony Books.

34. See, for instance, the Web site for SAGE, Services and Advocacy for Gay, Lesbian, Bisexual and Transgender Elders: www.sageusa.org/index.cfm. For the argument that this is already so, see Streib, Gordon F. 1968. "Are the Aged a Minority Group?" In Bernice L. Neugarten, ed. *Middle Age and Aging: A Reader in Social Psychology*. Chicago: University of Chicago Press, pp. 35–47. See also Rose, Arnold M. 1968. "The Subculture of the Aging: A Topic for Sociological Research." In Bernice L. Neugarten, ed. *Middle Age and Aging: a Reader in Social Psychology*. Chicago: University of Chicago Press, pp. 29–34.

35. Scott-Maxwell, Florida. 1973. *The Meaning of My Days*. New York: Alfred A. Knopf, p. 19.

36. Here too the intellectuals are quick to tell us that the sky is falling. See Keen, Andrew. 2008. *The Cult of the Amateur*. New York: Broadway Books.

37. See: www.raw42.com/cgi-bin/genre_guide.pl?refer=raw42.

38. Pareles, Jon. 2003. "That Blob of Multiplying Genres? It's Music." *New York Times*. February 23.

39. Anderson. Chris. 2008. *Long Tail*. New York: Hyperion. Schwartz, Barry. 2005. *Paradox of Choice*. New York: Harper Perennial. Tapscott, Don, and Anthony D. Williams. 2008. *Wikinomics: How Mass Collaboration Changes Everything*. New York: Portfolio. Shirky, Clay. 2009. *Here Comes Everybody: The Power of Organizing Without Organizations*. New York: Penguin. Weinberger, David. 2007. *Everything Is Miscellaneous: The Power of the New Digital Disorder*. New York: Times Books.

40. Marcus, Greil. 1995. "The Deborah Chessler Story." *The Dustbin of History*. Cambridge, MA: Harvard University Press, p. 234.

41. I want to point out that I am using the term "convergence" in a way quite different from the one employed by my MIT colleague Henry Jenkins. Cf. Jenkins, Henry. 2006. *Convergence Culture: Where Old and New Media Collide*. New York: New York University Press.

42. Stroh, Ann. n.d. *The Preppy Handbook and Other Myths*. This document may be found at www.sit.wisc.edu/%7Exanadu/preppy_handbook.html.

43. For the connection between the prep or yuppie movement and BMW, see Greyser, Stephen, and Wendy Schille. 1993. "BMW: The Ultimate Driving Machine Seeks to De-Yuppify Itself." *Harvard Business School Case Study*, No. 9–593–046, December 27.

44. Ebert, Roger. 1987. "Wall Street." *Chicago Sun-Times*, December 11. http://rogerebert.suntimes.com/apps/pbcs.dll/article?AID=/19871211/REVIEWS/712110302/1023.

CHAPTER 4: STATUS AND COOL

1. Kron, Joan. 1983. *Home-Psych: The Social Psychology of Home and Decoration*. New York: Clarkson N. Potter.

2. "These [class] behaviors involve matters of etiquette, dress, deportment, gesture, intonation, dialect, vocabulary, small bodily movements. . . . In a manner of speaking these behaviors constitute a social style." Goffman, Erving. 1951. "Symbols of Class Status." *British Journal of Sociology* 2, no. 4 (December): 300.

3. Luckmann, Thomas, and Peter Berger. 1964. "Social Mobility and Personal Identity." *Archives Européennes de Sociologie* 5: 338. Seeley, John R., R. Alexander Sim, and E. W. Loosley. 1956. *Crestwood Heights: A Study of the Culture of Suburban Life*. Toronto: University of Toronto Press.

4. Gans, Herbert J. 1967. *The Levittowners: Ways of Life and Politics in a New Suburban Community*. New York: Vintage. Martineau, Pierre. 1958. "Social Classes and Spending Behavior." *Journal of Marketing* 4, no. 3 (October): 121–130. Seeley, John R., R. Alexander Sim, and E. W. Loosley. 1956. *Crestwood Heights: A Study of the Culture of Suburban Life*. Toronto: University of Toronto Press. Warner, W. Lloyd, and Paul Sanborn Lunt. 1942. *The Status System of a Modern Community*. New Haven, CT: Yale University Press.

5. Fussell, Paul. 1983. *Class: A Guide Through the American Status System*. New York: Summit Books.

6. Bourdieu, Pierre. 1984. *Distinction: A Social Critique of the Judgment of Taste*. Richard Nice, trans. Boston: Harvard University Press.

7. McCracken, Grant. 2000. "J&B." *Harvard Business School Case Study*, No. 500051, May 16.

8. Lamont, Michele. 1992. *Money, Morals and Manners: The Culture of the French and the American Upper-Middle Class*. Chicago: University of Chicago Press.

9. Leavis, F. R. 1930. "Mass Civilisation and Minority Culture." *Minority Pamphlet*, no. 1. Cambridge, UK: Minority Press, p. 5.

10. Arnold, Matthew. 1993. *Culture and Anarchy and Other Writings*. Stefan Collini, ed. Cambridge, UK: Cambridge University Press, pp. 59, 100. Collini, Stefan. 1993. Introduction, in *Culture and Anarchy and Other Writings*. Cambridge, UK: Cambridge University Press, p. ix. Levine, Lawrence W. 1988. *Highbrow/Lowbrow: The Emergence of Cultural Hierarchy in America*. Cambridge, MA: Harvard University Press, p. 223.

11. McCracken, Grant. 2005. "Culture and Culture at the Royal Ontario Museum: An Anthropological Approach to a Marketing Problem." In *Culture and Consumption II*. Bloomington: Indiana University Press, pp.122–160.

12. Luckmann, Thomas, and Peter Berger. 1964. "Social Mobility and Personal Identity." *Archives Européennes de Sociologie* 5: 331–344.

13. Silverstein, Michael J., and Neil Fiske. 2003. *Trading Up: The New American Luxury*. New York: Portfolio, p. 54.

14. Borland, Sophie. 2008. "Open-Plan Living Leads to Death of Dining Room." *The Telegraph*, January 29.

15. Here's how I get the number 5,000. Some 5,000 paintings were submitted for consideration to the Salon of 1863. It is safe to assume that every artist in Paris wanted to be included. This would put the number of avant-garde artists at no more than this number (and, we can assume, many fewer). This is certainly true if an artist were allowed to submit more than one painting. We would also want to subtract the 1,000 paintings that were selected for inclusion in the Salon. These were mostly the work of artists who were conventional and academic.

16. I relied on Poggioli, Renato. 1968. *The Theory of the Avant-Garde*. Gerald Fitzgerald, trans. Cambridge, MA: Harvard University Press. Poggioli's work is sociological in nature, a discovery of ideal types in particulars fantastically particular. This makes my extraction from his abstraction an abomination, to be sure.

17. Anonymous. 1926. "Sad Young Man." *Time*, November 1. Henry James said most American art was now French.

18. Adler, Kathleen, Erica Hirschler, and H. Barbara Weinberg. 2006. *Americans in Paris, 1860–1900*. London: National Gallery. Lévy, Sophie. 2004. *A Transatlantic Avant-Garde: American Artists in Paris, 1918–1939*. Berkeley and Los Angeles: University of California Press. Seigel, J. 1986. *Bohemian Paris*. Baltimore: Johns Hopkins University Press. Adler, Kathleen. 2006. "We'll Always Have Paris." In Adler, Kathleen, Erica Hirschler, and H. Barbara Weinberg, *Americans in Paris, 1860–1900*. London: National Gallery, p. 16. Hirschler, Erica. 2006. "At Home in Paris." In Adler, Kathleen, Erica Hirschler, and H. Barbara Weinberg, *Americans in Paris, 1860–1900*. London: National Gallery, p. 59.

19. It was published in the fall of 1926 and by the end of the year was selling 5,000 copies a month. Reynolds, Michael. 1992. *Hemingway: The American Homecoming*. New York: W. W. Norton, p. 99.

20. The reader might learn the mischief with which Jake Barnes introduces a stranger as his fiancée and the searing honesty of Harvey Stone. And he would be warned not to be like Robert Cohn, that perfect captive of the bourgeoisie.

21. The following account of the beats is indebted to Watson, Steven. 1995. *The Birth of the Beat Generation: Visionaries, Rebels and Hipsters, 1944–1960*. New York: Pantheon Books.

22. Watson, Steven. 1995. *The Birth of the Beat Generation: Visionaries, Rebels and Hipsters, 1944–1960*. New York: Pantheon Books, pp. 3, 75–76. Burroughs later complained that Huncke could be relied upon to steal most from those to whom he owed most, and the title of Huncke's autobiography appears to accept the judgment: Huncke, Herbert. 1990. *Guilty of Everything*. New York: Paragon House. For more on the notion of "beat," see Mailer, Norman. 1957. *The White Negro: Superficial Reflections on the Hipster*. San Francisco: City Lights Books.

23. Hewitt, Nicholas. 1996. "Shifting Cultural Centers in Twentieth-Century Paris." In Michael Sheringham, ed. *Parisian Fields*. London: Reaktion Books, pp. 30–45.

24. In Watson, Steven. 1995. *The Birth of the Beat Generation: Visionaries, Rebels and Hipsters, 1944–1960*. New York: Pantheon Books, pp. 15, 16.

25. In Watson, Steven. 1995. *The Birth of the Beat Generation: Visionaries, Rebels and Hipsters, 1944–1960*. New York: Pantheon Books, pp. 138, 98, 127, 128.

26. *Atlantic* Editors. 1998. "In the Kerouac Archives." *Atlantic Online*, November. www.theatlantic.com/issues/98nov/kerouac.htm.

27. Sagan, Françoise. 1955. *Bonjour Tristesse*. New York: Dutton. This book was a literary sensation and best seller. It was written by a moody Paris teenager and begins, "A strange melancholy pervades me to which I hesitate to give the grave and beautiful name of sorrow."

28. The article might express an official disapproval, but the prose itself seemed to take on a hipster's rhythm and lingo. The only unambiguously scornful treatment came from Herbert Gold in *The Nation* and Norman Podhoretz in the *Partisan Review*. Gitlin, Todd. 1987. *Sixties: Years of Hope, Days of Rage*. New York: Bantam, p. 49. Podhoretz said, "What juvenile delinquency is to life, the San Francisco writers are to literature." The rest of the world couldn't quite conceal an admiration for these kids. The middle class managed somehow to stay in touch with its fearless vanguard.

29. David Halle has given us a glimpse into the motives of latter-day owners of modernist art. His respondents appear to say that it was precisely the ill-defined nature of the art that appealed to them. Abstract art permitted the imagination to wander and provoked creativity. Abstract art, they said, took you somewhere, away from conventional categories and conventions. This may have been the beat ideology at work. Halle, David. 1993. *Inside Culture: Art and Class in the American Home*. Chicago: University of Chicago Press, pp. 132–133.

30. Quoted in Caughey, John L. 1984. *Imaginary Social Worlds: A Cultural Approach*. Lincoln: University of Nebraska Press, p. 68.

31. In D. A. Pennebaker's documentary, Dylan is true to avant-garde form. He says, "If I want to find out something, I'm not going to read *Time* magazine. *Time* has too much to lose by printing the truth." "What is the truth?" a reporter asks him. He replies, "A plain picture . . . a tramp vomiting . . . into a sewer." Pennebaker, D. A. 1967. *Dont Look Back* (*sic*). n.p.: New Video Group.

32. "The only people for me are the mad ones, the ones who are mad to live, mad to talk, mad to be saved, desirous of everything at the same time, the ones who never yawn or say a commonplace thing, but burn, burn, burn, like fabulous yellow Roman candles exploding like spiders across the stars, and in the middle, you see the blue center-light pop, and everybody goes ahh . . . " Kerouac, Jack. 2002. *On the Road*. New York: Penguin Classics, p. 5.

33. See the entry for "hippies" in Wikipedia: http://en.wikipedia.org/wiki/Hippie.

34. See the list of best-selling albums by year on Wikipedia: http://en.wikipedia.org/wiki/Best-selling_albums_by_year_(USA).

35. Anonymous. 1967. "The Hippies: The Philosophy of a Subculture." *Time*, July 7. www.time.com/time/magazine/article/0,9171,899555–1,00.html.

36. Stewart Brand is a key figure in this transition. In the words of Kevin Kelly, "The WEC [Whole Earth Catalog] helped rid us of our allergy to commerce. Brand believed in capitalism, just not by traditional methods. He was the first person to embrace true financial transparency. His decision to disclose WEC's finances in the pages of the catalog had a profound ripple effect. A lot of those hippies who dropped out and tried to live off the land decided to come back and start small companies because of it. And out of that came the Googles of the world." Kotler, Steven. n.d. "The Whole Earth Effect." *Plenty Magazine* 24. www.plentymag.com/magazine/the_whole_earth_effect.php.

37. "Burning Man is an annual art event and temporary community based on radical self expression and self-reliance in the Black Rock Desert of Nevada." See the Web site at www.burningman.com.

38. Frank, Thomas. 1997. *The Conquest of Cool: Business Culture, Counterculture, and the Rise of Hip Consumerism*. Chicago: University of Chicago Press. Klein, Naomi. 2000. *No Logo: No Space, No Choice, No Jobs, Taking Aim at the Brand Bullies*. Toronto: Alfred A. Knopf .

39. Thus when Elvis Mitchell of the *New York Times* asked Steven Soderbergh how he prepared for the movie *Out of Sight*, the director replied that he said to himself, "If you blow this, you will be doing art-house movies for the rest of your life and that's as bad as doing big-budget things. I wanted to do both." We are stunned at how casually Soderbergh claims both sides of a distinction on which a previous generation of filmmakers crucified itself. And when David Brooks went to examine the suburbs he discovered "bourgeois bohemians," creatures like Soderbergh who refused to choose. Brooks, David. 2000. *Bobos in Paradise: The New Upper Class and How They Got There*. New York: Simon & Schuster. The great distinction was collapsing.

CHAPTER 5: PRODUCERS AND CONSUMERS

1. Wolk, Josh. 1999. "Victimless Crime." *Entertainment Weekly*, May 25. www.ew.com/ew/article/0,,84404,00.html.

2. Anonymous. n.d. "Through the Lens: The Look of Blue." Disc 4, Side B. *NYPD Blue*, Season 4. Steven Bochco Productions. 20th Century Fox. This wonderful little documentary appears on the DVD without attribution. I recommend it. There were lots of innovations on the show beyond the restless camera: the use of many light sources, mixing light temperatures, shooting from both above and below, running the gamut from near darkness to blinding overexposure. Wow. That's my anthropological assessment. Wow.

3. Dektor and I talked by phone on December 17, 2008, for about an hour. I thank him and Faith Dektor for giving me the time.

4. Just to be completely clear, everything from "Indeed, film cameras . . ." to the end of this paragraph is my surmise and my language. I hope it captures Dektor's intention, but it may not. Just so you know.

5. This sounded anthropological to me. That's the objective of the ethnographic interview, to be absolutely attentive to what the respondent is saying, to accept his or her terms, and to respond to them. What you don't want to do is manhandle the interviewee or "manicure" the interview. I said this to Dektor. There was a long pause. *Oh dear*, I thought. Then he said, "That sounds right." Whew.

6. Weinraub, Bernard. 2000. "A Gritty Portrayal of Police Life Gets a Kind of Closure." *New York Times*, February 6. http://query.nytimes.com/gst/fullpage.html?res=9E0CE0DC143FF935A35751C0A9669C8B63&partner=rssnyt&emc=rss.

7. "Leigh's distinctive film style—in which the commonplace is often tinged with the extraordinary—has been dubbed 'social surrealism,' or as Leigh prefers to call it, 'heightened realism.' He prefers to work without a script, writing the film as he rehearses with his cast, improvising and collaborating together." Simon, Alex. 2008. "Mike Leigh: The Lord High Executioner Speaks Out." *Hollywood Interview*, October 30. http://thehollywoodinterview.blogspot.com/2008/10/mike-leigh-hollywood-interview.html.

8. See the Wikipedia entry for Basil Exposition: http://en.wikipedia.org/wiki/Basil_Exposition#Allies.

9. *Buffy the Vampire Slayer*, "The Pack," season 1, episode 6. Source of these quotes is the Buffy Verse Database: http://vrya.net/bdb/index.php.

10. Wilcox, Rhonda. 2005. *Why Buffy Matters*. London: I. B. Tauris, p. 28. In a recent episode of *Psych*, psychic detective Shawn Spencer says, "One of those buildings is going to be targeted next by the arsonist." An attractive investigator from the arson squad asks, "Are you sure?" Spencer replies, "I'm Al B. Sure watching Diane Schuur apply Sure Roll-On . . . while viewing *The Sure Thing*." Arson investigator: "That's pretty sure." Spencer: "That's all-day sure." Al B. Sure is the stage name of Albert Joseph Brown III, an American singer and songwriter; Diane Schuur is a blind American jazz singer; Sure Roll-On is a deodorant; *The Sure Thing* is a romantic comedy directed by Rob Reiner; and "all-day sure" was a commercial slogan.

11. Stewart, James B. 2005. *Disneywar*. New York: Simon & Schuster, p. 437.

12. Chaffin, Joshua. 2006. "Hollywood's Blockbuster Budgets Leave the Chests Bare." *Financial Times*, July 17.

13. Rottenberg, Josh. 2006. "The Piracy Debate: The Rough Seas of the Upcoming 'Pirates of the Caribbean' Films." *Entertainment Weekly*, July 7. www.ew.com/ew/article/0,,1210875,00.html.

14. It would be wrong to give the impression that artists and other creative producers have limitless freedom, that they create our culture from their own instincts and without regard to external constraints. But I think it's fair to say

that there is new freedom and new expressive range. And this is an important part of the world that needs watching by the CCO; this is the thing that makes it more dynamic, more inventive, more dispersive, and more chaotic, and that makes the job of the CCO more difficult.

15. The first person I heard make this argument was writer and journalist Hargurchet Bhabra. I think if we wanted a single data point here it might be the career of David Milch. He has written for *Hill Street Blues*, *NYPD Blue*, and *Deadwood*. See the interview of Milch by David Thorburn in the MIT Communications Forum speaker's series called Television in Transition at http://mitworld.mit.edu/video/383/. See especially Milch's account of his work on *Deadwood*, beginning at the 17:55 mark. Thorburn's remarks suggest that Milch so wowed his teachers at Yale, they would have been happy to keep him on as a member of the faculty. That he found a career in TV writing, that he was able to write at the top of his literary ability and intelligence, is a mark of what has happened to popular culture. To be sure, *Deadwood* is a minority taste. *NYPD Blue* was not. Singer, Mark. 2005. "The Misfit: How David Milch got from 'NYPD Blue' to 'Deadwood' by way of an Epistle of St. Paul." *New Yorker*, February 14. www.newyorker.com/archive/2005/02/14/050214fa_fact_singer.

16. Jenkins, Henry. 1992. *Textual Poachers: Television Fans and Participatory Culture*. New York: Routledge. What Jenkins was doing with viewers, Susan Fournier was doing with consumers. Fournier, Susan. 1998. "The Consumer and the Brand: Developing Relationship Theory in Consumer Research." *Journal of Consumer Research* 24 (March): 343–373.

17. I am grateful to Andrew Zolli for his comments on this creation. See the Wikipedia entry for more details on *All Your Base*.

18. This paragraph was on the first page of the Web site http://xfiles.about.com/mbody.htm?once=true& as it appeared on July 22, 2001.

19. Fournier, Susan, and Lara Lee. 2009. "Getting Brand Communities Right." *Harvard Business Review*, April, pp. 105–111.

20. Jenkins, Henry. 2006. *Fans, Bloggers, and Gamers: Exploring Participatory Culture*. New York: New York University Press.

21. Remarks made at the MIT Futures of Entertainment Conference, November 16, 2007, Cambridge, MA.

22. From an interview I conducted with a consumer in 2007.

23. Locke, Christopher, Rick Levine, Doc Searls, and David Weinberger. 2000. *The Cluetrain Manifesto: The End of Business as Usual*. New York: Basic Books.

24. McCracken, Grant. 2005. "Cotton, Converse and Co-Creation." *This Blog Sits at the Intersection of Anthropology and Economics*, July 27. www.cultureby.com/trilogy/2005/07/i_had_drinks_wi.html.

25. I thank Ed Cotton of BSSP for an interview conducted in New York City July 21, 2005.

26. Taylor, Catharine P. 2006. "Chevy's Crash and Burn." *Adweek*, April 17, p. 14. McCracken, Grant. 2006. "Chevy Cocreation." *This Blog Sits at the Intersec-*

tion of Anthropology and Economics, April 26. www.cultureby.com/trilogy/2006/04/chevy_cocreatio.html.

27. McCracken, Grant. 2005. "Consumers or Multipliers: A New Language for Marketing?" *This Blog Sits at the Intersection of Anthropology and Economics,* November 10. www.cultureby.com/trilogy/2005/11/consumers_or_mu.html.

28. McCracken, Grant. 2008. "Story Time, aka Commerce Gets More Cultural." *This Blog Sits at the Intersection of Anthropology and Economics,* October 8. www.cultureby.com/trilogy/2008/10/lt-font-defin.html.

29. When Bud Caddell creates another character in the show, a character who lives outside the AMC program, he engages in something Henry Jenkins calls "transmedia," storytelling that takes place over more than one media. Jenkins, Henry. 2008. *Convergence Culture: Where Old and New Media Collide.* Rev. ed. New York: New York University Press.

30. For more on the Bud Melman experiment, see his Web site, We Are Sterling Cooper, at http://wearesterlingcooper.com/. The expert on fan fiction is the Convergence Culture Consortium, run by Henry Jenkins out of MIT. Jenkins, Henry. 2006. *Fans, Bloggers, and Gamers: Media Consumers in a Digital Age.* New York: New York University Press.

31. Johnson, Steven. 2005. *Everything Bad Is Good for You.* New York: Riverhead/Penguin, pp. 256–257.

CHAPTER 6: BUILDING A SECRET SNEAKER STORE

1. The store in question is called Bodega. I will not say where it is. But if you start in the shadow of the Christian Science complex, consider yourself "warm." Thanks to owner Jay Gordon for taking the time to chat. Thanks to John Deighton for the trip. Thanks to Leora Kornfeld for finding Bodega in the first place.

2. Staff. 2008. "Cassette Playa x Nike Sportswear Blazer Interview with Carri Munden." *Hypebeast,* December 11. http://hypebeast.com/2008/12/cassette-playa-x-nike-sportswear-blazer-interview-with-carri-munden/.

3. Demby, Eric. 2003. "Sneaker Stories: Following the Trail of a Cultural Shift." *New York Times,* September 28. www.nytimes.com/2003/09/28/fashion/28SNEA.html.

4. See www.steadyhustle.com/steadyhustle/index.html.

5. Taleb, Nassim Nicholas. 2007. *The Black Swan.* New York: Random House.

6. I am simplifying a little bit. See the IF version of what they do here: www.inferentialfocus.com/.

7. For more answers to this question, see McCracken, Grant. 2007. "The Charlie and Barney Show: Birth of a New American Male?" *This Blog Sits at the Intersection of Anthropology and Economics,* January 3. www.cultureby.com/trilogy/2007/01/the_charlie_and.html.

8. McCracken, Grant. 2005. "The 'Arrested Development' Case Study: Say You're Mitchell Hurwitz, What Would You Do?" *This Blog Sits at the Intersection of Anthropology and Economics*, November 25. www.cultureby.com/trilogy/2005/11/the_arrested_de.html. Snierson, Dan. 2005. "'Arrested Development' 2003–2005? We Say Goodbye to 'Arrested Development.'" *Entertainment Weekly*, November 18. www.ew.com/ew/article/0,,1131713,00.html.

9. Doctorow, Cory. 2009. "Crowdsourced Science: How to Do Agarose Gel Electrophoresis Using Nothing But a Drinking Straw, a 9V Battery and a Pair of Alligator Clips." BoingBoing.com, February 6. www.boingboing.net/2009/02/06/crowdsourced-science.html.

10. FitzGerald, Frances. 1987. *Cities on a Hill: A Journey Through Contemporary American Cultures*. New York: Touchstone, Simon & Schuster.

11. McCracken, Grant. 2006. *Flock and Flow: Predicting and Managing Change in a Dynamic Marketplace*. Bloomington: Indiana University Press. For other ways to read the diffusion effect, see McCracken, Grant. 1988. "Consumers, Goods, Gender Construction and a Rehabilitated Trickle-Down Effect." In *Culture and Consumption*. Bloomington: Indiana University Press, pp. 93–103. See King, Charles W. 1963. "Fashion Adoption: A Rebuttal to the 'Trickle-Down' Theory." In Stephen A. Greyser, ed. *Toward Scientific Marketing*. Chicago: American Marketing Association, pp.108–125. Rogers, Everett M. 1995. *Diffusion of Innovations*, 4th ed. New York: Free Press. Simmel, Georg. 1971. "Fashion." In *On Individuality and Social Forms: Selected Writings*. Chicago: University of Chicago Press, pp. 294–323.

12. McCracken, Grant. 2006. "The Artisanal Trend and 10 Things That Define It." *This Blog Sits at the Intersection of Anthropology and Economics*, November 9. www.cultureby.com/trilogy/2006/11/the_artisanal_m.html.

13. Transcribed from the La Brea Bakery Web site on August 21, 2008.

14. Consider this an anthropological sketch of the topic. I defer to the academic experts in this field, the likes of John Kotter, Rosabeth Moss Kanter, and Rakesh Khurana. On the consulting side, see Tom Guarriello, Patrick Lencioni, Niko Canner.

15. Langley, Monica. 2005. "Behind Citigroup Departures: Culture Shift by CEO." *Pittsburgh Post-Gazette*, August 24. www.post-gazette.com/pg/05236/559338–28.stm.

16. Bateson, Gregory. 2000. *Steps to an Ecology of Mind: Collected Essays in Anthropology, Psychiatry, Evolution, and Epistemology*. Chicago: University of Chicago Press.

17. Gray, David. 2003. "Wanted: Chief Ignorance Officer." *Harvard Business Review*, November.

18. McGovern, Gail, David Court, John A. Quelch, and Blair Crawford. 2004. "Bringing Customers into the Boardroom." *Harvard Business Review*, November.

19. Mandel, Michael. 2004. "This Way to the Future." *BusinessWeek*, October 11. www.businessweek.com/magazine/content/04_41/b3903402.htm.

20. Baghai, Mehrdad, Steve Coley, and David White. 2000. *The Alchemy of Growth: Practical Insights for Building the Enduring Enterprise*. New York: Basic Books.

21. Thompson, Stephanie. 2005. "Kraft Shows Late for Beach Party; Low Expectations for Low-Carb Line." *Advertising Age*, January 10.

22. Breene, R. Timothy S., Paul F. Nunes, and Walter E. Shill. 2007. "The Chief Strategy Officer." *Harvard Business Review*, October.

23. This work is from DDB, Chicago. Creative director was Mark Gross.

24. "Creative commons" refers to that body of intellectual property that is freely distributed and widely shared. The idea is promoted by a foundation of the same name that specializes in crafting and encouraging licenses that enable a content provider to gift his or her work to the public domain. www.creativecommons.org.

25. Blum, David. 2001. "Tired Joke or Cultural Touchstone: The Sitcom Clam." *New York Times*, December 9. www.nytimes.com/2001/12/09/arts/television-radio-tired-joke-or-cultural-touchstone-the-sitcom-clam.html.

26. As nearly as I can tell, the origin of the "third space/place" *term* is the sociologist Ray Oldenburg: Oldenburg, Ray. 2002. *Celebrating the Third Place: Inspiring Stories About the "Great Good Places" at the Heart of Our Communities.* New York: Da Capo Press. Oldenburg allows many institutions into this category, and I don't mean to imply that Starbucks is the only one. Starbucks multiplied and perhaps legitimized the third space by installing it thousands of times in American cities. It also must be observed that Starbucks discovered the "third space" *concept* when CEO Howard Schultz went to Italy in 1983 and examined café life there. Randle, Yvonne, Eric G. Flamholtz, and Howard Schultz. 1998. *Changing the Game: Organizational Transformations of the First, Second, and Third Kinds*. New York: Oxford University Press, p. 92.

27. Sahlins, Marshall. 1972. *Stone Age Economics*. Chicago: Aldine Transaction.

28. Bolter, J. David, and Richard Grusin. 1999. *Remediation: Understanding New Media*. Cambridge: MIT Press. Florida, Richard. 2002. *The Rise of the Creative Class*. New York: Basic Books. Jenkins, Henry. 1992. *Textual Poachers: Television Fans and Participatory Culture*. New York: Routledge. Jenkins, Henry. 2006. *Convergence Culture: Where Old and New Media Collide*. New York: New York University Press. Johnson, Steven. 2005. *Everything Bad Is Good for You*. New York. Riverhead. Lessig, Lawrence. 2008. *Remix: Making Art and Commerce Thrive in the Hybrid Economy*. New York: Penguin. Locke, Christopher, Rick Levine, Doc Searls, and David Weinberger. 2000. *The Cluetrain Manifesto: The End of Business as Usual*. New York: Basic Books. McCracken, Grant. 1997. *Plenitude*. Toronto: Periph.:Fluide. Shirky, Clay. 2008. *Here Comes Everybody: The Power of Organizing Without Organizations*. New York: Penguin. Weinberger, David. 2003. *Small Pieces Loosely Joined: A Unified Theory of the Web*. New York: Basic Books.

CHAPTER 7: HOW-TO

1. This definition is from the entry on "stimming" on Wikipedia.

2. Baudelaire, Charles. 1863/1972. "The Painter of Modern Life." *Baudelaire: Selected Writings on Art and Literature*. P. E. Charvet, trans. New York: Viking, pp. 395–422. Benjamin, Walter. 1999. *The Arcades Project*. Howard Eiland and Kevin McLaughlin, trans. Cambridge, MA: Harvard University Press. Georg Simmel, *The Metropolis and Mental Life*, D. Weinstein, adapt., Kurt Wolff, trans. In *The Sociology of Georg Simmel*. New York: Free Press, 1950, pp. 409–424. Sontag, Susan. 1977. *On Photography*. New York: Farrar, Straus, and Giroux.

3. For more on Morgan Friedman, see his Web site, www.westegg.com/. For another master noticer, see the blog of Nokia's Jan Chipchase: www.janchipchase.com/blog/archives/2006/06/watching_cities.html.

4. This passage is from a slide Friedman presented during his talk at Interesting2008 New York, at the Fashion Institute of Technology on September 13, 2008.

5. www.overheardinnewyork.com/archives/008930.html.

6. We must hope that one of these days, someone will do for American culture what Kate Fox did for the English. See her exemplary Fox, Kate. 2008. *Watching the English: The Hidden Rules of English Behaviour*. London: Nicholas Brealey Publishing.

7. Firth, Raymond, ed. 1957. *Man and Culture: An Evaluation of the Work of Bronislaw Malinowski*. London: Routledge, p. 19. Anthropologists are more likely to look for the *meaning* of a social practice than the function, thanks to the influence of people like Roland Barthes and Clifford Geertz. Barthes, Roland. 1972. *Mythologies*. New York: Hill and Wang. Geertz, Clifford. 1977. "Religion as a Cultural System." In *The Interpretation of Cultures*. New York: Basic Books, pp. 87–125.

8. Goleman, Daniel. 2006. *Emotional Intelligence: Why It Can Matter More Than IQ*, 10th ed. New York: Bantam, p. 96. See the entry "empathy" by Charles Edward Gauss in the *Dictionary of the History of Ideas*, vol. 2, pp. 87–89.

9. Brooker, Katrina. 2002. "The Un-CEO." *Fortune*, September 16.

10. These are guesses, but characteristics very different from these would make Mrs. Rios the wrong kind of candidate for this sort of interview.

11. Precourt, Geoffrey. 2003. "The Student of History." *Hamilton College Alumni Magazine*. Fall. www.hamilton.edu/magazine/2003/fall/lafley4.html. Jones, Del. 2007. "P&G CEO Wields High Expectations But No Whip." *USA Today*, February 19. www.usatoday.com/money/companies/management/2007–02–19-exec-pandg-usat_x.htm.

12. Sutherland, Rory. 2005. "The Campaign Essay: Adland's Hidden Talent." *Brand Republic*, January 14. www.brandrepublic.com/News/232515/.

13. Gladwell, Malcolm. 2008. *Outliers: The Story of Success*. New York: Little, Brown and Company.

14. I think we are well served by the "expansionary individualism" now evident in our culture. McCracken, Grant. 2008. *Transformations: Identity Construction in Contemporary Culture*. Bloomington: Indiana University Press.

15. For an extended treatment of empathy, see Patnaik, Dev. 2009. *Wired to Care: How Companies Prosper When They Create Widespread Empathy*. New York: FT Press.

16. Staff. 2008. "HBS Centennial Colloquia Reports: Harvard Business School Discusses Future of the MBA." *HBS Alumni Bulletin*, November 24.

17. Pink, Daniel H. 2006. *A Whole New Mind: Why Right-Brainers Will Rule the Future*. New York: Riverhead Trade, p. 14.

18. Bryant, Adam. 2009. "He Wants Subjects, Verbs and Objects." *New York Times*, April 26. www.nytimes.com/2009/04/26/business/26corner.html?th&emc=th.

19. Anonymous. 2007. "Fresh, Far from Easy." *The Economist*, June 21.

20. For more detail on the mechanics of the interview, see McCracken, Grant. 1988. *The Long Interview*. Thousand Oaks, CA: Sage Publications.

21. The empathy stuff can get tricky. I was doing research for an American client in China. On the local client team was a woman, a Chinese national, who hated the method. Sitting in the corner she gave off a constant signal of skepticism and contempt. The point of the method is to empathize, so I was empathizing with and thus internalizing her hostility. And that's a bad place to be. Internalizing someone's hostility to the method as you practice the method, really, it's just not good.

22. This is the holistic impulse students of culture draw from anthropology. See Parsons, Talcott. 1937. *The Structure of Social Action*, vol. 2. New York: Free Press, p. 478. Franz Boas insisted on structural coherence; Bronislaw Malinowski on functional coherence. Boas, Franz. 1887. "The Occurrence of Similar Inventions in Areas Widely Apart." *Science* 9, no. 226: 485. Malinowski, Bronislaw. 1931. "Culture." *Encyclopedia of the Social Sciences* 4: 625.

23. Improv is one of the great themes of contemporary culture. See my discussion of "involuntary improv" in McCracken, Grant. 2008. *Transformations: Identity Construction in Contemporary Culture*. Bloomington: Indiana University Press, pp. 236–253.

24. Surowiecki, James. 2005. *The Wisdom of Crowds*. New York: Anchor.

25. Further reading in this area: Kane, Pat. 2005. *The Play Ethic*. London: Macmillan. Johnstone, Keith. 1979. *Impro: Improvisation and the Theatre*. Boston: Faber and Faber. Lahr, John. 2000. "Making It Real: How Mike Nichols Re-Created Comedy and Himself." *New Yorker*, February 21 and 28, pp. 196–214. Pink, Daniel H. 2006. *A Whole New Mind: Why Right-Brainers Will Rule the Future*. New York: Riverhead Trade. Sweet, Jeffrey. 1978. *Something Wonderful Right Away: An Oral History of the Second City and the Compass Players*. New York: Avon Books.

26. Foust, Dean. 2004. "Gone Flat." *BusinessWeek*, December 20, pp. 77–82.

27. Vogt, Evon Zartman. 1955. *Modern Homesteaders: The Life of a Twentieth Century Frontier Community*. Cambridge, MA: Belknap Press of Harvard University Press.

28. Pendergrast, Mark. 1993. *For God, Country and Coca-Cola*. New York: Macmillan.

29. Anonymous. 2000. "Highlights in the History of Coca-Cola Television Advertising." http://memory.loc.gov/ammem/ccmphtml/colahist.html.

30. The ad in question, informally referred to as "Haircut," is the work of Foote, Cone & Belding, New York. The creative team was Gary Resch, Mark Warfield, Todd Eisner, Greg Wikoff, Kelly Fagan, and Robert Logevall.

31. For the model, see McCracken, Grant. 2005. "Meaning Management." In *Culture and Consumption II*. Bloomington: Indiana University Press, pp. 175–191.

32. For more on these approaches, see McCracken, Grant. 2008. "Branding Now Blog Compendium." www.cultureby.com/BrandingNowBlogcompendiu GrantMcCracken.pdf.

33. For the model, see McCracken, Grant. 2005. "Meaning Management." In *Culture and Consumption II*. Bloomington: Indiana University Press, pp. 175–191.

34. Aaker, David A. 1995. *Building Strong Brands*. New York: Free Press. Asacker, Tom. 2005. *A Clear Eye for Branding*. New York: Paramount Market Publishing. Baskin, Jonathan Salem. 2008. *Branding Only Works on Cattle: The New Way to Get Known*. New York: Business Plus. Gobe, Marc, and Sergio Zyman. 2001. *Emotional Branding: The New Paradigm for Connecting Brands to People*. New York: Allworth Press. Holt, D. B. 2004. *How Brands Become Icons: The Principles of Cultural Branding*. Boston: Harvard Business School Press. Keller, Kevin. 2007. *Best Practice Cases in Branding*, 3rd ed. New York: Prentice Hall. Koehn, Nancy F. 2001. *Brand New: How Entrepreneurs Earned Consumers' Trust from Wedgwood to Dell*. Boston: Harvard Business School Press. Kotler, Philip, and Gary Armstrong. 2007. *Principles of Marketing*, 12th ed. New York: Prentice Hall. Levy, Sidney J., and Dennis Rook. 1999. *Brands, Consumers, Symbols and Research: Sidney J. Levy on Marketing*. Thousand Oaks, CA: Sage Publications. Walker, Rob. 2008. *Buying In: The Secret Dialogue Between What We Buy and Who We Are*. New York: Random House.

35. Mau, Bruce, Jennifer Leonard, and Institute Without Boundaries. 2004. *Massive Change*. New York: Phaidon Press.

36. Bhide, Amar. 2008. *The Venturesome Economy: How Innovation Sustains Prosperity in a More Connected World*. Princeton, NJ: Princeton University Press.

37. www.cdf.org/issue_journal/interview_with_a.g._lafley.html.

38. Kelley, Thomas, and Jonathan Littman. 2005. *The Ten Faces of Innovation: IDEO's Strategies for Defeating the Devil's Advocate and Driving Creativity Throughout Your Organization*. New York: Broadway Business. Moldoveanu, Mihnea C., and Roger L. Martin. 2008. *The Future of the MBA: Designing the Thinker of the Future*. New York: Oxford University Press.

39. Jana, Reena. 2008. "IBM Reshapes Its Sales Meetings." *BusinessWeek: Innovation*, November 10. www.businessweek.com/innovate/content/nov2008/id20081110_227229.htm.

40. I am thinking of the work by Harley Earl in the 1950s and the more recent work of Richard Sapper and Lee Green for IBM.

41. For those who want to undertake their own education in design, the following books are recommended: Bierut, Michael. 2007. *79 Short Essays on Design*. New York: Princeton Architectural Press. Guarriello, Tom, and Jim Biolos. 2007. *Work Different: Design for the Rest of Us*. New York: TrueTalk. Heller, Steven. 1998. *Design Dialogues*. Allworth Press. LaConte, Vincent, ed. 2008. *Ninety Questions and Answers with Thirteen Design Thinkers*. Chicago: Illinois Institute of Technology Institute of Design. Lupton, Ellen. 2004. *Thinking with Type: A Critical Guide for Designers, Writers, Editors & Students*. New York: Princeton Architectural Press. Millman, Debbie. 2008. *The Essential Principles of Graphic Design*. New York: How. You might also keep an eye on David Armano's blog *Logic + Emotion*.

42. We could call this "phatic communication." Curry, Ian. 2007. "Twitter: The Missing Messenger." *Frogblog*, February 26. Demopoulos, Dino. 2007. "The Presents of Presence." *Chroma*, July 18. Earls, Mark. 2007. "Phatic Is Phat." *Herd, The Hidden Truth About Who We Are*, March 8. Reichelt, Leisa. 2007. "Ambient Intimacy." *Disambiguity*, March 1.

43. To which the answer is "read Danah Boyd," the Microsoft anthropologist and expert on this question. Boyd, Danah. 2008. *Taken Out of Context: American Teen Sociality in Networked Publics*. PhD diss., University of California-Berkeley, School of Information. The other indispensible source is the Pew Internet and American Life Project at www.pewinternet.org.

44. Dawkins, Richard. 1989. *The Selfish Gene*, new ed. New York: Oxford University Press, p. 196.

45. McCracken, Grant. 1998. *Plenitude 2.0*. Toronto: Periph.:Fluide, p. 126.

46. Rushkoff, Douglas. 1996. *Media Virus!* New York: Ballantine Books.

47. Florida, Richard. 2003. *The Rise of the Creative Class: And How It's Transforming Work, Leisure, Community and Everyday Life*. New York: Basic Books. Planners are the people inside advertising and marketing firms who know and speak for the consumer.

48. Baskin, Merry. 2000/2008. "What Is Account Planning?" at the Account Planning Group Web site in the form of a PDF. www.apg.org.uk/about-us/what-is-planning.cfm.

49. Davies, Russell. 2006. "How to Be Interesting." *Russell Davies* blog, November 6. http://russelldavies.typepad.com/planning/2006/11/how_to_be_inter.html.

50. Bullmore, Jeremy. 2003. *Behind the Scenes in Advertising*, 3rd ed. London: World Advertising Research Center. Lannon, Judie, and Merry Baskin. 2008. *A Master Class in Brand Planning: The Timeless Works of Stephen King*.

London: Wiley. Habberstad, Henrik. n.d. "The Anatomy of Account Planning: The Creativity Behind the Creativity." Available online at Faris Yakob's Web site: http://farisyakob.typepad.com/blog/2007/01/anatomy_of_an_a.html. Pollitt, Stanley. 1979. "How I Started Account Planning in Agencies." *Campaign*, April 20. Staveley, N. 1999. "Account Planning: A British Perspective." In John Philip Jones, ed. *The Advertising Business*. London: Sage Publications. Steel, Jon. 1998. *Truth, Lies and Advertising: The Art of Account Planning*. New York: Wiley.

51. Malbon, Ben. 1999. *Clubbing: Culture and Experience*. London: Routledge. See the blog by Faris Yakob called *Genius Steals*, Brand New by Gareth Kay, Chroma by Dino Demopoulos, Brand Tarot by John Grant, Experience Planner by Scott Weisbrod, and Noah Brier at noahbrier.com.

CHAPTER 8: PHILISTINES

1. Brodesser-Akner, Claude. 2007. "Eisner on Dentists, Topps and 'Foolish' Writers Strike." *Ad Age*, November 12.

2. McCracken, Grant. 2005. "When Cars Could Fly." In *Culture and Consumption II*. Bloomington: Indiana University Press.

3. Terlep, Sharon. 2009. "GM Product Chief Lutz to Step Down." *Wall Street Journal*, February 10.

4. Gladwell, Malcolm. 1997. "The Coolhunt." *New Yorker*, March 17, pp. 78–88. www.gladwell.com/1997/1997_03_17_a_cool.htm.

5. In Grossman, Lev. 2003. "The Quest for Cool." *Time*, September 8. Irma Zandl is president of the Zandl Group. www.time.com/time/magazine/article/0,9171,1005612,00.html.

6. Elliott, Stuart. 2009. "Tropicana Discovers Some Buyers Are Passionate About Packaging." *New York Times*, February 22. Levins, Hoaq. 2009. "Peter Arnell Explains Failed Tropicana Package Design." *Ad Age*, February 26. Zmuda, Natalie. 2009. "Tropicana Line's Sales Plunge 20% Post-Rebranding." *Ad Age*, April 2.

7. Helm, Burt. 2009. "Blowing Up Pepsi." *BusinessWeek*, April 27. www.businessweek.com/magazine/content/09_17/b4128032006687.htm.

8. Arnell's remark comes from his defense of the Tropicana design. See these remarks on the AdAge video at www.youtube.com/watch?v=WJ4yF4F74vc. February 26, 2009.

9. In Lyons, Daniel. 2009. "Mad Man." *Newsweek*, March 28.

10. The idea of phatic communication was shaped by several of the giants in anthropology: Malinowski, B. 1923. "The Problem of Meaning in Primitive Languages." Supplement to C. Ogden and I. Richards. *The Meaning of Meaning*. London: Routledge and Kegan Paul, pp. 146–152. Jakobson, R. "Linguistics and Poetics." In T. Sebeok, ed. *Style in Language*. Cambridge, MA: MIT Press, 1960,

pp. 350–377. Bakhtin, M. 1999/1986. "The Problem of Speech Genres." In Adam Jaworski and Nikolas Coupland, eds. *The Discourse Reader*. London and New York: Routledge, pp. 121–132.

11. Rivlin, Gary, and John Markoff. 2004. "Can Mr. Chips Transform Intel?" *New York Times*, September 12.

12. Edwards, Cliff, Kenji Hall, and Ronald Glover. 2008. "Sony Chases Apple's Magic." *BusinessWeek*, November 10, p. 48. www.businessweek.com/magazine/content/08_45/b4107048234222.htm?campaign_id=rss_daily.

13. Levitt, Steven D. 2005. *Freakonomics: A Rogue Economist Explores the Hidden Side of Everything*. New York: William Morrow, p. 139.

14. Ibid., p. 121.

15. Bourgois, Philippe. 1995. *In Search of Respect: Selling Crack in El Barrio*. New York: Cambridge University Press.

16. Forgive my daring paraphrase. In Smith's own words: "It is not from the benevolence of the butcher, the brewer, or the baker that we expect our dinner, but from their regard to their own interest. We address ourselves, not to their humanity, but to their self-love and never talk to them of our own necessities, but of their advantages." Smith, Adam. 1776/1904. *The Wealth of Nations*. London: Methuen, p. 44.

17. Braudel, Fernand. 1973. *Capitalism and Material Life, 1400–1800*. Miriam Kochan, trans. London: Weidenfeld and Nicolson. Brewer, John, and Roy Porter, eds. 1993. *Consumption and the World of Goods*. London: Routledge. Bushman, Richard L. 1992. *The Refinement of America: Persons, Houses, Cities*. New York: Alfred A. Knopf. Carson, Cary, Ronald Hoffman, and Peter J. Albert, eds. 1994. *Of Consuming Interests: The Style of Life in the Eighteenth Century*. Charlottesville: University Press of Virginia. McKendrick, Neil, John Brewer, and J. H. Plumb. 1982. *The Birth of a Consumer Society: The Commercialization of Eighteenth-Century England*. Bloomington: Indiana University Press.

18. For Lord Northcliffe's approach, see Carey, John. 1992. *The Intellectuals and the Masses: Pride and Prejudice Among the Literary Intelligentsia, 1880–1939*. London: Faber and Faber, p. 6. For Paley's approach, see Kammen, Michael. 1999. *American Culture, American Tastes: Social Change and the 20th Century*. New York: Alfred A. Knopf, p. 43. For the Revson quote, see Tobias, Andrew. 1976. *Fire and Ice: The Story of Charles Revson*. New York: William Morrow, p. 107.

19. "The Western conception of the person as a bounded, unique, more or less integrated motivational and cognitive universe, a dynamic center of awareness, emotion, judgment, and action organized into a distinctive whole and set contrastively both against other such wholes and against a social and natural background is, however incorrigible it may seem to us, a rather peculiar idea within the context of the world's cultures." Geertz, Clifford. 1979. "From the Native's Point of View: On the Nature of Anthropological Understanding." In Paul Rabinow and William M. Sullivan, eds. *Interpretive Social Science*. Berkeley and Los

Angeles: University of California Press, p. 229. Kroeber, Albert L., and Clyde Kluckhohn. 1952. *Culture: A Critical Review of Concepts and Definitions*. New York: Random House.

20. Cowen, Tyler. 2000. *In Praise of Commercial Culture*. Cambridge, MA: Harvard University Press. Cowen, Tyler. 2004. *Creative Destruction: How Globalization Is Changing the World's Cultures*. Princeton, NJ: Princeton University Press.

21. Christensen, Clayton M., Scott Cook, and Taddy Hall. 2005. "It's the Purpose Brand, Stupid." *Wall Street Journal*, November 29, p. B2.

22. Shakespeare, William. 1880. *King Lear*. 7th ed. Philadelphia: J. P. Lippincott. Act 2, Scene 4, lines 263 and 264.

23. Kotler, Philip, and Gary Armstrong. 1999. *Principles of Marketing*, 8th ed. Upper Saddle River, NJ: Prentice Hall. Levitt, Theodore. 1981/1986. "Marketing Intangible Products and Product Intangibles." *The Marketing Imagination*, new, expanded ed. New York: Free Press, pp. 95–110. Levy, Sidney J., and Dennis W. Rook. 1999. *Brands, Consumers, Symbols & Research: Sidney J. Levy on Marketing*. Thousand Oaks, CA: Sage Publications. Ries, Al, and Jack Trout. 1986. *Positioning: The Battle for Your Mind*, 1st ed., rev. New York: McGraw-Hill.

24. Sacks, Danielle. 2006. "Crack This Code." *Fast Company*, April. www.fastcompany.com/magazine/104/rapaille.html.

25. Ibid.

26. Zaltman, Gerald, and Lindsay H. Zaltman. 2008. *Marketing Metaphoria: What Deep Metaphors Reveal About the Minds of Consumers*. Boston: Harvard Business School Press.

27. Winsor, John. 2006. "Cracking the Culture." *Under the Radar Blog*, April 19. www.johnwinsor.com/my_weblog/2006/04/cracking_the_cu.html.

28. For an account of the bad writing contest, see Dutton, Denis. 1999. "Language Crimes: A Lesson in How Not to Write, Courtesy of the Professoriate." *Wall Street Journal*, February 5. http://denisdutton.com/language_crimes.htm. For more on the contest, visit www.denisdutton.com/bad_writing.htm.

29. Tyler, Stephen. 1986. "Post-modern Ethnography." In James Clifford and George E. Marcus, eds. *Writing Culture: The Poetics and Politics of Ethnography*. Berkeley and Los Angeles: University of California Press, p. 129.

30. Sahlins, Marshall. 2002. *Waiting for Foucault, Still*. Chicago: Prickly Paradigm Press. Douglas, Mary. 2002. *Purity and Danger: An Analysis of the Concepts of Pollution and Taboo*. London: Taylor.

31. Levine, George. 1992. "Introduction: Constructivism and the Reemergent Self." In George Levine, ed. *Constructions of the Self*. New Brunswick, NJ: Rutgers University Press, p. 1.

32. Lévi-Strauss, Claude. 1968. *The Savage Mind*. Chicago: University of Chicago Press.

33. This is intemperate of me. For a more thoughtful and elegant statement of pragmatism, see Haack, Susan. 2000. *Manifesto of a Passionate Moderate: Unfashionable Essays*. Chicago: University of Chicago Press; and Dickstein, Morris, et al. 1998. *The Revival of Pragmatism: New Essays on Social Thought, Law, and Culture*. Durham, NC: Duke University Press.

34. Morgan, Lewis Henry. 1970. *Systems of Consanguinity and Affinity of the Human Family*. Oosterhout, Netherlands: Anthropological Publications. Boas, Franz. 1995. *Race, Language, and Culture*. Chicago: University of Chicago Press. Lukes, Steven. 1969. "Durkheim's 'Individualism and the Intellectuals.'" *Political Studies* 17, no. 1: 14–30.

35. Vogt, Evon Zartman. 1955. *Modern Homesteaders: The Life of a Twentieth Century Frontier Community*. Cambridge, MA: Belknap Press of Harvard University Press. Warner, W. Lloyd. 1953. *American Life: Dream and Reality*. Chicago: University of Chicago Press. Warner, W. Lloyd, J. O. Low, Paul S. Lunt, and Leo Srole. 1963. *Yankee City*. New Haven, CT: Yale University Press.

36. Easton, John. 2001. "Consuming Interests." *University of Chicago Magazine* 93, no. 6 (August). http://magazine.uchicago.edu/0108/features/.

37. Barth, Fredrik. 1993. *Balinese Worlds*. Chicago: University of Chicago Press. Hannerz, Ulf. 1993. *Cultural Complexity: Studies in the Social Organization of Meaning*. New York: Columbia University Press.

38. Buford, Bill. 1991. *Among the Thugs*. London: Secker and Warburg. FitzGerald, Frances. 1987. *Cities on a Hill: A Journey Through Contemporary American Cultures*. New York: Touchstone, Simon & Schuster. Gans, Herbert J. 1967. *The Levittowners: Ways of Life and Politics in a New Suburban Community*. New York: Vintage. Huber, Richard M. 1971. *The American Idea of Success*. New York: McGraw-Hill. Katz, Donald R. 1993. *Home Fires: An Intimate Portrait of One Middle-Class Family in Postwar America*. New York: Perennial. Klein, Richard. 1993. *Cigarettes Are Sublime*. Durham, NC: Duke University Press. Klosterman, Chuck. 2002. "The Pretenders." *New York Times*, March 17. Lamont, Michele. 1992. *Money, Morals and Manners: The Culture of the French and the American Upper-Middle Class*. Chicago: University of Chicago Press. Marcus, Greil. 1995. *The Dustbin of History*. Cambridge, MA: Harvard University Press. Merelman, Richard M. 1984. *Making Something of Ourselves: On Culture and Politics in the United States*. Berkeley and Los Angeles: University of California Press. Some films: *Election* by Alexander Payne, *Metropolitan* by Walt Stillman, *Fast Times at Ridgemont High* by Amy Heckerling, *Mystery Train* by Jim Jarmusch, *Swingers* by Doug Liman, *Slacker* by Richard Linklater.

39. Morris, Betsy, and Patricia Sellers. 2000. "What Really Happened at Coke." *Fortune*, January 10.

40. Hays, Constance. 1999. "Variable-Price Coke Machine Being Tested." *New York Times*, October 28.

CHAPTER 9: CONCLUSION

1. McGirt, Ellen. 2009. "Boy Wonder: How Chris Hughes Helped Launch Facebook and the Barack Obama Campaign." *Fast Company*, www.fastcompany.com/magazine/134/boy-wonder.html.

2. Staff. 2009. "Lessons from the Trenches." *Fast Company*, www.fastcompany.com/magazine/134/lessons-from-the-trenches.html.

3. Ibid.

BONUS FEATURE A

1. Edward Tufte is professor emeritus at Yale University and author of several books. The one that features Charles Joseph Minard's map is Tufte, Edward R. 1992. *The Visual Display of Quantitative Information*, 2nd ed. Cheshire, CT: Graphics Press, pp. 40–41.

2. Young, George M. 1950. *Last Essays*. London: R. Hart-Davis.

3. Personal communication, January 26, 2009.

BONUS FEATURE B

1. Thanks to John Galvin for suggestions he gave me several years ago.

2. McCracken, Grant. 2007. "The Charley and Barney Show: Birth of a New American Male." *This Blog Sits at the Intersection of Anthropology and Economics*, January 3. www.cultureby.com/trilogy/2007/01/the_charlie_and.html.

3. Zoglin, Richard. 2008. *Comedy at the Edge: How Stand-Up in the 1970s Changed America*. New York: Bloomsbury.

4. Kozinets, Robert V. 2002. "Can Consumers Escape the Marketplace? Emancipatory Illuminations from Burning Man." *Journal of Consumer Research* 29 (June).

5. Chen, Andrew. 2009. "Why Metrics-Driven Startups Overlook Brand Value." Futuristic play by @Andrew_Chen. Andrewchenblog.com. June 18. http://andrewchenblog.com/2009/06/18/why-metrics-driven-startups-overlook-brand-value/.

6. Surowiecki, James. 2005. *The Wisdom of Crowds*. New York: Anchor.

7. I thank Noah Brier for a lively conversation on this topic.

8. For those prepared to create an enterprise here, I don't need to say that there is lots of talent out there. (Assuming, that is, we can find people who know the slow culture as well as the fast. No mere cool-hunters need apply.) I was just reading an article by Craig Fehrman in *Salon*, and I thought, "This guy would be perfect for a cultural McKinsey." The other day I was talking to Drake Bennett of the *Boston Globe*. Another sterling candidate. There are all those journalists now in transit as the newspaper and magazine industries decline. Indeed, there are easily five hundred people who could be recruited tomorrow (and we need only eight). They are superbly well informed about contemporary culture, and some of

them are distinctly underemployed. Tell me again why it is, in our world, we keep culture here and commerce there, as if their more witting interpenetration would expose us to the dangerous combination of unstable chemicals?

9. Jenkins, Henry. 2007. "From YouTube to YouNiversity." *Confessions of an Aca/Fan*, February 16. www.henryjenkins.org/2007/02/from_youtube_to_youniversity.html.

INDEX